PUBLICIZATION

Publicization

How Public and Private Interests Can Reinvent Education for the Common Good

Jonathan Gyurko

Teachers College Press
Teachers College | Columbia University
New York and London

For Donna, William, and Robert

Published by Teachers College Press,® 1234 Amsterdam Avenue, New York, NY 10027

Front cover image: ArtBoyMB / iStock by Getty Images.

Library of Congress Cataloging-in-Publication Data is available at loc.gov

ISBN 978-0-8077-6942-3 (paper)
ISBN 978-0-8077-6943-0 (hardcover)
ISBN 978-0-8077-8225-5 (ebook)

Printed on acid-free paper
Manufactured in the United States of America

Contents

It always seems impossible until it is done.

—Nelson Mandela

Acknowledgments

Publicization would not have been possible without insights learned from great teachers, mentors, and colleagues, including David and Hilary Matthews, Gail and Brian du Toit, Lettie van Antwerpen, Hester Smit, Monica Jacobs, Eleanor Moagi, Johann and Sandra Dorfling, Marius Moorcroft, Phil Price, Andy Taylor, and John Harwood; Harold Levy, Joel Klein, Burt Sacks, Beverly Donohoe, John Green, Matt Sapienza, Liz Sciabarra, Eric Nadelstern, Claire Sylvan, Monte Joffee, Stacey Gautier, Sy Fliegel, Harvey Newman, Michele Cahill, Rich Buery, Rich Berlin, Eve Colavito, Mimi Corcoran, Steve Zimmerman, Paul Hill, Robin Lake, James Merriman, Greg Richmond, Bob Hughes, Linda Brown, and John Chubb; Randi Weingarten, Michelle Bodden, Carol Gerstl, Ellie Engler, Steve Allinger, Mary Butz, Steve Barr, Fran Streich, Alan Cage, Nancy van Meter, Jessica Smith, and Deborah Meier; Jeffrey Leeds, George Bell, Rob Bernstein, Susan Cates, Paul Skordilis, Penny MacCormack, Brad Felix, Doug Saidenberg, Matthew Goldstein, Benno Schmidt, Eduardo Padrón, Molly Broad, Elmira Mangum, Rebecca Martin, Nancy Zimpher, Charlie Rose, Andy Stern, Kemp Battle, Brennan Brown, Farhad Asghar, Harry Williams, and Amy Goldstein; Stefan Pryor, Adam Goldfarb, and Liz Donohoe; Hank Levin, Tom James, Dorian Warren, Bob Jervis, Steven Cohen, Nancy Degnan, and Dan O'Flaherty; Chuck Lovelace, Megan Mazzocchi, Reid Barbour, and Milly Barranger; Lance Odden, Willy MacMullen, Jon Bernon, Robin Osborn, Bill Morris, Emily and Gordon Jones, John and Carol Sbordone, Rusty Davis, Linda Saarnijoki, and Jean Piacenza; Marie Carrubba, Louis Esparo, Marion O'Donnell, Cheryl Dwyer, Ronnie Santo, Dan Tokarz, Judy Pernal, Ann Gensch, and Mary Cianciolo; Charlie Sciabetta and the inimitable Deb Levitzky.

I am particularly grateful to John Ayers, Harry Brighouse, Leo Casey, Geoff Decker, Brian Ellerbeck, Jeff Henig, Kalila Hoggard, Aaron Pallas, Kevin Reilly, Charlie Rose, Carole Saltz, Chad Vignola, Phil Weinberg, Joe Williams, Jon Zimmerman, and anonymous reviewers for their manuscript feedback. The book is the better for it and, of course, the interpretations and unintended mistakes are mine.

—JG
Brooklyn, NY, and Goshen, CT
2023

Introduction

Not long ago I attended a discussion among nationally recognized leaders in education. It was held at an elite university, at its respected college of education, home to prominent scholars with a long history of researching schools and setting their agenda.

Toward the event's end the moderator asked, "What's the greatest threat to public education?" Without much hesitation, the first panelist answered in a word: "Privatization." The other speakers joined in, expanding the view.

I took a moment to read the room. Among the hundreds of attendees were teachers, administrators, policymakers, researchers, and union leaders. All seemed to have knowing smiles and nodded in agreement.

I was struck. Their reaction likely said more about the political leanings of the college, the panelists, and those willing to trek out on a cold November night to listen. No one seemed bothered by the question's gratuitous framing, as education politics are often discussed.[1]

I was most unsettled by a feeling that everyone seemed to share a common understanding of the word "privatization" and, for that matter, a shared definition of "public education." How could this be?

The moderator didn't press the point, nor did any attendees during the Q&A. But surely, in a nation of 100,000 elementary and secondary schools and 13,000 school districts, enrolling 51 million students across 50 different states, five territories, and the District of Columbia,[2] our notions of what makes for a public education, and what it means to privatize it, can't all be the same.

Had I broken the comfortable consensus and asked, "What do you mean by 'privatization'?," I suspect I would have heard a predictable list: vouchers, aid to private schools, charter schools, and at-will employment—a form of workplace privatization. Admittedly, the night's polite setting and the panel's remaining minutes would not have allowed for much elaboration.

Yet as early as the 1970s, some progressive academics recommended vouchers to augment and extend public education, by providing underserved students with opportunities to attend better-resourced schools.[3] Tax dollars have supported private schools for decades, to purchase textbooks, student lunches, transportation, and special services, originating in the logrolling to first pass the Elementary and Secondary Education Act.[4] Charter advocates vociferously defend the schools as public. Are they wrong?

That night in the wood-paneled auditorium, where did our experts draw the line between public and private? Where should *we*?

This book is about a definition: specifically, what we mean when we say "public education." Amidst intense national debates about our schools and children, and pervasive talk from the political left about the threat of privatization, it's necessary to first clarify what's being privatized. What makes an education "public"? And how might we get more of it?

These questions urgently need answering. Forty years ago, President Reagan launched a philosophical revolution by declaring that government—the public sector—was the cause of our nation's woes and that the private sector, powered by markets and competition, was the solution. The *nation was at risk*, as the eponymous 1983 report declared, and government-run schools were part of the problem.[5] It became a national creed.

As many have documented, this thinking came to dominate school improvement efforts. It was the era's gestalt, from the political center-left to the right, headlined in popular titles like David Osborne and Ted Gaebler's *Reinventing Government: How the Entrepreneurial Spirit Is Transforming the Public Sector from the Schoolhouse to Statehouse, City Hall to the Pentagon*, published in 1992.[6] These ideas did not go unchecked. They faced heated political opposition. But as I will show, most carried the day in school reforms adopted nationwide.

In this regard, I agree *conceptually* with the panelists in the opening vignette. Our public sector and its schools have been the object of a 40-year "privatization project."[7] It applied market-inspired reforms to schools, their districts, and state education systems. That project was led by a constellation of educators, philanthropists, policymakers, and politicians who shared a faith in private-sector superiority. Some genuinely believed that these ideas would do better by children; others were less well intentioned, aiming to advance private interests or a conservative agenda, or simply to make a buck.

Yet today, the national faith in markets and limited government has been called into question. Bookstores feature titles like Thomas Philippon's *The Great Reversal: How America Gave Up on Free Markets*, Jonathan Tepper's *The Myth of Capitalism: Monopolies and the Death of Competition,* Anand Giridharadas's *Winners Take All: The Elite Charade of Changing the World*, Jonathan Hopkin's *Anti-System Politics: The Crisis of Market Liberalism in Rich Democracies*, Ian Haney López's *Merge Left: Fusing Race and Class, Winning Elections, and Saving America*, and Thomas Piketty's *Time for Socialism: Dispatches from a World on Fire.*[8]

A new generation, outraged by racism, economic inequity, and environmental destruction, is looking *to* government for the changes they seek. Outspoken progressive leaders have been elected who share this belief that government can be a force for good in education and our economy and for our physical and social infrastructure. Local and global social movements, including Black Lives Matter and Fridays for Future, are demanding racial and environmental justice.

Although we are a deeply divided nation, the social and political forces in support of the public sector feel stronger than they've been in a long time. It is, possibly, an inflection point, away from an "economic style of reasoning" toward something new, argues Elizabeth Popp Berman in her persuasive *Thinking Like an Economist: How Efficiency Replaced Equality in U.S. Public Policy*.[9]

But toward what? And where does this leave America's schools? If, like a receding tide, the market-based philosophy underpinning decades of reform is washing out to sea, what will take its place?

My belief, and the impetus of this book, is that a restoration of public education can't be defined in the negative, merely an *undoing* of reforms broadly understood as part and parcel of the recent privatizing past. Again from Popp Berman: "Once a particular intellectual framework is institutionalized, it can take on a life of its own, defining the boundaries of what is seen as politically reasonable."[10] If so, we must first reckon with privatization's pervasiveness to understand how to replace it and with what. Otherwise, like sand rushing out from under one's feet, the absence of a coherent, affirmative view makes for unsteady footing.

This book aims to help those of us seeking to strengthen public education by providing a new intellectual architecture to replace the old. It offers a constructive vision, with a set of guiding principles, to better understand what makes an education public and how to advance it. Without this or another, similar conceptual framework, I fear that school improvement efforts risk being intellectually adrift and, as such, less likely to succeed.

Sounds overdrawn? "Public education" often goes undefined, or explained in the negative, in many scholarly texts, leaving it to readers' assumptions and biases.[11] The Spencer Foundation recently brought together scholars, educators, and activists representing charter and district schools to prompt their thinking about what makes a school public. It revealed that few had thought deeply about the question. They were clear about what makes a school private, but did not have nearly the same crispness on the question of what makes one public.[12] My experience is similar: Champions of public education are sure of what they're against, but given the national fights over schools, they can ill afford to be vague about what to do instead.

PRIVATIZATION'S ANTIDOTE: PUBLICIZATION

This book offers some answers, in an extensive critique and rejoinder to educational privatization, with ideas old and new, and under a new banner: *public*-ization. Admittedly, it's an unfamiliar, even hard-to-pronounce term:

puh·blick·eh·zay·shun. One has to do some etymological digging, beyond the marketer's act of *publicizing,* to find an older meaning: *that which makes something public.*[13]

Why a new term? At one time the word *privatization* was not part of the lexicon. Today it rolls off the tongue, giving voice to a generally understood set of ideas. Searching the word online yields 70 million results. As for "publicization"? A meager 112,000 hits, largely related to marketing. This means that now, to help turn the political tide, we again need new language, capturing the essence of its own set of ideas, to describe what's happening and achieve more of it.

THE PUBLIC GOOD

We can think of "publicization" as a retort to many of the parts of life and public policy that have been privatized over the past 4 decades. As it applies specifically to education, I define it both in *substance* and *process*: first, by the public goods that schools can (but don't always) produce and, second, through six domains of policy and practice discussed in the following chapters—the educational processes that garner more (or less) of these common benefits.

Historically, our country has looked to schools to "take a vast, heterogenous, and mobile population . . . and forge it into nation,"[14] able to

- sustain our democracy, by preparing the next generation of engaged **citizens;**
- serve our economy, by equipping productive **workers** with the knowledge, skills, and dispositions required to engage in the workforce; and to
- promote social cohesion, by cultivating shared norms across communities, among people living together as good **neighbors.**

To these three, we must now add a fourth, broad purpose of schooling: to also

- prepare **stewards** of our planet. Only a common commitment will arrest an ecological catastrophe that will exacerbate political authoritarianism, economic inequity, and societal injustice.

As a definition goes, I think it's reasonable to expect public institutions to produce public goods. I posit that an education should be considered "public" when a school prepares students to advance these four common goods.

Like so much of our nation's still-perfecting story, and despite these long-standing expectations, our systems of education have not always met the mark. More tragically, schools have been used at times to keep some Americans down and others divided. These are not the schools we want or need.

Plus, today, all four public goods are imperiled. Our polity is deeply divided, threatened most dramatically by an attempted coup encouraged by concerted efforts to delegitimize our elections; our economy is rife with inequity, slipping standards of living, and inflation that exceeds wage growth; the nation's original sin of slavery still manifests in racism in every quarter of society; and climate deniers found their way into our very language: we talk of "change" instead of "warming."

Did schools not do their job? In a way. It's absurd to place all of the responsibility at their feet. But as I will argue, privatization privileged self-interest over the common good. It gave moral authority to the individual at the expense of the community. The privatization project impaired schools' ability to do their part in advancing a political, economic, social, and environmental way of life that all can enjoy and to which all can contribute. So how do we undo the damage?

CRITERIA OF A "PUBLIC" EDUCATION

Schools do either a good or a bad job at producing the aforementioned common goods, what I define as the *substance* of an education we should consider "public." The outcome depends on our priorities, values, and the choices we make about how schools operate, the *processes* of schooling.

This book presents six criteria by which to a) examine how well schools produce the collective goals we've long expected of them and b) how to get more of these goals from our schools. These familiar categories can be considered the constitutive processes of schooling. What may be novel is examining them together by the degree to which each advances private or public aims.

The criteria address the following core dimensions in the delivery of an education:

1. **Funding,** specifically the extent to which education is free and provided by tax-funded schools that have the resources necessary to meet society's expectations of them for all children, with resources comparable from one school to the next, including what it takes to educate children who need more support.
2. **Facts and beliefs,** specifically the degree to which educational aims are based on an underlying philosophy of facts, determined through collective processes that separate fact from fiction, while honoring and contextualizing values and opinions.
3. **Governance** that brings society's stakeholders into dialogue regarding what is taught and how, through processes that hear and

heed different views, within deliberative rules of the road that guide when some voices have more say than others. Just as democracy is theorized at its best when participation is robust and respectful, so too should be the governance of schools.
4. **Standards and testing** that, respectively, articulate the results of deliberative and participatory governance as to what it means to be an educated American and what we expect schools to address, with processes to determine if such expectations are met, answering the all-important question: How do we know?
5. **Accountability** that is mutual among all of society's stakeholders, on the basis of evidence fit for each purpose, which holds one other to a good-faith standard of effort and, in doing so, deepens schools' legitimacy.
6. **Equity**, first, from the equity-advancing effects of these first five domains and, second, by replacing the current industrial paradigm in which today's schools operate—which inequitably pits students against one another—with an intellectual-emotional paradigm. Such a new conception promotes human flourishing and depends less on where a child starts in life and, by schooling's end, produces results indistinguishable by race, ethnicity, class, gender, or sexual orientation.

A POLITICAL PROJECT

My aim is not simply to better define a public as opposed to a private education, although clarity we very much need. This book is also a call to action, for a political project that makes schools more effective at meeting civic, economic, social, and environmental imperatives. Doing so will require a campaign as well organized as the privatization project of the past 4 decades. Like any movement, this new *Publicization Project* needs its own constellation of ideas around which individuals and institutions can rally. Presented here is one such vision, intended to inspire a coalition that is clear in its aims, with policies and programs aligned to the goals of making schools more public.

In this regard, the leaders and yeomen of a Publicization Project have much work to do—much more than repealing privatizing policies of recent decades. They must first abandon any romantic notions about America's schools and come to terms with the deeper structural expressions of private interests that eclipse the common good. Such interests have controlled schooling for far longer than the current era of market-based reforms, determining the purposes, funding, and operation of schools, exacerbating disenfranchisement and injustice.

Simply, champions of a Publicization Project must first admit that what many consider to be some of America's best public schools, when judged against our criteria, aren't all that public. Harder still, the project must learn and co-opt lessons from privatization efforts that can, counterintuitively, strengthen schools' ability to produce the common goods we need. This book offers some guidance.

Such a Publicization Project is also political in the best sense: of organizing interests and building coalitions, of determining the quality and character of schools through deliberative, rather than market, processes. It is also political in that it must outcompete, in the long-game of democratic processes, privatization's own well-established coalition. As Popp Berman concludes, building this new intellectual framework and the institutions to support it is an "all-hands-on-deck *project*."[15]

What's "in it" for anyone? Those seeking to turn the tide in American politics, who are concerned about our democracy, economy, society, and environment, are natural allies; this book aims to meet their need for new ways of thinking and talking about the change they seek. Education reformers, fatigued by past disappointments and looking to move beyond political gridlock, are another constituency. Throughout the book, I show how a Publicization Project is in the particular interest of one group or another. But it bears emphasizing: My aim is to inspire common cause around the self-evident value of *shared* interests that need not be defended solely on the basis of private or group interests. At its core, *Publicization* asks us to care as much about what we share as what we keep to ourselves.

* * *

In the rest of this Introduction I preview a diverse range of somewhat unique professional experiences that inform my take on things, to be elaborated on in later chapters. I then argue that schooling is neither "public" nor "private"—the binary in which debates are typically framed and scholarly literature sometimes presented. Rather, I posit that schools live on a spectrum of "publicness," in service of public aims (at one end) and private interests (on the other). Finally, a proposed exclusion test is introduced as a tool with which to determine where schools land on this spectrum.

Then, in Part I, I examine each of the six dimensions of a Publicization Project, building an interdependent case as I go along. Ideas and modes of analysis, like the proposed exclusion test, get introduced early on and are woven throughout chapters. My style is dialogic, acknowledging and addressing anticipatable objections. I draw on the history of U.S. education and the research literature with illustrative examples. My necessarily brief sketches of admittedly complicated topics inevitably omit competing claims and historiographical debates. Guilty as charged. Instead, I've endeavored to make the narratives sufficiently on-point to credibly apply the exclusion test, expose the pervasiveness of private interests in schools, and propose how to make education more public than private.

Thinking about publicness or privateness as a matter of degree serves a practical purpose, too. It allows a Publicization Project to work progressively over time, step-by-step, moving schools toward greater degrees of common purpose, in service of the public good. This dynamic framing creates room for more people to join the effort. It welcomes those who may not have fully appreciated the privateness of their views and who may seek to promote more public-oriented change. It also asks those with strong views about what isn't public to revisit their beliefs and, as I will show, find publicness where they had once assumed only privateness.

For these reasons, I judiciously use the words "public" and "private," as well as "public education." For example, in most instances I refer to "tax-funded schools." This is not meant as a pejorative, as the label "government schools" is sometimes brandished.[16] Rather, I refer to tax-funded education for sake of discipline. Given that I seek to better define public education and provide recommendations on how to strengthen its publicness, I can't responsibly use the same terms, circularly, in my analysis.

Similarly, I refer to "district schools" rather than public schools to identify those tax-funded schools operated by school districts, governed by local boards of education, and overseen by state education agencies. This descriptor is particularly helpful in distinguishing these schools from "charter schools," which are also tax-funded but operate differently. In doing so, I ask readers to suspend their own notion of a public school, which may be based more on a legal type of institution, and instead join me in evaluating schools' publicness through our six criteria, with the exclusion test, and by the degree to which common political, economic, social, and environmental goals are advanced.

As readers will find, examining the story of education in America through the lens of publicness and privateness exposes the pervasiveness of private interests in schools. It challenges what many consider to be emblematic of the best of public education. But this is no jeremiad; rather, it is a critique coming from loyal dissent. Only by acknowledging the depths of any challenge can we understand why the privatization project took such a powerful hold and what a Publicization Project must do to succeed it.

* * *

In Part II I apply the six criteria to two cases of particular relevance to a Publicization Project: charter schools and the teacher unions. Both are emblematic of the major fault lines in American education politics, and a Publicization Project must seek new ways forward with both.

Since the first charter school opened in Minnesota in 1992, these institutions have been a leading vehicle for market-based ideas of choice and competition as championed by the privatization project. They are also a favorite target of self-described defenders of public education. Yet today, millions of students are enrolled in charters. They've cultivated a political bloc of loyal parents and are defended by a well-funded lobby. As such, it's foolish to treat them as anything other than a permanent feature of the American educational landscape, and a Publicization Project ignores them at its peril. Instead, how might it strengthen charter schools' *publicness*?

The second case applies the six criteria to the teacher unions and their role in the publicness of tax-funded schools. The unions are among the least understood stakeholders in education, perceived with little more than superficial impressions of political power.[17] Their history and purpose, the specifics of what they do and why, along with detailed knowledge of collective bargaining and due process, are not well known by education leaders and policymakers. This second case seeks to broaden understanding of the unions, analyze their impact on the publicness of schools, and present changes that a Publicization Project must demand if schools are to be more public.

WHAT MAKES A SCHOOL "PUBLIC"? SOME PERSONAL PERSPECTIVES

What is public education? For most Americans, I suspect the answer is uncomplicated: The school down the street, where my kids go. Where I went years ago. Pressed for a little more: Paid for by my taxes and run by the town's board of education.

I grew up in such a place: Torrington, Connecticut. A former mill town in the state's northwest corner, it had six elementary schools that fed into a middle and high school. They had a great reputation, too. Favorite teachers, like Mr. Chretien for history and Ms. Pagano for art, had taught my parents. It's where Sally Reis, a founding researcher on talented and gifted students, got her start.[18] Torrington had a couple of parochial schools, but enrollment was dwindling. There was a state-run technical high school, too, but this was long before any charters.

These schools would have been my understanding of public education were it not for some fortunate events. A middle school counselor suggested I apply to one of New England's prep schools, where I boarded for 4 years. Although private, its motto of "not to be served but to serve" was rich in public spirit. A scholarship then sent me to a state university in the South, placing a young Yankee into a decidedly different milieu.

After college I taught at Tiger Kloof School in Vryburg, South Africa.[19] Founded in 1904 by the London Missionary Society (LMS), Tiger Kloof was the region's most important educational institution for Black South Africans. It graduated the first two democratically elected presidents of Botswana and a founder of the African National Congress (ANC) Women's League, among other notable leaders.[20]

But Apartheid forced Tiger Kloof's closure. The racist 1953 Bantu Education Act severely limited what could be taught to Black South Africans. In an act of conscience, LMS withdrew from the school. After a short period of state operation, it closed. For the next 40 years its stately stone buildings were left to decay. Classrooms that had launched southern Africa's leaders were used by a local farmer as pens for sheep.

Apartheid's death brought Tiger Kloof back to life. In 1995, I joined a team of educators, philanthropists, and community leaders reopening the storied institution. Efforts were led by Ruth Mompati, a prominent ANC leader and "Old Tiger" alumna; George Mosiapoa, another alum and owner of the local bus company; Wally Brink, a prominent citizen and rancher; and David H. Matthews, a celebrated South African educator and co-founder of the progressive Maru-a-Pula School in Botswana.[21] Tiger Kloof's resurrection, within a rural and conservative part of the country, was rich in significance. Rededication proceedings were led by Archbishop Desmond Tutu, whose mother was an Old Tiger. Curious educators visited us from around the world, including Ted Sizer, on one of his tours of interesting schools that inspired his writings.

Unbeknownst to me at the time, but key to my education about schooling, was the founders' decision to reopen Tiger Kloof as a hybrid: a public school, open to students of all races, but located on private property. It offered a mix of government-resourced and privately supported services. About half of our students lived on campus, while others arrived each morning from Huhudi, the nearby Black township.

Its charitable board was responsible for modest scholarships to cover student expenses. It supervised senior leadership, maintained the physical plant, and provided supplemental programs, including the drama enrichment program that I led. A second board, including teachers, parents, and community leaders, was constituted by South Africa's 1996 Schools Act. It was responsible for oversight of the state-required curriculum, administration of national matriculation exams, and management of teachers deployed by the town's district office.

Not quite private but not fully public, Tiger Kloof provided a valuable conceptual model for my return to New York City, where I fell into the nation's emerging charter school movement. I brought no ideological predilections to the work, no free-market buccaneering. Rather, there was an opening in the city's charter school office. I knew there was something happening there. What it was wasn't exactly clear to me, but I wanted to be a part of it.

I served as Director of Charter Schools in two administrations, first for the late Chancellor Harold O. Levy, who was mildly anti-charter, and then for Chancellor Joel I. Klein, who was wildly pro. The contrast was an education in and of itself. I was responsible for district oversight, funding allocations, and operational support to 32 schools educating about 8,000 students, a small slice of the city's 1,700 schools and 1.1 million students.

I then went to work for the United Federation of Teachers (UFT), the city's teacher union local, and became one of only a handful of educators who have worked on both sides of the management-labor divide.[22] The UFT was led at the time by Randi Weingarten, who now serves as president of the national American Federation of Teachers (AFT). She wanted to open UFT-run charter schools, and I offered to help. The experience provided an up-close understanding of teacher unionism and collective bargaining.

My perspective on the publicness and privateness of schools was also informed by state-level work with Connecticut's then Governor Dannel Malloy and his education commissioner, Stefan Pryor. Together we developed, negotiated, and passed the state's education reform statute. The effort was prompted by federal Race to the Top grants and waivers from provisions of the No Child Left Behind act.

This work coincided with a short chapter advising the Abu Dhabi Education Council on its implementation of learning standards, student-centered pedagogy, and dual-language instruction in government-run schools. The experience challenged many assumptions about how change happens (or doesn't) in the bureaucracy of an autocratic government. It was also a chance to work alongside the late John Chubb, who led our consultancy. Chubb co-authored the highly influential *Politics, Markets, and America's Schools,* a touchstone for the school voucher and choice movement. John also served as chief academic officer of Edison Schools, the for-profit school management company that became a poster child of privatization.[23] All the while, my wife and I guided our two sons through New York City's public schools. Its complex processes for middle and high school admissions included ability tests, interviews, written applications, and art portfolios.

What is "public education"? With more than a few perspectives on the question, my answer is: It depends. On the issue. On the criteria of schooling that one considers by which to judge a school's publicness or privateness. Ultimately, answering this question is the purpose of this book, to provide readers with a more nuanced way to think about schooling and to give those who seek to strengthen public education new perspectives on which to act.

A PRIMER, A MEMOIR, AND A PLAYBOOK

One writes for one's self, to clarify one's thinking, with the hope that others find it helpful. In this regard, I've written for my *younger* self the book I wish I had read when just getting started. Consider it a resource for the up-and-coming generation of educators, policymakers, and reformers—particularly champions of public education—to help them better engage with the ideas that animate our enterprise.

If, at times, it feels like a primer, the description is fair. I trade off complexity for the benefit of accessibility, to introduce readers to major themes and debates for which there are few easy answers. But hopefully this is a sufficient foundation to build one's own understanding and make more informed additions to the work. Where I cite key thinkers, books, and studies, I hope readers will seek the primary source to learn more. My failures to mention notable citations and scholars is only a result of having spent more time in the field than in the stacks. And although examples are largely from experiences in New York City, readers will likely find applicability to their own context.

Another rule of writing is to first make readers *care* about your character and then make them *worry* about your character. I suspect that anyone who picks up this book already cares about public education. There is much reason to worry, too. Just prior to the pandemic, the Fordham Institute lamented "America's 'Lost Decade' of educational progress," based on "extremely disappointing" trends in reading and mathematics achievement as measured by the National Assessment of Educational Progress. Post-pandemic scores showed the largest decline in 30 years, with continued "backsliding."[24] Schools remain highly segregated by race and ethnicity, mirroring larger and long-standing patterns of community segregation and racist housing laws.[25] Plus, reform efforts have flagged in the still waters between changing intellectual tides: more than one foundation program officer has commented to me that not much is happening right now.

This last detail may come as a relief to those who believe that recent foundation-funded reforms were dangerous elements of the privatization project. But there's no time for inaction. The nation's intense political partisanship, coupled with social media's overwhelming amount of mis- and disinformation, put an even greater burden on schools to prepare future citizens who can sort out fact from fiction. The clicking tock of global warming does not cease. Further delay to racial and economic justice is justice denied.

The Exclusion Test

What is "public education"? We'll examine six criteria that help us answer the question. But it's useful to first establish education's two "faces": one public, the other private. Doing so clarifies that education is not necessarily one or the other. Rather, it lives on a spectrum from public to private, susceptible to operating choices that move it in one direction or the other.[1]

Economists provide a helpful way to think about this, in the distinction they make between public and private goods. A public good is something that can't be excluded from others. Think of the air we breathe. If it's clean, we all benefit. If it's polluted, we all choke. A park or library, when open to all, is a public resource.

By comparison, a private good is *excludable* from others, with the benefits flowing only to the owner, such as most consumer goods. When I buy and eat an apple, the nutritional benefits are all mine. If I belong to a members-only nature preserve, some people are excluded from the trails.

Let's call this the *exclusion test*. When something is excluded from others, we should consider it a private good (such as my apple). When something is shared, either because it's unexcludable (like air) or by choice (like a park, open to all), it's public.

So far so good. But as with many simplifying models, the distinction between public and private goods blurs quickly in everyday life. If I buy a home air filter, I can improve the quality of the air that I breathe, turning fresh air into my own private good. A roadside apple tree planted centuries ago for any hungry passerby is something of a public good—no one is excluded from its benefits. Yet by fall's end the tree is bare, having only fed those who walked by first. It ceases to be a public good until the next season.[2]

It's in this blur that we find education, as it's both a public *and* a private good.[3]

Our country was founded on a belief that democracy requires an educated citizenry.[4] Washington thought it "essential that public opinion should be enlightened." Jefferson warned: "If a nation expects to be ignorant and free in a state of civilization, it expects what never was and never will be."[5] As the argument goes, well-informed voters will elect good stewards of our government, with civic benefits flowing to all citizens. The implication is that no one should be excluded from education—a public good—so that uneducated voters don't put the commonweal at risk.

A similar argument is made for commerce. An economy functions best when goods and services freely flow through trade and when everyone can sell and buy their wares or labor. For this to occur, everyone must have a common understanding of arithmetic and value, with shared norms respecting agreements and transactions. Again, this provides a rationale for education to be delivered as a public good, without exclusion, to equip everyone with the skills, knowledge, and dispositions necessary for economic activity. Those without such an education are at an economic disadvantage and may limit (or even harm) the entire system.

As introduced above, a third public good is social cohesiveness from broadly shared values held not by some exclusive group, but by the vast majority of Americans. Many values come to mind and some conflict—from our love of competition and rugged individualism to our sense of fair play, eagerness to help a neighbor, and narrative of diversity as a source of strength. Such national values are passed from one generation to the next by families, in churches, through the arts, on sports teams, by media, and elsewhere. But we've also looked to tax-funded schools to inculcate these ideals because of a desire for social stability, through shared norms, among *all* Americans. To wit, the earliest teacher preparation colleges were called *normal* schools.

Producing these public goods required that *education itself* become a public good, excluded from no one. In later pages we'll examine how well it has lived up to this commitment. But in the simplest terms, as measured by the exclusion test, mass schooling in American through 12th grade is "a signal accomplishment in the history of education," concluded Richard Hofstadter in his landmark *Anti-Intellectualism in American Life*.[6]

Alongside education's service to these three public goods we must now add a fourth: environmental stewardship. The climate crisis is *unexcludable*. Carbon released in the United States or China causes life-threatening weather events around the world. Only collective action on a global scale to preserve the ultimate public good—a habitable planet—can minimize predicted disasters that will harm everyone, and unequally harm the global poor.[7] Looking to schools to prepare stewards of our planet strikes me as a legitimate, albeit newer, common purpose of education.

This public good "face" of education serves shared, common interests: good government, a functioning economy, a cohesive society, and a habitable planet. But education serves private interests, too. This is when its face as a private good comes into full view.

At the most biological level, education is intrinsically a private good. What I learn gets encoded into my synapses. My thoughts are entirely *excludable* from others. I can gain private benefits from education that I may decide to share with no one. For example, by becoming a math whiz I might use my skills in the stock market to make a lot of money. Education gives me this personal, private advantage.

The degree to which education is a private good, advancing private interests, is both personally advantageous and necessary for a modern society. Virtually every walk of life, from lawyer and artist to builder, farmer, and cook, relies on expertise—a form of private knowledge and skill. We would not seek advice from an attorney untrained in the law. We risk starvation if farmers have no unique understanding of the land. The private benefits of education allow people to specialize, cultivate innate talents, and pursue their passions to everyone's benefit in our interconnected world.

But here's the point: the public and private nature of things isn't fixed, as the air and apple examples show. In important instances, like education, we get to decide, individually and collectively, the degree to which something is a private or public good. I can share my apple with others. I can invite neighbors to breathe easier in my home. I can teach others my financial insights or farming innovations. And we can suss out the degree to which I do or don't with the aid of our exclusion test.

For example, if communities choose to invest in their water systems, then potable water is available to all—another classic public good. New York City is famous for its delicious water, right from the tap. Alternatively, some people may prefer bottled water and have less desire to pay taxes for treatment facilities. The events in Flint, Michigan, show the life-threatening and discriminatory effects of treating safe water as an exclusive, private good.

Similarly, many of New York's majestic parks and beaches built in the early 20th century by Robert Moses are accessible resources exclusive to none.[8] But decades of neglect, alongside the rise of recreation clubs and resident-only beaches, show their eclipse by private alternatives. Nor can we ignore Moses' highways, tearing through poor communities to access those very same parks and beaches, or his overt racism: overpasses built too low for buses to exclude those without cars: "the poor Blacks and Puerto Ricans [who] Moses despised."[9]

By seeing that the publicness or privateness of a good depends on our choices, our question changes. We no longer should ask: What *is* public education? and search for it in one *type* of school or another.

Rather, if we agree to define education as public when a) schools produce public goods and b) don't exclude (i.e., they are public goods themselves), we can instead ask: *How public* is education? and use the exclusion test to find answers.

This framing gives us the power to decide. It understands education as something dynamic and responsive to our individual and collective will. How public do we *want* schools to be, meaning, how *much* of these four public goods do we wish schools to produce? Regardless of their type: district, charter, nonprofit, or proprietary?

Considering *how public* schools are (or aren't), and what we can do to strengthen their publicness, asks that we reflect on our values, the kind of society and planet in which we want to live, and the schools we need to prepare children to create and sustain that world. As the next chapter shows, this question of publicness begins with the first of six criteria: funding.

Part I

CRITERIA

If we have no criteria for evaluating answers to certain questions, then we should stop asking those questions until we do.

—Richard Rorty, *The Linguistic Turn: Essays in Philosophical Method*[1]

CHAPTER 1

Funding

> Star English teacher Ruby Ruf has sent teaching fans into a frenzy: "I am taking my talents back to New York City." PS431 made Ruby an offer she couldn't refuse: $80 million guaranteed over six years, with another $40 million in incentives based on test scores.
>
> —*Key & Peele*, "If We Treated Teachers Like Pro Athletes"[1]

In considering the publicness of education, the most basic criterion is funding: To be defined as "public," schools must be free to all and paid for by tax dollars. Otherwise, they fail the exclusion test by not being public goods in and of themselves. Tuition, even if modest, may exclude the poorest. Charitable scholarships, however generous, may fade in time or benefit some over others.

But here is where the simplicity ends. This chapter's brief history of school funding shows the large extent to which private interests have a controlling influence on the resourcing of tax-funded schools—resulting in more privateness than publicness. This chapter also draws on lessons from New York State's fiscal equity campaign, to illustrate the success of judicial remedies as well as their limitations, absent a broader political coalition that a Publicization Project must assemble.

* * *

To begin, consider the little red schoolhouses of the late 18th and early 19th centuries.[2] In our popular imagination, they are America's earliest, even iconic form of public education. One such building still stands down the road from where I write. Built in 1840, its façade is graced with two white doors, one for boys and one for girls. Peering through its closed shutters, you can still find rows of antique desks bolted to the floor and an old potbelly stove, long unused.

But these schools weren't free or tax-supported. Nearby families pooled their resources to hire an itinerant teacher. Poorly paid educators, immortalized by Washington Irving's Ichabod Crane, traveled the country looking for work. Teaching held little prestige, a mere "way station in life for a man of real ability and character."[3] The schoolhouse itself was built by the cooperating families, often on an unproductive parcel of donated land.

This financial arrangement more closely resembles tuition than a tax, a private rather than collective commitment, given that there were likely neighbors without children who did not contribute. Nor were cooperating families compelled by any government authority to stand up a school. They chose to, out of a desire to see their children learn the basics of reading, writing, and arithmetic. These early grammar schools were indicative of the voluntary, private associations that Tocqueville considered a defining feature of early American life, more creatures of civil society than the state.[4]

Plus, parents were in control. They hired and fired the teacher. They decided when children could be released from family duties to attend lessons. They set the curriculum, telling teachers what they wanted their children to learn. Contributing families also decided if and when to improve schoolhouse conditions, which were famous for disrepair and lack of heat. Other community members may have had a view on what constituted good schooling, but likely did not have much of a voice in decisions.

These factors suggest that *schooling* in early America was a *private* concern. Without question, the historical record indicates that our forebearers shared a commitment to *education*, given high rates of literacy, the cultural value placed on reading (in particular the Bible), and lofty sentiments that an "educated citizenry is a vital requisite for our survival as a free people."[5] But early schools were not the romanticized places of learning as often imagined. Nor were any such opportunities provided to the children of enslaved Americans; in much of the South, educating slaves was illegal.[6]

Only in the middle decades of the 19th century do we begin to see tax-funded grammar schools, brought about by concerns over the quality of education and social cohesion. The Common School movement, led by Horace Mann, Catherine Beecher, Henry Barnard, and others, sought to combine the tumbledown one-room schoolhouses into larger consolidated schools, funded by local taxes, with curriculum and hiring controlled by locally elected boards. During the same era, a nativist movement raised alarms about the perceived negative effects of Irish, German, and other immigrants on American culture. Tax-funded and locally governed schools were expected to acculturate these recently arrived neighbors.[7]

But we shouldn't look back on Common Schools as something foreordained. They took a movement to create. A *project.* In 1837 Mann wrote that "neglectful school committees, incompetent teachers, and an indifferent public, may go on degrading each other" until the notion of free education would be lost.[8] Moreover, taxpayer commitment was limited to *elementary* schools for most of the 19th century. Secondary education, beyond the basics, was provided nationwide by about 6,000 private academies.[9] They operated on tuition paid by families and were governed by non-elected boards or the academy's proprietor. Some received limited government financial support, such as a grant of land to sell or use. Some academies were constituted by a state authority, similar to charters granted to railway and canal companies and other privately operated enterprises deemed to provide civic benefits. Such state sanctioning could be considered a marker of publicness. But the limited financial support or oversight, and exclusion to those who paid tuition, made these academies more private than public.

Not until Progressive movements at the turn of the 20th century were tax-supported secondary schools created.[10] Inspired by Fredrick Winslow Taylor's notions of productive efficiency, and in an effort to get ward politics out of education, a loosely affiliated nationwide group of Administrative Progressives championed junior and senior high schools. Like their feeder elementary schools, these free and taxpayer-funded schools were governed by locally elected boards. They put most tuition-dependent academies out of business, too. Unable to compete with a free alternative, some academies relinquished private control and converted into locally governed high schools. Many closed, while a few, like Deerfield and the Phillips academies, reinvented themselves as privately operated, tuition-dependent boarding schools for America's elite.

By 1953, 86% of White students and 82% of "Negro and other" teenagers were enrolled in a free, tax-funded high school.[11] Resources varied widely, and de jure segregation created parallel and fiscally inequitable systems. In Atlanta, for example, per-pupil spending on White students averaged $570 as compared to $228 for Black children, with similar inequality in other segregated systems.[12] These discrepancies are significant, persistent, and should not be trivialized. But as this admittedly brief history indicates, by the middle of the 20th century a *minimal* definition of "public" had been met: free, tax-supported education was available to all American children from their early ages through adolescence.

PRIVATE INTERESTS REMAIN ENTRENCHED

Free and accessible by all still does not mean fiscally fair. Like our roadside analogy, some apples are fresh and delicious, while others are covered with flyspeck and sooty blotch. To this day, deeply embedded private interests continue to be expressed through school funding, providing some students with more than others. It is a direct inheritance of this history, and it undermines the publicness of tax-funded schools.

America's early structuring of school spending by schoolhouse and, later, by town reflected the fiscal preferences of parents and communities. For example, a farming community could support agricultural studies. Nineteenth-century urban schools, particularly those with an Americanizing agenda, could emphasize English and civics. Teachers may have been respected and well paid in some places, but more often, and later into the 19th century, women were hired at low wages.[13] The racism of segregation resulted in resource inequities—separate but by no means fiscally equal.

This arrangement works to the extent that families and communities have a legitimate interest in cultural reproduction—as they define it—by paying for the education they see fit. This arrangement does *not* work when power arrangements discriminate fiscally against some members of the same community. And beyond the fit, or "policy responsiveness,"[14] between the empowered community's interests and its funding of schools, such localization tied school resources to the wealth of a particular community. The founding fathers may have extolled the importance of nationwide education, and states prioritized education in their constitutions. But the cost was a local responsibility. Such a fiscal choice was consistent with early America's limited appetite for taxation, traditions of local control, and the absence, prior to the 20th century, of centralized state and national bureaucracies.[15] But this decision cast a long shadow on the operation of tax-funded schools.

For example, once-prosperous industrial towns funded well-resourced schools with modest taxes on their vibrant economies. Such was the case up and down Connecticut's Naugatuck River Valley during the 19th and early 20th centuries in cities like Bridgeport, Waterbury, and my hometown, which was world-famous for precision manufacturing of lathes and bearings.[16] Here and in communities across the country, no tax expense was spared in building prominent schools adorned with marble trim and neoclassical touches, whose teachers, teams, clubs, and graduates to Ivy League schools were a source of civic pride.

But following World War II—as industry changed, capital fled South and then overseas, and these towns rusted—school resources were cut, and a larger tax burden was placed on remaining businesses and residents. In Torrington, the high school recently risked losing its accreditation due to deferred capital improvements.[17] There and elsewhere, a reputation for high taxes, diminished economic opportunity, and underresourced schools caused a downward spiral. Families of means moved out. Left were (and are) families with fewer options, who send their children to schools that, perhaps superficially, are considered not that good.

Meanwhile, wealthier suburbs became home to upwardly mobile, white-collar professionals. They finance their schools with property taxes that are high but may be comparable to or even a lower percentage of household income relative to taxes in neighboring communities. The schools are well resourced and considered better than those in the former mill towns. Additional support is provided by affluent parent-teacher organizations.

When we apply the exclusion test, we find that the better-resourced schools are available only to students lucky enough to live on one side of a town line. Plus, the high price of suburban real estate and zoning restrictions on rental and multifamily homes further exclude lower-income families. A vicious cycle emerges as the suburb gets more and more exclusive. Although its schools are free, tax-supported, and open to anyone living along its leafy lanes, they have become, essentially, a private good only for the benefit of its fortunate residents.

We can find the same privateness *within* communities, too. Elementary school attendance zones often determine where young students study based on where they live. If one school gets a good reputation, parents may flock to live in that zone. It puts upward pressure on real estate, pricing out families with less income. Meanwhile, attendance zones in neighborhoods with lower household incomes and fewer community resources—vibrant parks, good transit, libraries, and supermarkets—may give those schools a bad reputation, regardless of the quality of teaching and learning.

This is often the case across New York City. Families go to great lengths to live in some of the city's 32 Community School Districts instead of others, and the cost of apartments is appreciably different. The small size of my family's home was a trade-off we were able to make for our sons to attend Brooklyn's William Penn Elementary School, better known as the sought-after PS 321.

These lines on maps protect the private interests of families (mine included) with the means and desire to live in places that provide a higher-resourced education to their children—to the exclusion of others. Such schools are free and tax-funded, and therefore public on this most rudimentary criterion. But just as in the suburbs, these schools, too, are private in that they are only available to the residents of that attendance zone. Looking around the ballroom of PS 321's annual gala, where the PTO raised tens of thousands of dollars, it even felt like a club.

Nor are attendance zones drawn at random. They are the result of decades of political processes in which some constituents have greater influence than others. These lines often separate communities by race, ethnicity, and class, creating government-sanctioned, market-reinforcing structural inequity. A no more dramatic case can be found than in Greenwich, Connecticut. Home to billionaires, since 2012 its schools have been cited by state authorities for "racial imbalance." At two elementary sites, the percentage of the minority population is 25 percentage points different from comparable schools in the same town.[18]

THE STRENGTHS AND LIMITS OF JUDICIAL REMEDIES

We can appreciate that parents have every desire to live in a place where they believe their children will receive the best education. Harder to defend, if education is to be a public good excluded from none, is "the best education" *that parents can afford,* as measured by the cost of real estate and local taxes. Indefensible is when racism and classism create geographic financial boundaries that *effectively or intentionally exclude* some children from better-resourced opportunities. That is what we have today. America's schools are more segregated than they've been in 50 years,[19] a clear manifestation of privateness endemic to America's tax-funded schools.

Compounding matters, the privatization project has sought tax funding *for* privately operated, tuition-dependent, and often denominational schools (i.e., private schools). Voucher programs have operated in Ohio, Wisconsin, and elsewhere. The conservative turn of the United States Supreme Court continues to build a body of case law to find these programs constitutional.[20] Nor has tax funding of private schools strengthened their publicness; these institutions typically do not admit all comers and forswear associated accountability to pursue collectively determined goals, have publicly accountable governance, or meet other defining characteristics of public schooling (that we will discuss in later chapters).

Champions of "public education"—the parents, teachers, and other stakeholders of tax-funded, district-operated schools—object to any such funding of private schools as a diversion of much-needed resources. In places where reasonable people would agree that district schools are underresourced to meet expectations, the protest is warranted. But it bears remembering that private schools only enroll about 10 percent of America's students.[21] This figure would likely grow if tuition were free or subsidized, due to a voucher, but not in all cases. Some private schools don't want government funding for fear of government control. Arguably, the amount of political energy spent fighting vouchers greatly exceeds the actual size of the issue.

By comparison, a Publicization Project should focus on the amount and fairness of funding to the tax-supported schools that educate 90 percent of the country's children. Given the strong degree to which private interests control how these schools are resourced and made inaccessible, the debates over vouchers are, to some degree, penny-wise and pound-foolish. Purely by the magnitude of the problem, a Publicization Project should redress fiscal inequities *between* one *tax-funded* school to the next, from town to town, and state to state. How might this look?

Since the 1960s, proponents of more equitable funding have turned to state courts. Legal efforts aimed to compel state governments to increase school spending, with arguments based on a child's right to an education as established in state constitutions.[22] But merely defining fiscal equity has proved challenging. Debates and decisions have turned on interpretations of the resources necessary to provide an "adequate," "basic," or "sufficient" education. Lawyers have parsed terms based on originalist interpretations from when the state's constitutional right was first established versus what is necessary to prepare students for today's knowledge-based economy.

Lawsuits seeking increases in state funding have also aimed to send more resources to poorer communities to address relative difference in resources from town to town. Such reallocation of state tax revenue aims to level the financial playing field, such as when one community can afford to offer higher salaries and recruit better teachers. Such formulae can also direct resources to schools that enroll children who will benefit from additional services, such as students with learning disabilities.

New York provides an example of the rewards and risks of this approach. Organizers of its Campaign for Fiscal Equity (CFE) sued and negotiated with the state government for nearly 30 years and with five different governors. The legal work was substantial: From 1996 to 2001 alone, the effort cost $14 million in pro bono services from the venerable firm of Simpson Thatcher & Bartlett. It deployed a team of eight attorneys led by Joe Waylan and the firm's chairman, Richard I. Beattie.[23]

CFE's victory was appealed by the state until a 2007 legislative commitment to "fully fund" the state's school aid budget. But enforcement challenges ensued and promises went unfulfilled. The 2008 recession strangled state coffers. Only recently, and as a result of federal pandemic aid and better than expected state revenue, did New York again pledge billions in additional school funding.[24] Yet Michael Rebell, who litigated CFE with noted educator Robert Hughes on behalf of plaintiff Robert Jackson, was less than sanguine. "Plagued by a sense of déjà vu," Rebell noted that New York may not honor its future commitments because "political winds can shift rapidly."[25]

Meanwhile, and despite decades of attention, within-state fiscal inequities persist. In Bedford, an exclusive town in New York's wealthy Westchester County, the school district spends about $17,500 per general education pupil and nearly $40,000 per special education pupil.[26] Fifty miles away, in the similarly named Brooklyn neighborhood of Bedford-*Stuyvesant*, the city's education spending averages $13,200 for general education—25% less—and $32,800 on special education.[27] These figures likely *understate* discrepancies, given additional resources available to students in Westchester from their families and community. The gap also does not address differences in educational needs: in the suburb, 23% of students are eligible for free and reduced-price meals, the federal indicator of poverty; in New York City, this figure is 73%.[28]

CFE is a cautionary tale. New York's litigation was like many others nationwide, including prominent efforts backed by the Ford Foundation in the 1960s and 1970s.[29] Typically, lawsuits are advanced by activists, private philanthropy, and groups with vested interests, including the teacher unions. New York's experience was also dependent on the largesse of a major law firm that, luckily, was led by prominent citizens committed to education.

But judicial remedies are not self-enforcing. Nor would any litigant want (or plan) for funding to depend on *force majure,* as recently delivered in the form of pandemic relief dollars. Plus, one can just as easily imagine a state's legal community unwilling to sue its own elected leaders, given their dealings with state government and desire for friendly relations.

Moreover, CFE lacked a broad coalition of New York's rich and poor, upstate and downstate, suburb, rural, and urban, all advocating for a common goal: educational funding sufficient to reasonably believe that all schools can meet the state's expectations of them, universally for all students, without *exclusion* by a student's race, ethnicity, gender, ability, family income, or place of residence. Absent such broad and popular demands, legislative and executive branches have less incentive to act; they can—and do—wait for the wind to shift.

This presents the first major task for a Publicization Project seeking to achieve greater fiscal equity across all tax-funded schools: It must build a broad political coalition of rich and poor that finds common interest in the education of one's children *and one's neighbors*, both next door *and in the next town over*. Doing so adds necessary *political* enforcement to judicial remedies. It can turn shifting political winds into steady streams of support.

Low-income families, who can only afford to live in communities with underresourced schools, have an obvious interest in joining the project. But given the many demands on their time, it takes constant attention to assemble and maintain such coalitions. This is the work of organizers—community, political, and labor—another key constituency of the project. It is exhausting work, too, such as the round-the-clock hours of calls and meetings spent by my late acquaintance John Kest, who helped to build the progressive Working Families Party, in concert with Bertha Lewis of the Association of Community Organizations for Reform Now (ACORN), later known as New York Communities for Change.[30]

What's "in it" for the middle and upper class? When Horace Mann was selling the idea of common schools—arguably the first great educational project in our nation's history—he emphasized democracy and prosperity. As Hofstadter wrote: "to the rich, who were often wary of its cost, [reformers] presented popular education as the only alternative to public disorder, to an unskilled and ignorant labor force, to misgovernment, crime, and radicalism."[31] Surely those old chestnuts are as persuasive today, to those who have more, in their relations with those who have less.

Readers sympathetic to this argument should take heart. Time and again, political coalitions have been built that are strong enough to advance a public purpose over private aims. The Progressive campaigns in the early 1900s and the Civil Rights Movement of the 1960s come to mind. In education, land-grant colleges took 50 years to gain traction.[32] Mann's concern about the prospects of his own project no doubt give us pause, but also argue for bottom-up collective action led by educators, students, parents, and communities. Such an approach is also called for by scholars Sonya Douglass Horsford, Janelle T. Scott, and Gary L. Anderson, who see "signs of coalitions forming." They astutely note that when such advocates galvanize, "the politicians will follow."[33]

Amidst our intense political polarization, such a prescription may seem naïve. It's worth remembering that Common School reformers advanced their project during the divided decades that led to the Civil War. Nor did our present polarization happen by accident. It is the result of its *own* coalition and campaign—the many formal and informal efforts over decades of the privatization project, emphasizing personal rights, interests, and grievances over collective responsibilities, shared sacrifices, and the public good. It may sound counterintuitive, but the success of *that* project suggests that the prospect of a countervailing Publicization Project is just as bright, if enough people enliven its organizing ideas with the same vigor.

Statewide campaigns, coalitions, and remedies can assure *within-state* fiscal equity across tax-funded schools. But a Publicization Project should set its sights higher, with a commitment to equitable funding of tax-supported schools *nationwide*. Doing so ensures that the material resources available to educate students in one state are not excluded from those in another, thereby strengthening the publicness of schools regardless of where a child is born.

At present, spending varies widely from state to state. New York leads the country in average spending per pupil, at $24,000. By comparison, Texas ranks 41st in the nation, spending $9,600 per pupil, with Utah in last place at $7,600.[34] Furthermore, states are pitted against one another when they seek to fund schools adequately and equitably. When New York increases taxes, it risks losing taxpayers who, out of financial self-interest, are able and willing to move to a place that taxes residents less. This leaves a greater financial burden on those who choose, or have no choice, to stay.[35]

Perhaps these discrepancies were tolerable when education served more local needs such as different labor demands of one state from another. This federalist approach also allows each state to express its own fiscal preferences and decide to what degree, as measured in tax dollars, it prioritizes education. Regional differences in the cost of living also explain some, but not all, of the gaps.[36] Plus, execution matters, tremendously: children in New York are not three times smarter than their peers in Texas.

But today our country faces political, economic, societal, and environmental issues of national and global concern. These issues know no state boundaries and require informed responses from future citizens comparably prepared to understand and address them, through schools that are comparably resourced to do so. The dire alternative remains as Mann warned: civic, economic, social, and environmental disorder.

Only much greater *federal* funding can address state-by-state fiscal inequities. Today about 8% of school funding comes from Washington.[37] The remaining 92% is supported about evenly by state and local taxes. In contrast, a true *national* commitment to free and fair tax-funded education, excluded from none, would see these figures flip.

If this, too, sounds naive, given the nation's hostility to taxes, consider this: In 2021 the IRS failed to collect $600 billion in owed taxes—from tax laws already on the books—due to understaffing.[38] That's roughly $12,000 per America's 51 million students. It's *more* than what's spent on each student in about half of the 50 states.[39] Meaning, a Publicization Project could substantially increase school funding in many states, and decrease local and state fiscal burdens in others, simply by demanding that *due* taxes get collected and spent on education.

I suspect there's a political deal to be made here. Benefits would reach North to South, applicable to all Americans regardless of political stripe. It requires greater federal support, but not necessarily new taxes. It would close tax "back doors," ensuring a collective, national commitment to education, and decouple the structural inequity that ties spending to where one lives, with its concomitant racism and classism. In wealthy communities, who wouldn't want to see property taxes go down? In low-income communities, who wouldn't want to see an influx of resources comparable to what the affluent already enjoy?

A QUESTION OF FAIRNESS

As I've presented, the most basic criterion of a *public* school is that it is free to all, excluded from none, and paid by tax dollars. But the core of *fiscal* publicness goes beyond the mere source of revenue. It is a question of resource *fairness*, not dissimilar from the conception of justice offered by philosopher John Rawls.[40] In a variation on his famous "original position" hypothetical: If your child, prior to her birth, were to be randomly assigned to a school somewhere in your town or state or the country that she *must* attend, what would you want the material conditions of her education to be, regardless of your own ability to pay for such schooling? (As we'll see later, the thought experiment of such random assignment is not so far-fetched.)

I doubt we'd find a parent who wouldn't desire a safe, clean, and up-to-date building, with relatively new computers and books, rich in curricular resources including the "extras" like art and music and athletics, able to offer attractive salaries to well-educated, skillful, and caring teachers and staff, responsible for no more students than those with whom they can reasonably develop a trusting, personalized relationship. Or as the most famous philosopher of education, John Dewey, put it: "What the best and wisest parent wants for his child, that must we want for all the children of the community. Anything less is unlovely, and left unchecked, destroys our democracy."[41]

The extent to which such an opportunity is freely offered to all young people is not a fiscal matter. It is only the difference between our private means and public spirit. It requires, as Horsford and colleagues conclude, the "political will to change how we finance schools, allow students to cross district boundaries, and provide more equitable ways to distribute resources."[42] Inspiring and mobilizing that will is the necessary work of a Publicization Project.

CHAPTER 2

Facts and Beliefs

> First, get your facts straight. Everyone is entitled to his own opinion, but not his own facts. Second, decide to live with the facts. Third, resolve to surmount them. Because fourth, what is at stake is our capacity to govern.
>
> —U.S. Senator Daniel Patrick Moynihan, 1983[1]

Means are for ends. With equitable funding of tax-supported schools sufficient to achieve desired ends for every student, what aims should a Publicization Project seek? What does it mean to receive a *public* education? To be an *educated American*?

As introduced above, we've long expected tax-funded schools to produce three overarching public goods, by preparing young people to sustain our democratic form of government, engage productively in the economy, and share values that promote a cohesive society. To these I've added a fourth—environmental stewardship—as the first three do not necessarily guarantee this shared and existential good. We should consider a school "public" when it advances these aims.

Over the course of the American saga, we can see how far we've come in pursuing these goals, how fragile they are, and just how much more we must do if these are the truths by which we wish to live.[2] Rhetoric about an "arc of history" may be inspiring, but there's no guarantee that it bends toward justice.[3] Nor is it surprising, given our still-perfecting union, to find a problematic history in the state's use of power to pursue these goals. In a country that so prizes liberty, one can point to this troubled past as reason to abandon broader expectations of schools and, instead, only look to them to develop the private interests of families and students. This line of thinking animates the school choice movement: Amidst differences that seem irreconcilable, simply let families decide.

Yet such an individualistic approach presents real dangers to a functioning democracy, fair economy, inclusive society, and habitable planet. Although the exercise of state power is imperfect, a Publicization Project should still work to strengthen schools' ability to prepare future adults who will embrace and advance these four essential public goods. It can do so by ensuring that schools' underlying philosophy—their epistemology—is based in facts and the norms by which we decide what constitutes a fact. More simply, for a school to be considered "public," it must advance facts.

SCHOOL CHOICE, PRIVATE BELIEFS, AND THE RISK TO PUBLIC GOODS

Let's start with an extreme scenario: if education were merely a private concern serving personal goals. In other words, a *private* good. Schools would not be expected to *directly* prepare citizens, workers, neighbors, or stewards of the planet. This might still happen as a *by-product* of formal education and other influences on children from family, community, church, culture, and elsewhere. But they would not result from intentional choices that make these aims explicit purposes of tax-funded schools.

In such a paradigm, families would find a school that serves what they seek: perhaps one that emphasizes the basics of reading, writing, and arithmetic, or more classical studies, or culturally relevant topics and content, or career-related subjects, or the arts, or sports. Alongside academics and extracurriculars, they'd also pick the values they want their children to develop: a family that prizes community and collaboration might not send their child to a school that emphasizes competition and rugged individualism. Absent compulsory education laws, families would also decide *how much* schooling their child needs and, importantly, the school's underlying philosophy: from the given wisdom of religions to the accumulated knowledge of science. This list of options goes on, and one of the promoted benefits of school choice (unrelated to theorized effects of competition) is for parents to freely find the best fit between their *own* interests and what a school offers.

Yet this approach risks underproducing our four public goods. Children in a family that prizes respect for authority might not develop an appreciation for the value of dissent in a democracy and may even learn that disagreement is unpatriotic. Children in wealth-motivated families might not learn about inequities that flow from unbridled capitalism and that threaten an entire economy and society. Children in homogenous communities may not learn to see diversity as a source of strength or be prepared to engage in different social settings. Families who are resigned to climate change, perhaps in locales removed from its more immediate effects, may pick a school focused on other things. As philosopher Harry Brighouse pointedly writes: Parents can choose from among schools that are "reliably left-wing, reliably racist, or reliably Christian" to reinforce, rather than challenge, their attitudes.[4]

Privileging the interests of families through school choice, a view celebrated by the privatization project, assumes that schools only *take* the pre-existing educational goals of families, to develop them further in their children. Such narrowly defined cultural reproduction is another way that the privateness of schooling gets emphasized over its publicness; by design, competing goals are excluded. But as political scientist Jeffrey R. Henig explored in *Rethinking School Choice,* this view underestimates, or even rejects, schools' ability to also *make* preferences that may differ from the interests, ideas, biases, insights, or misinformation that students bring to class.[5]

Think of a financier who wants to prepare her child for a career on Wall Street, only to find that he comes home from school with a passion for social work. Or parents who prize collaboration but see their student become more competitive by the day: she wants to be first in her class, the star of the play, and win every match. Or the industrialist whose son learns to protest the company's pollution. Or religious parents, whose children get exposed to the scientific method and question the authority of knowledge based on sacred texts. Or the child of a White supremacist whose best friend is Black.

If faced with such preference-*making* experiences—and if the purpose of schooling were to advance only private interests—parents could withdraw their children and find a school that teaches only what they want their children to know, do, and become. Alternatively, some parents might want their children to encounter new and different ideas. But this is by no means guaranteed.

If this all sounds theoretical, take the example of school choice in the 1950s and 1960s. As professor and civil rights activist Steve Suitts shows in *Overturning Brown: The Segregationist Legacy of the Modern School Choice Movement,* choice was a central strategy of those fighting racial integration. Seven Southern states passed voucher and tax credit plans to subsidize the cost of private, segregated schools. By 1956—still within living memory—about one million students were enrolled in these private schools; nearly all were White.[6] State-sponsored school choice, hardly a force for greater social cohesion, protected racism.

But if the decision of what schools are to teach is *not* left to parents, given that it risks underproduction of public goods such as a more tolerant society, how else can we justify the knowledge and values that schools choose to cultivate?

THE STATE'S DISREPUTABLE HISTORY IN "MAKING" AMERICANS

The preference-making power of tax-funded schools to pursue some goals and beliefs over others has its own controversial history. Immigration in the first decades of the 19th century raised concerns among influential educators and popular protest among nativists that the American way of life was at risk.[7] They turned to tax-funded schools to forcibly assimilate immigrants into their politically dominant culture. One of the biggest fault lines was religious, as large numbers of Catholics were entering the predominantly Protestant country.[8] At the time, there was little separation of church from state, with Protestant religious instruction and Bible reading a part of schools' curriculum. In intent and effect, the power of the state—funding and operating schools—was used to acculturate the children of families with a preference—their faith—different from those in power.

The educational enforcement of a Protestant way of life drove Catholics out of tax-funded schools. They built and operated their own schools at their own expense. They needed *private* recourse to educate children according to their own conscience. At their peak, these schools enrolled half of all Catholic children in America; today they still annually teach 1.6 million Americans.[9]

Ironically, this issue of religious liberty has come full circle. The privatization project, in its advocacy of school vouchers, has argued that decades of case law separating church and state equate to a state-imposed agnosticism. Vouchers to faith-based schools should be constitutional, they argue; otherwise the state is unconstitutionally imposing a limit on the free exercise of religion. It is a "persecution narrative," with the government "stomping all over the rights of Christians," writes journalist Linda Greenhouse, who covered the U.S. Supreme Court's decades-long conservative turn, including its "inclination to find anti-religious discrimination" at every opportunity.[10] Or, as Katherine Stewart argues in *The Power Worshippers: Inside the Dangerous Rise of Religious Nationalism,* Christian nationalists aim to convert "America's public schools into conservative Christian academies."[11]

A more heinous abuse of state power was the atrocity against Native American children who were forced by the federal government to attend hundreds of government-run schools between 1819 and 1969. As journalist Nick Martin reported, "instructors sought to strip Indigenous youth of their languages [and] traditions." The founder of Pennsylvania's Carlisle Indian Industrial School coined the phrase "kill the Indian, save the man," intending nothing less than cultural genocide. In 2021, U.S. Secretary of the Interior and the first-ever Native American cabinet member Deb Halland directed her department to undertake a full investigation. It found "instances of beatings, withholding of food, and solitary confinement." Investigators also identified burial sites: 19 of the schools "accounted for over 500 American Indian, Alaska Native and Native Hawaiian child deaths."[12]

While in South Africa, I learned how the racist Bantu Education Act was intended by the Apartheid government to keep black South Africans subservient. Under totalitarian regimes, tax-funded schools are used to indoctrinate. In capitalist economies, Marxist scholars argue that state-supported schools acculturate for a life of consumerism.[13] Any schooling, argued Ivan Illich, has dehumanizing and institutionalizing effects, in his famous call to "de-school" society.[14]

Collectively, these wide-ranging examples seem to strengthen the privatization project's case against state power in schooling: In an open society, people should be free to learn and become what they want. Let the chips fall where they may.

THE RISK OF "WORKING IT OUT AT THE POLLS"

Where, then, does this leave a Publicization Project that defines "public education" by the public goods that education should produce? One that seeks schools that prepare a citizenry to preserve our democracy, expand prosperity, nurture a cohesive society, and heal the planet?

A Publicization Project might conclude that *any* education is sufficient. Such a pluralist view holds that people should be free to get the education that they desire, without state interference, as long as it is *some* education. In such a scheme, debates and differences of values get worked out through the political process and in civil society, not inculcation via schools. Education could still be tax-funded, and even compulsory, but its goals would be for families to decide.

But this view is flawed. First, we know that political processes alone are insufficient to address societal differences, as not all voices are equally heard. From discriminatory gerrymandering and voter suppression, disproportionality in Congress, and unequal representation in the Electoral College, to the outside influence of special interests through unlimited campaign donations, we know that the chorus of democracy sings, as political scientist E. E. Schattschneider famously said, "with a strong upper-class accent."[15] Given that wealth and power are distributed along racial lines, the tone of voice is decidedly White.

We further know that educational opportunity, if measured by spending on schools, is not equitably distributed across towns, cities, states, and the country. Even were educational resources to become sufficient and fair nationwide, families still differ in the degree of importance they place on education. This could be mitigated by compulsory education laws, but disparities exist: Today, some states require that schooling begin by age 5 while others state no later than age 8, and until age 19 or as early as 16.[16] All told, these factors limit the ability of *any education,* writ large, to produce the common goods a Publicization Project seeks.

The particular risk to our democracy of an educationally pluralist approach, catering to diverse and privately held beliefs, was dramatically (if indirectly) shown on January 6, 2021. The insurrection at the United States Capitol was an existential threat to our form of government. If successful, it would have had harmful consequences on our society, economy, and environment. Although causes will be studied for years, a known factor was denialism and its assault on fact. Or, more precisely, how insurrectionists judged and weighed information to determine what they believed, and on which they took violent action.

Tragically, it was another disgraceful exercise of state power—cheerleading from the President of the United States—that legitimized fictions about election fraud. Although not officially delivered by the federal government through tax-funded schools, it nonetheless substantiated what insurrectionists unquestioningly wanted to believe—their *private* truths—despite all evidence to the contrary. What the insurrectionists "knew" about the workings of our government, and how their formal schooling prepared them to think about the election's events and evidence, was clearly insufficient. Scholar Mark Danner described it as an absence of any "shared reality."[17] Republican Senator Ben Sasse, echoing Daniel Patrick Moynihan, warned just a few years prior: "A republic will not work if we don't have shared facts."[18]

FACTS AS A MEASURE OF A SCHOOL'S PUBLICNESS

This brings us to a second major objective for a Publicization Project and the next criterion of a school's publicness. The Project must ensure that the epistemology of tax-supported schools is based in facts and the shared norms regarding what we constitute as facts.

Why? All four public goods—democracy, prosperity, comity, and habitability—require that people can judge fact from fiction. These common aims occur when members of a community can discern strong from weak evidence, understand what's adequate to defend a claim, and weigh competing evidence through modes of analysis and deliberation. It also requires a comfort with ambiguity, given the many complexities of life, and an ability to moderate one's understanding in the face of new, emerging information.

Learning all of this, what journalist Jonathan Rauch calls the "Constitution of Knowledge" shouldn't be left to chance, through informal education alone. Nor can establishing facts and preserving fact-making norms be left primarily to scholars, researchers, journalists, lawyers, and civil servants—the keepers of Rauch's "reality-based community."[19] A Publicization Project must insist that teachers and school leaders are part of this community, too, given their unparalleled opportunity to help young people become the informed skeptics that an open society requires.[20]

This asks more of schools than we do today. It expects educators to help students recognize and overcome the cognitive distortions to which we are all prey. These are the mental shortcuts, or "heuristics," identified by psychologists Amos Tversky and Daniel Kahneman, that we use to think fast but not necessarily accurately.[21]

Schools must also teach that knowledge is not one's tribal truth versus another's, but rather a social construct, collaboratively created within certain fact-making norms. Rauch lists two: the "fallibilist rule," in which a claim of established knowledge is debunkable and can withstand attempts to debunk it; and the "empirical rule," which rests on no personal authority, but rather on statements that establish knowledge developed through methods that "give the same result regardless of the identity of the checker or source of the statement."[22]

This asks schools to teach that "objective knowledge is inherently social," as first conceptualized by the 19th-century pragmatist philosopher Charles Sanders Peirce.[23] In this frame, facts are what can be validated by others, are put to the test, and survive falsification. "Unless truth be recognized as *public*," Peirce wrote (emphasis added), "as that of which any person would come to be convinced if he carried his inquiry, his sincere search for an immovable belief, far enough—then there will be nothing to prevent each one of us from adopting an utterly futile belief of his own which all the rest will disbelieve."[24] Except, perhaps, the members of one's own tribe, the very alarm raised by philosopher Hannah Arendt, when "gigantic lies and monstrous falsehoods can eventually be established as unquestioned facts."[25]

Herein lies a puzzle as old as Western thought. People do accept gigantic lies. They do so because the beliefs work for them. Their truths explain, to their satisfaction, the world and their place in it. Ironically, this pragmatic standard—what works—is the same for champions of a "reality-based community" like Rauch. In his tribe (of which I consider myself one), observations and evidence "work." They explain our experiences, until they don't anymore, and new facts come to replace the old, through the fact-making process.

It makes one wonder: What makes one worldview better than the other? Nothing, I suppose. Societies continue to organize themselves around different belief systems. Some are based on infallible totalitarian or religious authority. Others are loyal to folk traditions and conventional wisdom. Some operate in the tradition of Western liberal thought. Aren't they all, on some level, equally legitimate epistemological tribes of one kind or another?

Not if we again apply the pragmatic standard of *what works*. For example, the facts of mathematics are true because the discipline's laws, operations, and internal logic produce reliable and repeatable results. It works. As I've argued, "reality-based" facts are also needed to sustain our democracy, economy, society, and planet. If these four public goods are core to the purposes of a *public* education, a fact-based education *works best* to achieve them. In a fitting parallel, we should consider schools *public* when they teach the knowledge and knowledge-making process that are themselves, per Pierce, open to *public* scrutiny. In doing so, schools bequeath these social, fact-making norms to generation after generation, growing membership in the reality-based community.

* * *

In our diverse and divided country, it remains unclear how an educational philosophy premised on widely accepted facts, alongside knowledge-making norms of evidence, fallibility, and anti-authoritarianism, becomes *the* underlying philosophy of tax-funded schools. No school should do so on my or Rauch's or Pierce's authority, which would violate the empirical rule. Plus, not all schools have to; private institutions exist and educate students according to the dictates of their conscience. But in regard to an education we'd consider public, must the question simply be left to tribal politics? With a Publicization Project coercing schools through pressure, laws, and lawsuits into the reality-based community? Is this the one allowable authoritarian exception, because it protects against all other forms of intellectual authoritarianism?

Or is there some deliberative process around which we can agree to this view? Can the Constitution of Knowledge become the dominant paradigm through the same public and collaborative processes that are its own hallmarks?

This line of questioning rapidly leads us to the question of control: Who decides? If parental control runs the risk of emphasizing private interests over public purposes and state control has its own checkered past, how might an epistemology that advances common purposes be embraced? To make schools more public, particularly in our politically polarized age?

To these questions of governance, I turn next.

CHAPTER 3

Governance

> I'm not going to let parents come into schools and actually take books out and make their own decision . . . I don't think parents should be telling schools what they should teach.
>
> —Former Virginia Governor Terry McAuliffe in debate with (then-candidate) Governor Glenn Youngkin, 2021[1]

> Parents have a right to say that no teacher paid by their money shall rob their children of faith in God and send them back to their homes, skeptical, infidels, or agnostics, or atheists.
>
> —William Jennings Bryan, Scopes Monkey Trial, 1925[2]

So far, I've presented four overarching goals and two criteria, applied with the aid of our exclusion test, by which to judge the publicness of schools. But there's no guarantee that your neighbor wants to pay higher taxes to better educate children in another town or state. Nor is there any guarantee that facts and fact-making norms serve as schools' epistemology, to guide curriculum and content and better produce common benefits. Nor can we be assured that the facts get responsibly situated within competing values in a free exchange of human concerns, as Nel Noddings advocated in her classic *Educating for Intelligent Belief or Unbelief*.[3]

Even if the preceding chapters are persuasive, what students learn and how well their learning is resourced remain choices, issues of governance. Specifically: who controls these choices and how decisions get made. Progressive reformers in the early 20th century succeeded in taking patronage politics out of educational governance. In doing so, they made tax-funded schools less responsive to civic discourse and more under the exclusive control of professional educators.[4] But the long-term effects of this change have debilitated schools' legitimacy and emboldened the privatization project. In response—in order to make school governance more public—a Publicization Project must reverse this 100-year-old arrangement and put deliberative politics back *into* educational decision-making.

A FRAMEWORK FOR DEMOCRATIC EDUCATION

Political scientist and University of Pennsylvania president emerita Amy Gutmann's *Democratic Education* remains the best guide to understanding the publicness of school governance.[5] My critique in the preceding chapter of educational pluralism, with its inherent privateness through a market-based approach dominated by parent choice, draws inspiration from what Gutmann calls a "state of families" of education. In such an arrangement, parents are in control. It risks an education that merely reflects and reproduces parents' private interests, beliefs, and prejudices, regardless of facts and fact-making norms. Absent from this scheme are collective mechanisms to discuss and define the public goods and choice of competing goals that schools might also produce and how best to do so.

Gutmann also describes the undemocratic nature of a "family state" of education, in which those who control the levers of power dictate what children should learn in state-supported schools. Coerced acculturation of Catholics, the abuse and deaths of Indigenous students, and the use of vouchers to sustain racism are all examples of this autocratic and unilateral approach, serving the private interests of those in power. This, too, offers no governing mechanisms to identify and expect schools to produce collectively agreed-upon goals.

Alternatively, in a "democratic state" of education, Gutmann advocates for shared control of schooling among three stakeholders: families, elected officials, and education professionals. The rationale for each? Parents have an intrinsic interest in what their children learn and the values they develop. Elected officials, such as a governor, state education commissioner, members of a board of education, or mayor can mediate the competing interests of families with a community's larger needs, resources, and interests. In doing so, elected officials can ensure that public goods—be it greater economic development or more mutual understanding or however a community defines its particular collective concerns—are served by its tax-funded schools. Moreover, as the duly elected representative of these shared interests, they are held accountable at every election to represent them well (at least in theory).

Third, education professionals, including teachers, administrators, researchers, and subject-matter experts, can ensure that schooling is kept within professional norms and standards. As experts, they represent their field's current consensus, based on facts and mindful of areas of professional interpretation and disagreement (present in the knowledge-making process). They can also ensure that curriculum is taught with profession-accepted best practices.

Gutmann's book-length treatment fully interrogates this useful model. She further requires that deliberation among stakeholders, as they make governing choices about schooling, be respectful and tolerant of divergent views, meeting her proposed standards of "nonrepression" and "non-discrimination." In both we can see the exclusion test, ensuring that ideas and people are not excluded from decision-making, thereby making schools themselves more of a public good.

But just like the economists' simplifying model for public and private goods, things get complicated quickly when Gutmann's framework is applied to the way in which America's 100,000 tax-funded schools are governed today. To begin, where might such deliberation occur? In the absence of a national system of education, there is no formal *national* venue for parents, elected officials, professionals, and, I'd add, a fourth group—ordinary citizens and residents—to deliberate and decide what it means for schools to prepare educated Americans.

At the state level, departments of education have taken responsibility for setting the academic standards that students are expected to meet by different grades. These standards, which govern many school decisions, vary state-to-state, despite recent efforts to have common national expectations. Such standards are often developed by committees of experts and professionals and adopted by elected officials through regulations and laws. These standard-setting processes *may* include civic and parent representatives, but it's hard to identify examples of states having robust and respectful dialogue among stakeholders, à la Gutmann, as to what it means to be an educated Texan or New Yorker. More often it's only a controversial topic, like the teaching of evolution, or how to address racism, or the absence of non-European or European literature on reading lists,[6] that foments general (or gadfly) interest from time to time. Even then, this may occur *after* the standards are developed and adopted.

At the local level, meetings of boards of education are the idealized governance venue for families, elected officials, education professionals, and citizens to come together to voice their views and make decisions about their community's schools. But the governing authority of local boards to take action on these matters has been limited over the years by the growing influence of state and federal regulations that "constrain the potential for community engagement and democratic practice," note Sonya Douglass Horsford and others.[7]

As a result, board meetings more often focus on local, and limited, issues of funding and budgets, high-profile hirings and firings, and student conduct, among other topics unrelated to the broader purposes of education and how these goals translate into content and instruction. Even when curriculum, pedagogy, and learning standards are a topic of discussion, parents may not be aware of alternatives for which they might advocate. Add polarization and fear into the mix—about climate degradation, public health mandates, and our fractured national narrative on race—and these meetings have devolved into ungovernable screaming matches; some board members have even received death threats.[8]

Another governing body, of a sort, where the purposes of education *might* be addressed are school leadership teams in which administrators, teachers, and parents interact. But, again, the topics over which they have control are similarly constrained by federal, state, and district regulations and limited to the interests of those *inside* the school. Parent-teacher conferences, a smaller venue still, typically provide 10-to-15-minute updates on how one's child is doing, not in-depth conversations about goals, content, and approach. Curriculum nights, with presentations by teachers, do more *informing* about activities than dialogue and decision-making.

Two related concepts help to explain this frustrating state of play. First, the notion of "loosely coupled" systems, developed by Karl Weick, describes organizations with numerous parts that are only loosely connected and without clear mechanisms for decision-making and control.[9] American schooling fits this bill, with its layers of federal, state, and local bureaucracy; legal mandates; and rule-based operations. Competing traditions of professionalism, giving administrators and teachers a degree of autonomy, further "loosen" the arrangement.[10]

The second is David Tyack and William Tobin's notion of the underlying "grammar" of schooling. Like a sentence, and despite infinite combinations of words, the underlying syntax doesn't change. Similarly, the structure of schooling rarely changes—and is hard to change—in part because there is no clear locus of control or venue for deliberation.[11] Absent such deliberation, stakeholders may not learn about alternatives or see much reason for children's experience to deviate from their own. Case in point: Sorting students into age-based grades started in the 1820s, was prevalent by 1860, and remains how most schools operate today.[12]

So, imagine a group of parents familiar with project-based learning, in which older and younger students collaborate, who want to see more of it in school assignments. Or teachers who want to add more diverse authors to an English curriculum that's set by the district. Or math education experts who identify a better, research-based way to teach mathematics that's different from the current approach. Or local employers who see that statistics and quantitative reasoning prepare better employees than calculus. Or child development specialists, who find that the structure of schooling, with 50-minute blocks and crack-of-dawn arrivals, conflicts with how the brain learns and the adolescent body works. Or, simply, parents who *don't* have suggestions, but *do know* that the current approach didn't work for them and isn't working for their kid.

To where do they take their ideas? To venues that have the governing authority to make change? In dialogue with other parents, professionals, elected leaders, and citizens? Moreover, who decides on the rules of the road governing such decision-making? To identify matters where it might be appropriate to defer to teachers, such as the best methods of instruction? Or when elected leaders may have the final say, such as the kind of mathematics needed to meet a community's employment needs? Or to parents, on a dress code policy, with its conflicting messages of equality versus uniformity? Or those topics that rightly need the consensus of all stakeholders?

GETTING POLITICS OUT OF EDUCATION

Layers of bureaucracy and loosely coupled structures—that effectively exclude parents, citizens, and civic leaders from democratic governance—are no accident. Education administrators in the early 20th century represented a new, male-dominated managerial class. They aimed to get politics *out* of education by creating, and then running, a "one best system" of education across states and localities, as ironically dubbed by Tyack. These bureaucratized systems intentionally centralized control, impeded deliberation, and insulated self-defined experts from parents and politicians—to do what the administrators knew to be best. Horsford and colleagues show that this mostly White "administrative regime" was "hierarchical and authoritarian," creating solidarity among top leaders to the exclusion of women and people of color.[13] Their education reforms were part of a general rise in the role and prestige of Progressive experts in service of "the people," on taxation, regulation, social welfare, and other policies.[14]

Among Gutmann's three stakeholder groups, this regime made *education professionals* the most decisive, controlling voice in American schools. This governing arrangement persists to this day. Teachers have classroom authority to decide on learning activities and develop lesson plans with their colleagues and leaders. School district employees and curriculum specialists select textbooks and curricula. State education officials set learning standards, define certification requirements, and promulgate other regulations. The arrangement more closely tracks to Gutmann's authoritarian family state than a democratic one, with education experts, like Plato's philosopher kings, determining what children should know and be able to do, along with the content and instructional methods to achieve these objectives.

In fairness, these professionals *do* have more training and educational expertise than most parents or elected leaders. It's an example of the specialization needed in a modern society. As noted earlier, when we're in need of medical attention, we expect doctors to diagnose and treat our condition, and we defer to their expertise.

But unlike medicine, with its grounding in the natural sciences and empirical research, not all of the decisions regarding the purposes and processes of schooling are educators' to make alone. These choices—as to what it means to be an educated American—involve judgments over priorities that have lifelong and community-wide consequences. If, for instance, educators set expectations too low, students' life prospects may be forever limited. Their decisions are imbued with values, too, such as pedagogical approaches that range from team-based collaboration to authoritarian "chalk and talk." This choice of values influences what kind of polity and society students go on to make, an unexcludable, shared concern.

But let's assume, for sake of argument, that education professionals *can* perfectly gauge the will of the people, mediate conflicting interests, and translate this into goals, standards, curriculum, and pedagogy, with nary any meaningful deliberation with other stakeholders. Parents are happy to leave their children at the schoolhouse door and employers are eager to hire well-prepared graduates, trusting that educators are getting it right. Each new generation of citizens does its civic duty, gets along with others, and lives a productive, carbon-neutral life.

Even under such fanciful circumstances, school governance would still not model the deliberative processes that allow leaders, citizens, professionals, and parents to come together to define, *and commit by virtue of their participation* to the private and public purposes of education. It risks turning political, social, economic, and environmental goals into the private—and thereby politically vulnerable—interests of experts, rather than broadly shared commitments. Nor would schools, under such circumstances, be holding their own work accountable to the same collective, open processes through which knowledge gets built. If we use the exclusion test to judge the publicness of educational governance by the extent to which it involves stakeholders in decision-making, today's tax-funded schools fall short.

PRIVATE INTERESTS FILL THE VOID

In the absence of local, state, or national systems of governance empowered to hear, mediate, and heed input from stakeholders to organize a working, if provisional, consensus as to what it means to be an educated American, the void has been filled from time to time by one group or another. For example, in the 1980s and early 1990s, private associations of educators aimed to define what every American should know and be able to do, producing standards intended for voluntary adoption by states (that would, in turn, be *required* of districts and schools).

Their work responded to the 1983 report *A Nation at Risk,* which caused broad concerns about America's international economic competitiveness. It placed much of the blame on America's schools for failing to prepare students to win this global race.[15] Among the many reactions it spurred, the National Council of Teachers of Mathematics developed and released math standards in 1989. The National Center for History in the Schools published history standards in 1994. The National Council of Teachers of English recommended theirs in 1996.[16]

Standards are particularly relevant to issues of governance, given the large degree to which they control what happens inside schools. From the standards flow curriculum, learning materials, assessments, staffing decisions, and priorities both educational and fiscal. As such, the manner in which standards are authored directly relates to the publicness of education control.

As historian and activist Diane Ravitch notes, all three sets of standards became victims of the era's culture wars.[17] The history standards were attacked as politically biased. The English standards were challenged for their lack of rigor and preponderance of fashionable concepts. Even the math standards, which found early success, were later questioned for giving insufficient attention to basic skills. The associations behind these standards were no doubt well intentioned and public spirited. But the standards' fate shows the *political* risk of experts privately deciding in relative isolation what Americans should learn.

Plus, academic disciplines are famously divided. Even if their standard-setting process achieved a level of *disciplinary* consensus, the result was clearly out of step with major segments of society. The authoring process did not organize others' understanding and support. Instead, it mobilized opposition. The experts certainly knew their subject better than ordinary Americans. But they miscalculated in believing that Americans would accept their prescription on their authority, underestimating the country's long history of anti-intellectualism, fickle relationship with experts, and belief that government is, at best, a "necessary evil."[18]

A more recent effort to define and control what Americans should know and be able to do was the Common Core State Standards Initiative. Launched in 2009, the effort was led by the National Governors Association and the Council of Chief State Schools Officers.[19] Leading subject-matter experts were tasked with developing standards in English and mathematics. Teachers served on working and feedback groups. Draft standards were released for public comment and, following review by a validation committee, the final versions were released a short 14 months from the official start of the process. Common Core staff then promoted the standards through videos, meetings, and conferences to inform students, parents, teachers, administrators, and citizens of their content and purpose.

This process gets closer to Gutmann's envisioned democratic state of education, with dialogue among key stakeholders intended to cultivate a shared understanding of what it means to be an educated American (at least in literacy and numeracy). Governors and state education executives are the duly elected and publicly accountable representatives of the polity and its education professionals. Subject-matter experts had a strong voice in the process, commensurate with their knowledge of English and mathematics education. Efforts to inform parents and teachers acknowledged, to some degree, that their buy-in was key.

But the Common Core, like its predecessors in the 1990s, also engendered opposition. One reason was the outsized, some said coercive, role of the federal government in its adoption. Amidst the Great Recession, much-needed Race to the Top school funding from the Obama administration was implicitly tied to states' adoption of the Core.[20] Not surprisingly, 45 states and the District of Columbia had complied by 2013, adopting the Core or modifying their existing state standards to show sufficient alignment.

Some did so under duress, describing the link to funding as unconstitutional "federal overreach."[21] Horsford and colleagues are less generous, calling it an "unabashed attempt to pressure states to align their policies with the administration's federal reform agenda."[22] The Core also engendered right-wing opposition from conservative champions like Phyllis Schlafly, called "Obama Core" a "comprehensive plan to dumb down schoolchildren so they will be obedient servants of the government and probably to indoctrinate them to accept the left-wing view of America and its history." Glen Beck added: "this is the progressive movement coming in for the kill."[23] The Common Core was also opposed by the political left, when teachers and parents objected to the administration tying it to state tests and teacher evaluations.

Any dialogue about the quality of the standards themselves, as reasonable learning goals for all young Americans, was drowned by a hastily pushed system interlocked with unpopular assessments and high-stakes teacher accountability, all developed in perceived isolation by state and federal bureaucrats. The rushed timeline also resulted in precipitous drops in test scores, drawing the ire of politically powerful "White suburban moms."[24] The Core became emblematic of all of this controversy and an easy political target by "one sprawling octopus of an adversary," as then Secretary of Education Arne Duncan later described it.

As I observed Common Core advocates at meetings in New York and Washington, DC, they earnestly defended the quality and value of the standards. Yet too often it seemed as if they were explaining something big, new, and *fixed*. I shared as much, in a large meeting led by a deputy director for the Bill and Melinda Gates Foundation. In Tyack's term, it was yet another "one best" set of standards being imposed on families, children, employers, and taxpayers by a private coterie of experts, rather than as a starting place on which to build and grow over time.

But Core developers like David Coleman, who is now chief executive of the influential College Board, didn't want "too many cooks in the kitchen," for fear of standards being "a mile wide and an inch deep."[25] Inasmuch as brevity is a virtue, Coleman's attitude fails the exclusion test. His sentiment is profoundly undemocratic when setting the expectations that will govern the education of every American student, at each and every grade level, in every tax-funded school.

Secretary Duncan conceded as much: "In the midst of so much rapid change, we proved to be terrible" at explaining to teachers, parents, and students Race to the Top's aims of higher academic standards, use of data, focus on failing schools, and teaching evaluations based on student learning.[26] Indeed. These stakeholders are not a "sprawling octopus." They are Americans, with a legitimate interest in what it means to be an educated American.

Despite initial opposition, the Common Core survived in some shape or form. Controversy subsided when teacher evaluations were detached from student assessments of Core content. Under new names, Core expectations can be discerned in state learning standards, state assessments aligned to the Core, commercial products like Coleman's Scholastic Aptitude Test (the SAT), and publishers' textbooks. Perhaps this represents a win for the one best/knows best experts: Despite all of the sturm und drang, the education industry has coalesced around it.

But on a measure of publicness, the Core is a failure. Duncan missed an opportunity to lead the country in conversation toward a shared understanding of why *any* standards matter, the public and private aims that standards seek to achieve, and what we can agree on, collectively, to govern what schools do. Instead of coalition-building around a core understanding of what American children are taught, the country has become more divided in the decade since the Core was introduced, and student achievement has flagged. Nor can any reasonable person believe that the process was anything but coercive. States aggressively competed for Race to the Top funding, an "infusion of cash like they had never seen before," but not, notably, to the universal benefit of all students. Rather, it was doled out exclusively to states most aligned to the reforms that Duncan "craved."[27]

Even U.S. Senator Lamar Alexander, who in the 1980s was a founding champion of learning standards, pulled his support. Yet Duncan misreads the significance. Alexander's decision did not "exemplify what [is] so often broken in DC politics."[28] Alexander's decision *was* DC politics. What champions of the Core ultimately failed to appreciate is that nothing is more *political* to the publicness of tax-funded schools than what they teach. It is an elementary lesson, apparently learned the hard way by folks in Washington who are supposed to be the political pros.

"EXIT" IS NOT "VOICE"

Right-wing opposition to the standards of the 1990s and the Common Core reaffirmed that the privatization project has little need for deliberative governance structures that identify a common vision of the public and private goals that schools should pursue. It even benefited from the controversy, pointing to yet another failed effort by Big Government.[29] Rather, the privatization project's response remained the same: *Let parents decide.* Let school choice be the way parents control what they want in their children's schooling; it's a simple matter of individual liberty.

In concept, perhaps. Parents might have more say in their child's education when they can choose a good fit between their personal preferences and what a school offers. Such choice is also defended on equity grounds so that no child is forced, by a government-created attendance zone, to enroll in a "bad" school captive to unresponsive professionals who fail to hear or heed the voices of parents, community leaders, and elected officials clamoring for change.

But *choice* as a form of *voice* is limited, at best. As noted above, more choices are inequitably available to families that have the means to move to towns or attendance zones with the tax-funded schools they desire. Within-district systems of choice are only a muted expression of voice, as no district, even one as large as New York City, can cater to every parental preference.

If parents are unhappy with the school they chose, they may speak up and try to effect change via their parent-teacher association, a school leadership team, or some other venue. But within choice schemes, schools have less incentive to respond. Their leaders can conclude that the school is simply not the right "fit" and advise the unhappy family to go elsewhere. Only when large numbers of families leave a school, or the school is unable to recruit enough students to fill its seats, is the market signal loud enough for the school to hear and take corrective action. Sometimes it's too late for a school to recover, when steps could have been made sooner had deliberative processes been in place for stakeholder input, feedback, and change.

In the typology developed by economist A. O. Hirschman,[30] school choice is "exit," not true "voice." It is the method of the market, as when consumers go from one vendor to the next to get what they want. With commercial goods, exit has the virtue of ease: rather than asking Colgate to change its toothpaste recipe, I can simply switch to Crest. Exit is not, by definition, a mechanism for deliberation and an envisioned dialogue among stakeholders about the means and ends of schooling. That requires *voice*—the mechanism of politics.

Nor, in education, is exit all that easy. In economists' parlance, it's full of transaction costs. Students make friends they don't want to lose. Parents are reluctant to disrupt schooling in the middle of the year or outside of breaks between elementary, middle, and high schools. Transportation may be an obstacle. A family may be dissatisfied, but with no meaningful venues to voice concerns, they may choose to stay put and muddle through in silence.

Moreover, exit invites a concentration of similar private interests, as families freely sort themselves, by choice, into schools that reflect their *own* group interests and possible prejudices. As discussed in the preceding chapter, this runs the risk of schools underproducing public goods that are identified through collective deliberative processes—particularly when such goals run counter to parents' individual, private interests. Not interested in an inclusive democracy and society? Or a belief system based on facts instead of sacred texts? Or think that the climate crisis is a hoax? No problem—choose a school that agrees with you, to ensure that your children think the same.

PUTTING POLITICS BACK *INTO* EDUCATION

If, at present, governance of tax-funded schools resembles an exclusionary "family state" with decision-making largely controlled by professional educators, and the privatization project prizes a "state of families," with parents in control via school choice and regardless of the risk to public goods, what are self-described champions of "public education" left to do? In the simplest terms: *Undo* the "one best system," created a hundred years ago by education administrators and that closed off governance from parents and others, and put deliberative politics and decision-making *back into* education.[31]

Supporters of a Publicization Project—those who believe in the public purposes of schools and that schooling must itself be a public good—must engage in dialogue where it exists and demand dialogue where it doesn't. It must actively work to broaden the dialogue, by encouraging others to engage, particularly those with divergent views, so that decision-making is informed by the full range of voices and perspectives among parents, education professionals, employers, citizens, and elected officials. Advocates of this project must be particularly attentive to those who have been blocked out of the conversation. As scholars Gloria Ladson-Billings and William F. Tate wrote, "without authentic voices of people of color . . . it is doubtful that we can say or know anything useful about education in their communities."[32] When this occurs, the exclusion test tells us that schools are simply less public.

Such inclusivity mitigates against any one well-organized special interest—an expression of privateness—from dominating the discussion. Such interest groups, be they champions of computer science, social-emotional learning, or career readiness, hailing from private philanthropy, the teacher unions, or civil society, may *sincerely believe* that they represent more than a vested, private interest. They may present that the makeup of their constituency, or the nature of their cause, serves a larger *public interest*. But this violates Rauch's warning against authoritarianism, in which no one person or group can claim complete perfect knowledge. This particularly applies to claims of knowing the public interest, which is notoriously elusive.[33]

As such, a Publicization Project should encourage participants to defend the publicness of their views by subjecting their ideas to competing claims. By simply asking "Why?" and "What do others think?," the project honors Rauch's two useful rules of deliberation: the need to defend one's knowledge on the basis of reliable evidence (the "empirical rule") and to consider that one's view might be wrong (the "fallibilist rule").

This kind of deliberation is an attitude, an orientation. Rather than trying to win, it seeks to learn and improve one's views by engaging with the thoughts of others. Its venues must be opened up, from state, district, and charter school board meetings to think tank gatherings, policy conferences, and elsewhere. This approach, championed by pragmatist philosophers, asks us to look around rooms and ask: Who's not here? How can we bring them, and their perspective, in? It takes organizers, trained in turning out the *voice*, so to speak. As sociologist Elizabeth Popp Berman notes, it will also require institution-building, of the organizations that nurture and advance this approach. No one entity is responsible for managing it; rather, it's up to advocates of a Publicization Project to live by the values that make school governance more public. Education scholar Marilyn Cochran-Smith and her co-authors describe this as nothing less than "the democratization of power relationships."[34]

RULES OF THE ROAD

Champions of a Publicization Project must also ensure that deliberative governance establishes and honors rules of the road, "jointly determined by relevant stakeholders," adds Cochran-Smith. Such procedures identify the categories of decisions in which some stakeholders have greater expertise and therefore greater say, or greater responsibility and therefore more authority. One such helpful framework to achieve both authentic and functional forms of deliberative decision-making was proposed by Gary L. Anderson. In it he distinguishes between micro- and macropolitical considerations, with degrees of "broad" versus "relevant" participation, mindful of local conditions and processes.[35]

Such frameworks and procedures, once established and honored, can help facilitate dialogue on what issues are of local, state, or national interest and therefore decision-making. For example, I don't have a strong feeling if parents one school or town over want their children to wear uniforms; I do have an opinion on whether my state's standards (and related college admissions criteria) privilege calculus over statistics; by comparison, how slavery and the Civil War are taught is an issue of national concern, if tax-funded schools are to promote a more cohesive country; and I do believe that every student in every class must learn the evidence of the climate crisis and the need to act now.

How might such an inclusive dialogue look? In the above case of learning standards, one could imagine regularly revisiting these educational goals every 5 or 10 years, with town halls and gatherings in every county, enabled by social media, aggregating search engines, and AI technology, informed by research, with input taken seriously.[36] Such an inclusive process would *itself* help to legitimize tax-funded schools. More open deliberation, with greater participation, deepens consensus and builds a broader coalition in support of learning goals. It can inspire greater confidence in educators and generates a wider understanding of the role of schools in the civic, economic, social, and environmental vitality of communities. Generating such trust is also necessary to deepen taxpayers' willingness to commit sufficient resources to the schools in one's own community, and one's neighbors'.

The benefits of greater trust and legitimacy rebut complaints by education professionals that such processes—involving multiple stakeholders, layers of decision-making, and varying degrees of authority depending on the topic—is simply too messy. That it's *unmanageable.* "Just let us run our schools—we know what to do," they say, with a "one best," "triumphant managerialism," notes political philosopher Leo Casey, a longtime union activist and leader at the American Federation of Teachers.[37]

Such a view only sees schooling as the transmittal of knowledge privately defined by experts, rather than in service of public goods that are identified and committed to in collective ways. Such inclusive governance, as messy as it may be, is part of a student's education and society's too. It makes schools more public than private.

FOLLOWING THE RULES OF THE DEMOCRATIC "GAME," OVER AND OVER

Recall that Gutmann calls for such governance to happen through respectful dialogue that doesn't repress or discriminate. It's hard to see this happening today, given that opinions count as facts and that norms of civil discourse are undermined by partisanship, tribal epistemologies, and overt racism. School board meetings, historically "sedate affairs," have become venues for scorched-earth rhetoric.[38] Groups like Moms for Liberty have attacked choices of curriculum, demanding removal of books from reading lists, like Toni Morrison's *Beloved* and Art Spiegelman's *Maus,* that make students "feel discomfort, guilt, anguish, or . . . psychological distress on account of his or her race or sex." Over 900 school boards have been the object of recent right-wing campaigns guided by template language, webinars, and model legislation from the conservative American Legislative Exchange Council (ALEC) on "reclaiming education and the American Dream."[39]

The New Yorker describes it as a "war on public schools" by "partisan saboteurs."[40] But education historian Jonathan Zimmerman, personally outraged by such bans, wryly asks: "Where were you when *Huck Finn* was going away? [It wasn't] because of Ron DeSantis or Moms for Liberty. It went away because of censors on my side of the [political] aisle."[41] The lesson? These are organized groups exercising their democratic rights. They're putting *their* politics into education, to see schools advance what they seek for their children. Ad hominem judgments about their intentions only imply that their voices should be silenced instead of engaged.

The task for a Publicization Project is to organize other voices, countervoices, and get them more robustly into the dialogue. It must stand not only for the books that it believes help to advance the public purposes of schooling, but also for the principles and practices of deliberative dialogue. It takes effort, patience, and courage to hear and harmonize different voices, particularly when some voices, due to the evidence, must change their views more than others.

Turning *down* the rhetorical heat, by modeling these norms, exemplifies the character of conversation that democracies need. It is an act of civil *obedience.* Epistemologically, it shows that acquiring knowledge—in this case the deliberation by which we determine what knowledge *children* must acquire—is "a conversation . . . a journey we take together, not alone," as separate tribes.[42] It's also the simple act of responsible adults showing children how to respectfully engage with others, amidst strong differences of opinion. Educators Ted and Nancy Sizer put it well: *The students are watching*.[43]

Civility can also be nurtured if advocates of a Publicization Project embrace a belief that decisions are only temporary, to be revisited again and again, in an ongoing and inclusive conversation about what it means to be an educated American. Famous experiments in game theory provide empirical, if tangential, proof: Cooperation increases *over time*. When two players keep playing, their behaviors change, from seeking large- and short-term gains to overall larger *and mutual* benefits. A "tit-for-tat" pattern emerges that creates accountability when one player acts selfishly, and builds the trust needed for longer-term collaboration.[44]

As applied to the history of learning standards, Americans have largely been offered a single round of play, like my experience in meetings where the Common Core was presented as fixed—a one-and-done. State officials, professional associations, and advocates suddenly introduced *their* definitive statement of what American students should know and be able to do. Under such conditions, and per game theory, competing interests are highly motivated to play as vigorously as they can to see their point of view written into the standards or see the standards defeated. They are responding as expected within a one-time, winner-takes-all event.

Alternatively, if stakeholders know that the process governing learning expectations will be repeated over time, we find ourselves in multiple rounds of play. Standards defined in any one round are, by definition, provisional, to be revisited and updated regularly. Stakeholders have current *and* future opportunities to win and get their point of view memorialized, for a time, in the school expectations. Repetition also decreases the stakes in any one round, creating room for more civil discourse—a precondition to persuading others to change their minds.

In fairness, the applicability of game theory is not perfect. It assumes the same players, round after round, which is not the case in schooling. Parents' and students' time in a school is limited compared to educators'. Principal and superintendent turnover is high. Such turnover can also work to one party's advantage—like the flashy superintendent who launches a lot of initiatives and then moves on to a new post, or a teachers' union that learns how to successfully play the long game with a revolving door of novice administrators.

Nor should an agreement ever be final. As political theorist Danielle S. Allen argues in *Talking to Strangers: Anxieties of Citizenship Since Brown v. Board of Education*, recurring processes are "the central project of democracy." She shows how distrust is overcome "when citizens manage to find methods of generating mutual benefit despite differences of position, experience, and perspective."[45] She cautions, though, not to expect perfect agreement. "An honest account of collective democratic action must begin by acknowledging that communal decisions inevitably benefit some citizens at the expense of others, even when the whole community generally benefits." Those who lose in one round of play "nonetheless accede to those decisions [and] preserve the stability of political institutions." It is this sacrifice that makes *democracy* possible along with, I would add, *schooling* that is public.[46]

I can't help but wonder if the Common Core, and its subsequent linkage to student assessments and teacher evaluations, would have been more positively received if the Core's proponents had presented a *process* rather than a *product*, with a planned, ongoing dialogue among stakeholders to revisit, revise, and recommit to what we expect of tax-funded schools. In other words, if the Core were construed as a *political* rather than *educational-technocratic* objective, designed to grow and sustain a supporting coalition. Some members of Duncan's own team advocated for an incremental process, and Duncan later conceded that doing so would have built more confidence in public education. But at the time, he didn't agree, saying there would always be "plenty of political pushback" no matter the pace. That "it was all or nothing." In other words: a single round of high-stakes play that united the left and right in opposition. When this happens, it can't simply be chalked up to "strange bedfellows."[47] It's a sign that things have gone horribly awry. You can't blame the politics; you have to *do* the politics.

Is the lesson learned? Advocates of a Publicization Project must demand more inclusive mechanisms in the decisions that govern tax-funded schools. It can make processes more collaborative, over the long term, by convening stakeholders through durable representative organizations. In education at the national level, such groups exist in spades, old and new: the National Education Association was founded in 1857, the National Parent Teacher Association in 1897, the National Governors Association in 1908, the National Association for the Advancement of Colored People in 1909, and the American Federation of Teachers in 1916. Recent upstarts include the National Alliance of Public Charter Schools founded in 2005, Chiefs for Change in 2010, and Black Lives Matter in 2013. The list goes on. Bellwether, an education reform consultancy, lists over 600 educational organizations that share a "commitment to improving education and advancing equity for all young people."[48] Yet many are still entrenched with other like-minded tribes that don't speak across divides. They must.

TRUST OVER TIME VERSUS WINNER-TAKES-ALL

In late 2020, we witnessed the tragedy of a winner-takes-all approach to educational decision-making. The horrific murders of Breonna Taylor and George Floyd were moments of national disgrace. In response, Black Lives Matter amplified its calls for justice, equity, and anti-racist policies, including anti-racist pedagogy and curriculum. This involved legitimate demands to revise the dominant historical narratives taught in schools on matters of race and racism.

Nativist backlash was swift, led by the White House, which called for "Patriotic Education" that excused founding fathers for owning slaves and characterized calls for change as "left-wing indoctrination in our schools," with outrageous comparisons to European fascists.[49] Allied right-wing think tanks took up their pens, arguing that liberal educators "were manipulating students into thinking of America . . . as a shameful embodiment of white supremacy." They found a "perfect villain" in Critical Race Theory (CRT), which examines the systemic ways racism has shaped American society, as an "existential threat" to children and the American way of life.[50] The well-organized response was indicative of the institutions and infrastructure built over decades to advance the privatization project.

Such inflammatory rhetoric is categorically different from how the developers of CRT describe the theory's collection of ideas in understanding American society. As philosopher and legal scholar Kimberlé Williams Crenshaw notes, CRT is "a method that takes the lived experience of racism seriously, using history and social reality to explain how racism operates in American law and culture, toward the end of eliminating the harmful effects of racism and bringing about a just and healthy world for all."[51] De jure and de facto school segregation are examples.

But the issue became so politicized, so quickly, that Texas's Republican-controlled state legislature banned the teaching of CRT. It also required the State Board of Education to draft new teaching curriculum standards for the teaching of slavery and racial subjugation. Other states followed suit, including Arkansas, Florida, Idaho, Iowa, New Hampshire, Oklahoma, and Tennessee, with, at the time of writing, more bills and gag orders on statehouse floors. Across higher education, more than 30 bills in Republican-led states aim to restrict or ban diversity, equity, and inclusion efforts.[52]

Both sides approached the issue as a high-stakes, single-play moment. This does not mean that both sides were equally justified: Nothing is more high-stakes than the life and death issue of race relations, given our nation's racist past and present, as evidenced in the higher rate of violent death among Black and Latinx people, particularly at the hands of police power.[53] How could racial equity advocates *not* seize a moment of national outrage to advance their cause, with demands to replace one historical and educational narrative with another?

But intellectual and social paradigms rarely shift rapidly, as Thomas S. Kuhn carefully examined in his classic *The Structure of Scientific Revolutions*.[54] First, there is often not agreement on the problems to solve. Then we try to solve them within existing paradigms. Once a new paradigm is proposed, it's typically opposed by defenders of the status quo due to their vested interests. Nor is it immediately clear if the new paradigm solves as many of the existing issues as well as the old paradigm.

Some*one's* embrace of a new paradigm, given how different it is from the existing worldview, is "like the gestalt switch, it must occur all at once . . . or not at all."[55] But a *community's* embrace is necessarily gradual, with "the transfer of allegiance . . . a conversion experience that cannot be forced." It's here that Kuhn's title of a scientific "revolution" is unhelpful as popularly understood. Although new, paradigmatic *ideas* are revolutionary, they are adopted by accretion and through the traditional methods of experimentation and persuasion. *Political* revolutions, by contrast, occur when traditional political recourse fails. They are sudden and, dangerously, are often by force.

Pressure politics are an instance of such force. Inasmuch as they seek rapid civic change, they can be stopped in their tracks when the status quo powers are stronger. The backlash to the Black Lives Matter movement—with its greater power to enshrine its will into law—is another tragic example of structural racism. The success of the backlash also illustrates the need to remain within the bounds of "traditional political recourse," characterized by steady organizational and institutional change over time. In other words, a game of repeated play, rather than winner-takes-all. A Publicization *Project.*

Such a decidedly *un*revolutionary approach to advancing revolutionary ideas gets criticized as too incremental, such as by historian and activist Ibram X. Kendi, or as insufficiently structural, as legal scholar Derek Bell (another CRT originator) came to believe.[56] But if we pragmatically judge a tactic by its outcome, it is very hard to conclude that recent demands for anti-racist curriculum were a success.

Danielle Allen helps to explain why. The sacrifice that "is ubiquitous in democratic life" makes "learning how to negotiate the losses . . . fundamental to becoming a political actor."[57] In America, political minorities have learned, all too inequitably, how to accept their losses "without violence or rebellion." In doing so, they grant fellow citizens social "stability, a gift of no small account." In stark contrast, it is the political majorities, all too unpracticed at loss and threatened in winner-takes-all moments of history, who are unwilling to make the same sacrifice. Such refusal to give the gift of stability is seen in ways large and small: from the attempted coup at the United States Capitol to menacing disruption of school board meetings.

"The real project of democracy" writes Allen, and, I'd add, of a Publicization Project for schools in service of our democracy, "is neither to perfect agreement nor to find some proxy for it, but to *maximize agreement while also attending to its dissonant remainders:* disagreement, disappointment, resentment, and all the other byproducts of political loss," by moving "beyond the idea of the zero-sum political game to a conception of reciprocity so fluid that even a winner doesn't expect to stay a winner for long."[58] Because the game doesn't end.

Moving to this mindset, this attitude, in the governance of schools is not a revolutionary event. It requires patient work for decades to come. It asks advocates of a Publicization Project to do the same political organizing that achieved the *Brown v. Board of Education* decision, the Civil Rights Act, and, importantly, their actual enforcement.[59] More recently, it was long-term planning and organizing that equalized marriage, considered one of the most dramatic and swiftest changes in American culture and law.[60] That coalition's project was durable enough to withstand the conservative right's own 50-year, planful effort to control the United States Supreme Court. When, in 2022, the constitutional basis of marriage equity seemed at risk, the coalition mobilized to pass, on a bipartisan basis, the federal Respect for Marriage Act, mandating federal recognition of same-sex marriages.[61] Projects succeed. Their example should give us reason for hope.

PRESSURE POLITICS: HOW DO WE KNOW?

There is a final reason why a Publicization Project should lean into a long-term movement of direct actions and durable governing processes through inclusive, deliberation-based change, rather than winner-takes-all pressure politics. It's also the question that should nag the conscience of every educator: *How do we know*? How do I know if my preferred paradigm is better than another? When I am, for example, as convinced about the sin of racism as White nationalists are in their righteousness?

If my view prevails, how do I know if it's merely the result of my political coalition, in a window of opportunity, being stronger than another? Or because of long-term advantages in traditional power structures, or from newly built barricades? In winning, have I left the other side feeling like it's lost, resentful, and with what consequences? How different are the hard-charging politics that rushed to impose the Common Core through federal coercion from the well-organized local politics driving a nativist backlash to anti-racist pedagogy? Or partisans in the fight over books—with some calling for bans while others, like the group of self-styled "suburban woman" Red Wine & Blue, work to "ban book busters"?[62] Aren't both sides equally convinced they're right? How does *anyone* know?

Amidst such ambiguity, schools sometimes present a consensus view of a topic. But textbooks famously truncate debates.[63] Watered-down accounts minimize dissenting views and disagreements that depend on perspective and context, particularly for the most controversial and, arguably, important topics. For example, I am old enough to remember that states' rights was presented in my Advanced Placement U.S. History class as the prevailing reason for the Civil War. Nor was my experience unique: Historian Donald Yacovone examined hundreds of textbooks published by leading houses from the early 1800s to the 1980s, concluding that schooling has consistently served "the needs of white supremacy."[64]

Today, the states' rights narrative has largely been replaced with a new generation of scholarship concluding that slavery was, in fact, the war's root cause. Historians have archival evidence on their side. Their revised view was responsibly vetted through the collective, public processes by which new knowledge displaces the old. Yet the slavery narrative is likely still rejected in many parts of the country. Simply trying to impose a new narrative, on the basis of expert authority, does not succeed, nor should it. Doing so flies in the face of the healthy skepticism that a democracy requires. It violates Rauch's anti-authoritarian rule.

My highly charged example further shows the special responsibility, and extraordinary burden, on a Publicization Project in rejecting pressure politics: *It cannot force a side.* It cannot simply choose one side's facts and, in doing so, alienate another side's truths. Doing so privileges one private point of view—however mainstream or evidence-based—over another. Doing so only hardens the "congealed distrust"[65] that leads to political failure. Picking a side undermines tax-funded schools' ability to reproduce our democracy for the simple reason that citizens will "no longer think it sensible, or feel secure enough, to place their fates [and the fate of their children] in the hands of . . . strangers."

This is hard to stomach. *It is even hard to write*, particularly when faced with deniers: of climate change, the 2020 election, the Holocaust, institutionalized racism, and other instances where the evidence is incontrovertible and the issues painful, even fatal, to others. Rauch asks, rhetorically, "Aren't those debates settled and far past the point of where airing them does any good? Doesn't continuing them only force [people] to relive pain and suffer indignity?"[66]

Sadly, the mere persistence of the debates shows they are not. Champions of a Publicization Project must accept this, if it is to bring people into a shared narrative and thereby make schools better able to produce the public goods we need from them. As Rauch continues, suppressing ideas doesn't defeat them. Competing ideas win by "holding false claims up to the light of evidence and argument": by teaching the debates—the history *and the historiography*—the facts *and the evidentiary standards*. Rauch, a leader of the marriage equality movement, admits it "stung" every time he was told he could never marry, but found that "every foolish or bigoted claim was an opportunity to make [his] case," respectfully listening and talking, sometimes using humor and the full range of his rhetorical gifts, to change minds.

Otherwise, rejection casts the holder of an idea out of the intellectual, cultural, and political community—in a dangerous form of banishment. It fails the exclusion test by which we measure what makes something more public than private. It is political warfare, waged "on those with whom one will not share a polity," leaving a mob outside of the discourse and a "permanent threat to the public sphere."[67] Hannah Arendt warned of this "great danger," from "people forced to live outside the common world," who are "thrown back, in the midst of civilization, on their natural grievances . . . [who] lack that tremendous equalizing of differences which comes from being citizens of some commonwealth."[68]

We need not take deniers' unsubstantiated *ideas* seriously, nor give any more weight to their views than the evidence allows. But to minimize dangers within our midst, a Publicization Project must take *them* seriously, to understand what is at the root of their beliefs and how they might, willingly, change them. We treat dissenters properly, adds Allen, "because the process of negotiating differences allows for social stability," the same argument made by Mann nearly 200 years earlier. It is the only *political* recourse; the alternative is civil war, "in major or minor keys."[69]

It is possible, and work is already under way. Stanford's Center for Deliberative Democracy convenes hundreds of students and dozens of higher education institutions to collaboratively "shape the future."[70] The University of Virginia's Democracy 360 gathering by the Karsh Institute of Democracy is another. Groups like the Constructive Dialogue Institute, the Deliberative Citizenship Initiative, the Kenen Institute for Civil Discourse, the Bipartisan Policy Center, and Bridging the Gap are advancing this mode of politics, efforts that a Publicization Project must grow.

A more transformative example remains South Africa's Truth and Reconciliation Commission.[71] Its hearings followed the most violent, final years of Apartheid. It gave voice to past atrocities, made space for collective grieving, and brought races together into a new national narrative, both of the past and for the future. Not every perpetrator or victim made this story their own, but enough did to give the new country the much-needed gift of stability. To a young American raised in the North, educated in the South, and mindful of my own country's damaged history of race, watching all of this, up close, was inspiring.[72]

In closing, advocates of a Publicization Project can take further inspiration in guidance from the pragmatist philosopher Richard J. Bernstein, who eloquently describes the attitude that the Project requires. He asks that we

> [take] our own fallibility seriously . . . [be] willing to listen to others without denying or suppressing . . . [and] seek out commonalities and points of difference and conflict . . . [to] genuinely seek to achieve a mutual reciprocal understanding—an understanding that does not preclude disagreement, [and] begin with the assumption that the other has something to say to us and to contribute to our understanding. The initial task is to grasp the other's position in the strongest possible light . . . [and] attempt to be responsive to what the other is saying and showing. This requires imagination, sensitivity, and [interpretive] skills . . . One does not seek to score a point by exploiting the other's weaknesses; rather one seeks to strengthen the other's arguments as much as possible so as to render it plausible.[73]

How do we know? If a Publicization Project is to know *only one thing*, it can be that it lives, and engages with others, by these values.

CHAPTER 4

Standards and Testing

> Young men make wars . . . Old men make the peace.
>
> —*Lawrence of Arabia,* 1962[1]

The question "How do we know?" serves a double purpose for a Publicization Project. As discussed above, it guides the open process by which we collectively and collaboratively determine what we seek students to learn and be able to do, based on what we broadly consider to be of value. In other words, the ongoing publicization of the knowledge and skill expected of tax-funded schools to cultivate in educated Americans.

But the question is also an educator's conscience: *How do I know* if my students met these standards and learned what I intended to teach? If they've mastered a body of knowledge and skill, to engage with even more demanding material? Or if I need to revisit a topic, to clear up misunderstandings? For my students to meet our shared expectations and be prepared in the ways we seek?

Enter what is among the most controversial topics in education: testing. "CANCEL THE F**KING TESTS," read the subject line of an email sent by John Merrow, former *PBS NewsHour* education correspondent, to his large network of prominent friends.[2] Merrow, and other self-described champions of public education, have their reasons. Testing and student data were co-opted by the privatization project in a regime of punitive top-down accountability on schools and teachers. But state tests, and the education standards they intend to measure, have a public-spirited origin worth revisiting for the instructive lessons to advocates of a Publicization Project.

This chapter chronicles how the privatization project misused standards and tests. (Yes, it takes an entire chapter). What a Publicization Project needs to do about it, I discuss in the next.

A NATION AT RISK AND THE RISE OF STANDARDS

In 1989, George H. W. Bush did what presidents had only done twice before in American history: He gathered the nation's governors and, in a first, on the issue of education.[3] Among the 49-plus attendees was future secretary of education and South Carolina governor Richard Riley; soon-to-be education secretary Lamar Alexander, who was then president of the University of Tennessee following 8 years as the state's governor; and an ambitious governor from Arkansas, Bill Clinton.[4]

The convening was a bipartisan response to *A Nation at Risk* and another example of how the influential report stoked fears that America was falling behind because of failing schools. The meeting built on foundational work led by the National Governors Association and was followed by months of discussions, culminating in educational goals announced by Bush in his 1990 State of the Union address.[5]

Bush's goals did not set national learning standards, given doubts about his constitutional authority and lack of political appetite to take this step. Rather, through presidential encouragement and governors' initiative, states picked up the work.[6] Over the next decade, nearly every state set educational standards, providing teachers and administrators with common, statewide learning goals. For the first time, educators could align courses, lessons, and materials to their state's expectations. Common goals for every student irrespective of race, class, gender, or ability could also combat the entrenched injustice of holding groups of students to different expectations.

States also had a growing financial interest in school outcomes, given increased state funding resulting from public pressure and fiscal adequacy lawsuits. *But how would they know?* How would state leaders confirm that standards were being met? If increased funding was having the intended effect? And, collectively, if the nation was less "at risk"?

The solution was state tests, typically multiple-choice, with answers famously filled in with a #2 pencil. Perhaps because it was so novel, I remember when my 4th-grade teacher, Mrs. Minnerly, passed out test booklets and bubble sheets, explaining that it was something new from Connecticut's Department of Education. She encouraged us to do our best and calmed our fears: It would not affect our report cards.

At about the same time, the National Assessment of Educational Progress (NAEP) gained greater prominence. NAEP was created in 1969 with funding from the Carnegie Corporation to randomly sample and test students nationwide on different subjects. In 1988, Congress gave NAEP a formal governing board. Two years later, states began voluntarily administering NAEP tests to a sampling of students before adopting, in 1996, its biannual cadence. Its results are considered the "Nation's Report Card," used by educators, policymakers, researchers, and gadflies to draw conclusions and make prescriptions, like Fordham Institute's pronouncement of a "lost decade of educational progress."

Champions of standards, including Senator Alexander and prominent commissioners like Connecticut's Gerry Tirozzi, encouraged NAEP testing despite a perceived federal encroachment on states' rights. NAEP would give governors data to compare their state's performance to others, they argued. In lower-performing states, the data would strengthen governors' calls for greater investment in education to attract residents and businesses, and to increase economic vitality. It would engender a healthy competition, "in the best sense," to have great schools.[7]

This perspective viewed standards and their associated tests as a valuable *political* tool: to rally citizens and grow within-state coalitions supporting tax-funded schools. Test data could also serve the cause of equity—exposing within-state achievement gaps between wealthy suburbs and poor cities and between students of different race, class, or gender. The political project around this thinking culminated in bipartisan support for No Child Left Behind (NCLB), the 2001 Elementary and Secondary Education Act (ESEA) reauthorization. Learning standards, and their associated tests, were still for states to set. But unlike NAEP's biannual sampling of 4th and 8th graders, NCLB required testing *every* year, in *every* state that accepted federal education dollars, of *every* student in 3rd to 8th grade.

How would states know? The testing mandate—a quid pro quo for federal funding—generated mountains of data to determine how well standards were met. It spurred a cottage industry of data analytic businesses, too, like SchoolNet, The Grow Network, and others. Teachers organized "data study groups" to make sense of it all. How *much* anyone could know from the tests, and how well the data could be used for management and decision-making, remained an open question. The assessments were, and remain, criticized for their poor quality and the limited value of multiple-choice questions scored and returned months after their administration. The tests did at least confirm persistent and pernicious achievement gaps among students by race and class and between states.

If Alexander's *political* prediction had been right, standards and testing would have been a boon for public education, awakening citizens to inequity and an inability to compete economically, allowing leaders to mobilize their support. It would have brought people into a then unnamed Publicization Project, to ensure, as President George W. Bush declared, that no child would be left behind. But the mood of the moment—our national turn toward markets, freedom, and individual liberty—wasn't about shared civic responsibility.

TAXES VERSUS ACCOUNTABILITY

With state testing came accountability. No longer was achievement a local matter, measured by school-developed exams, accountable to the varied expectations of local communities, in the context of an industrial economy where someone without a high school degree could still find middle-class employment. Rather, state standards and tests allowed achievement to become a matter of broader concern—*as intended.* Knowing *what* to expect (the standards) and *how well* expectations were being met (from test data) allowed a conversation regarding *what to do* when they weren't and *who* to hold responsible.

In the 1970s and 1980s, as states were sued to increase funding for tax-supported schools, economists turned their attention to the relationship between school resources and student outcomes. One of the most prominent leaders in this work was Erik Hanushek, whose influential meta-analyses did not find a connection between more spending and stronger achievement.[8] High-profile examples, like New Jersey's numerous *Abbott* fiscal equity court rulings,[9] and its city of Newark, which had some of the highest per pupil spending in the country yet some of the lowest test scores, sowed further doubts as to whether more money was necessary.

This kind of cost-benefit analysis came to dominate U.S. policymaking in the 1970s, particularly in center-left and economics-oriented think tanks like the Brookings Institution, alongside conservative groups like the Hoover Institute, where Hanushek is still a senior fellow.[10] As Popp Berman shows, this approach is embedded within an overall "economic style of reasoning" that values market principles like choice, competition, and especially efficiency—its "cardinal virtue." Institutionalized in policy schools and think tanks, legal frameworks, administrative rules, and evaluation requirements, these economic values eclipsed competing values of rights, universalism, and equality as alternate and legitimate bases for public policy as well as the kinds of arguments made when suing to fund an equitable education.[11]

In education, Popp Berman points to the 1965 Elementary and Secondary Education Act (ESEA), with its universal funding to all schools that enroll low-income students, as in keeping with the tradition of New Deal and Great Society policymaking on the basis of rights and fairness. Yet by 1972, champions of cost-benefit analysis, notably then-Assistant Secretary for Planning and Evaluation Alice Rivlin, demanded a cost-effectiveness study of ESEA's Title I spending.[12] Rivlin went on to create the Congressional Budget Office and receive high-level appointments in Democratic and Republican administrations.[13] Only a few short years would pass before President Reagan's full-throated embrace of markets, deregulation, and privatization.

This emphasis on efficiency is prominent in Hanushek's famous paper, "The Economics of Schooling—Production and Efficiency in Public Schools." His and others' findings allowed a perception that states and localities were *already* providing adequate financial resources. Exaggerating this allowed elected leaders to "preach that resources don't matter."[14] Rather, the arguments went, funding was not as relevant to meeting state standards as how well—*and on whom*—school funding was spent. The sentiment also allowed efficiency-minded policymakers to dodge the damaging effects of poverty on learning, first shown in the 1966 *Equality of Educational Opportunity* report by James S. Coleman and colleagues.[15]

Instead, the privatization project, with its economic style of reasoning, engineered an astonishing reversal: Rather than a nation at risk *that only a nation could save,* by directly tackling poverty, decreasing income inequality, and stopping the flight of capital eroding communities, *schools* were expected to save the nation. Rather than sustain the progress of Great Society legislation and policies (which on the whole are considered a success[16]), the national mood was a callback to the nativist 1800s: It was up to educators to protect the country from the current threat. And if the problem wasn't funding—meaning taxes didn't have to rise—failing to meet state standards must have been a problem of "productive efficiency"—in the *quality* of schooling, and particularly the "economic incentives" of its educators.

ECONOMICS INVADES EDUCATION

Thus began a top-down "era of accountability," explain Marilyn Cochran-Smith and colleagues, on teachers, their education colleges, and the profession.[17] The idea that teachers were not sufficiently incentivized to leave no child behind, and needed to be held more accountable, took extraordinary hold. Teacher tenure, characterized as a "job for life," was maligned as the ultimate disincentive, allowing teachers to slack off. It was, and largely remains, a "failure narrative," expressed in "inflammatory, condescending, or alarming rhetoric."[18]

The era's union animus also played a part, starting with Reagan's busting of the air traffic controllers' union in 1981—a bellwether event in the decline of private-sector unions and attacks on their public-sector brothers and sisters.[19] School districts were maligned as "captured" by the unions—another element of the economic style of reasoning—with administrators unable to fulfill their management and oversight responsibilities. Dating to the 1950s and 1960s, legal and rational choice scholars believed that government regulatory agencies had become "subservient to the needs of business."[20] Their recommendation, for industry and later for education, was *less* regulation and more competition, to let markets work their efficient, quality-enhancing "magic."

It's worth taking a moment to remember that state tenure laws were originally championed in the early 1900s by Administrative Progressives (the reformers of their day) and by teachers to get patronage politics out of education.[21] More concerned about quality than efficiency, tenure aimed to stop the firing of teachers, capriciously or *en masse*, with the spoils of every election.

Tenure laws, often synonymous with a "just cause" employment standard, establish a demanding burden of proof that must be satisfied in cases of workplace discipline and termination. Think of it as being on one end of a spectrum. On the other end is "at-will" employment, preferred by the private sector for the power it gives management to terminate a worker at any time, for a stated reason, or for no reason at all. Management can also treat labor as a variable resource—efficiently raising or lowering staffing levels as the market demands. At-will employment also assumes that employees are mostly incentivized by extrinsic sticks and carrots. Take away the threat of termination, the argument goes, and workers will slack off. Make it harder to fire someone, as does tenure, and educators won't be accountable to work hard and ensure that their students meet learning standards, as measured by the tests.

This reasoning, core to the privatization project, follows yet another economic idea: alignment. Absent alignment of interests, desired outcomes such as better teaching to meet state standards won't be achieved. It's an application of economists' theorized principal-agent problem. A principal hires an agent to perform a task. Short of continuous monitoring, the principal has no way of knowing if the agent is doing the work, on the assumption that the agent has interests different from the principal. In response, the principal clarifies expectations, often in a verbal or written contract, to increase the likelihood of getting what she wants. The contract might specify terms and conditions of employment, like when to report to work and when to clock out. It might include various deliverables to be produced by specified times. The principal then holds the agent accountable to meet these contractual expectations.

The contract might also include performance incentives for further motivation. If a firm's obligation to shareholders is to maximize profits, it can align an employee's interests by sharing the gains. The firm might award bonuses based on performance targets, to get staff to work harder. Continued employment is likely dependent on meeting contractual goals, with the threat of termination believed to be key to aligning a person's individual incentives with the firm's.

Among teachers, this threat is only credible if they are readily firable. This somewhat dismal view of human nature assumes that absent specific expectations, extrinsic and aligning incentives, and high-stakes accountability, teachers won't be as productive as they could be, to maximize production of learning to standards as efficiently as possible. They might, unaccountably, free-ride on the labor of others. The proof? Low test scores.

* * *

Having personally put the privatization project's economic style of reasoning into policy, I've come to believe that "alignment" is a very odd concept to apply to education and, more broadly, the helping professions. Generally, those called to careers in the public and nonprofit sectors are *already* motivated by the mission of the work. As a member of a profession, they are further moved by a professional identity to meet peer expectations. They find *intrinsic* value in the work and are compensated both economically and psychologically by a job well done. In such situations, a worker's personal motives are typically, and *already*, well aligned with the goals of the enterprise. My sister, for example, is proud to *be* a hospice care provider and, despite the low pay, goes above and beyond for her clients and their families.

More often it's *outside* the helping professions, particularly when profit is the goal, where better alignment is necessary for stronger performance. For example, it's the rare salesperson who wakes up every morning with an overwhelming desire to sell as many shower curtain rings as possible.[22] The job is a means for more satisfying pursuits, like having time to serve one's community or church and spend time with family and friends. Regardless of occupation, pioneering research by psychologist Edward Deci and others shows that *intrinsic* incentives are most motivating.[23] Extrinsic incentives can generate short-term changes in behavior. But it's our sense of mission, purpose, and identity that provides the most durable reasons for doing what we do.

Yet by 2009 the privatization project's economic mode of reasoning, wrapped in the politically popular banner of accountability, had embedded "alignment" into the standards and testing movement. With so many test scores, it was conceivable to develop statistical models that would efficiently determine the putatively precise impact of a particular teacher on his students. Being evaluated by these test scores would motivate teachers to work harder and get more students to meet standards. Findings from new value-added algorithms could then be used in employment decisions, particularly to get "bad" teachers out of schools.

This view was bolstered by studies, including work by economist William Sanders, that found that teachers have the largest effect on student test scores among other *within-school factors*, such as class size and spending per pupil. Also influential was John Hattie's review of over 800 meta-analyses of 50,000 research articles, finding that the "teacher–student relationship had one of the powerful influences on student achievement."[24] Meaning, if there was one high-leverage input to focus on, teacher quality was it.

Scholars Andy Hargreaves and Michael Fullan take exception, describing this as the most outdated and "abused educational research finding" to guide recent policymaking.[25] They note that student test scores against standards is a "cumulative effect" from *many* teachers, who exist in professional and employment cultures that need transforming. It also ignores Coleman's findings and later research noting that that *out-of-school factors*, like family income, still have the largest *overall* effect on academic outcomes.

But poverty is harder to tackle, especially amidst a going belief that schools should save the nation and being poor is your own fault.[26] Instead, reformers extolled the extraordinary positive effects of simply firing the lowest-performing 10%, or "teacher deselection," as Hanushek euphemistically argued in *Creating a New Teaching Profession*.[27] States developed value-added statistical models to analyze test data, measured attainment against standards, and identified the unique effects of individual teachers on their students. Laws made these analyses a formal part of teachers' annual evaluations. Extrinsic rewards—but mostly punishments—were adopted to correct teachers' otherwise misaligned interests, in an overall approach that epitomized the privatizing, economic style.[28]

A REFORMER'S CONNECTICUT ADVENTURE

The statistical models and the overall commitment to "alignment" collapsed under their own weight. Value-added analyses were so riddled with methodological problems and margins of error as to make findings useless.[29] Implementation was rushed by arrogant reformers who did not engage with stakeholders—Duncan's "octopus." Teachers avoided getting assigned to grades with state tests, if they could, or focused on students "on the bubble"—those close to meeting standards versus those simply too far behind. It invited "moral hazard"—another anticipatable economic idea—conspicuously in Atlanta, where 44 schools inflated and altered test results within a district culture of "fear, intimidation, and retaliation." All told, it was another chapter of a "recurring factor in American education," in which the "techniques of testing . . . [get] exalted into a faith . . . by those hungry to find its practical application and eager to invoke the authority of science on behalf of their various crusades."[30]

I experienced such a collapse firsthand, and bear some responsibility for it, when I advised Connecticut's then-governor Dannel Malloy and his education secretary Stefan Pryor on their school reforms. It was 2011, in the heady days of policies demanded by Race to the Top (RTTT) funding. In such a blue state, Malloy knew that teacher union support would be key. Pryor's natural instinct is for dialogue, to find and create common ground. I was engaged given my experience on both sides of the educational divide, with charter school reformers and teacher union leaders.

The administration got off to a good start—negotiating a tenuous agreement on new teacher evaluation regulations with a large cross-section of stakeholders, including the unions. Malloy wanted student test scores to weigh the most among other metrics. A compromise was reached around a majority composed of scores from a teacher's own students as well as whole-school performance. The enabling state regulations asked teachers and administrators to co-develop and agree on personalized student learning objectives, or SLOs, against which a teacher would be evaluated. The approach was working well in New Haven, which had made national headlines for its innovative approaches.[31]

But the fragile coalition fell apart, and acrimony quickly ensued, when the governor introduced legislation linking evaluations to the process by which teachers would earn and retain tenure. Against our counsel, but in keeping with national rhetoric, Malloy pointedly attacked tenure in his address opening the state's 2011 legislative session.[32] His bill, which I had a hand in drafting, was like others sweeping the nation: another tightly interlocking system to fully align teacher incentives around student achievement.

Given the state's distressed finances, Malloy's speech and bill was a bit of a desperate advertisement for much-needed RTTT funding. We also, naively, believed that a political window had opened to lock these reforms into law. Instead, the situation degenerated into a single-round game of pressure politics. The Connecticut Education Association (CEA) and the American Federation of Teachers-CT (AFT-CT) mobilized teachers and parents against the bill. Malloy faced angry crowds in town hall after town hall. The bill was lambasted by pundits as "corporate reforms"—an anti-privatization project phrase that caught on nationwide.[33] Nor could the state's anemic community of education reformers mobilize supporters in anything close to equal numbers.

Well-organized opposition weakened the resolve of state legislators from Malloy's own party, who held majorities in both houses. A placeholder bill, which made no mention of the most controversial proposals, was passed by the education committee to save the governor from the embarrassment of a bill not reaching the Assembly floor.[34] Weeks of negotiation ensued. One memorable session between the governor's staff and legislative leaders occurred inside the state capitol as teachers rallied outside.[35] Their chants of "we need a voice" echoed throughout the building. The demonstration strengthened the unions' already dominant bargaining position, enthusiastically represented by then-state senate leader Donald Williams (who now serves as the CEA's executive director). The chanting provided negotiators with a much-needed, if brief, moment of levity, as the irony wasn't lost on anyone.

We ultimately came to an agreement in the early-morning hours of the last day of the legislative session. The final version of Connecticut's 2012 education reform law passed unanimously in its House of Representatives. Described as a "centerpiece" achievement, it included greater state financial support and oversight for struggling districts.[36] It created a "Commissioner's District" to help the most troubled schools. The process by which teachers achieved tenure was left unchanged. Plus, the seeds of challenges to other provisions still disagreeable to some stakeholders were planted during the bill's final floor debate. Carefully phrased questions and answers about legislative intent were written into the official record.

The experience was humbling, to say the least. We passed a good law that allowed state education officials like Andrew Ferguson, who directed strategic initiatives, to provide meaningful support to Connecticut's most struggling schools. Nuanced teacher evaluation regulations, clarifying how to co-develop and implement SLOs, were adopted thanks to the tireless public service of noted educators Diane Ullman and Emily Byrne.

But we were also young men and women waging the reform war. We were witting contributors to the privatization project, caught up in the moment of a governor trying to make a national mark and a federal government aggressively asserting its agenda. We were convinced by the virtues of economic reasoning—if we ever really understood those assumptions—and failed to heed Professor Bernstein's assumption of fallibility. Nor did we take sufficient time to deliberate with stakeholders to hear their differences in a belief that their ideas could improve our own. We could have, at a minimum, better gauged the limits of our political strength. Instead, we were small boats riding an intellectual wave, crashing into political shoals. But now that we are older, and perhaps wiser, what kind of peace do we want to make?

THE WRONG LESSON TO DRAW FROM A MODEST VICTORY

Defenders of public education were emboldened by Connecticut's experience. It indicated that the privatization project's corporate-style reforms and market-based theories were not invincible—at least in this one deep-blue state.

But standards and tests aren't going away, no matter how much John Merrow and others may wish to see them canceled. Nor should they. The four public goods that we need schools to produce are themselves overarching expectations—standards—through which a Publicization Project must strengthen schools' publicness. Many other standards, of a smaller, more measurable scale, are needed to know that these larger aims are being met. Simply defeating how standards were *used* by the privatization project is insufficient, as standards will remain full of private interests if not commonly developed in ways that rally collective will.

The same must be said for testing. A Publicization Project should object to the narrow use of multiple-choice tests as the sole, sine qua non of acceptable data. Knowledge about student learning, the quality of teaching, and arguably any social phenomenon is best constructed from multiple sources of information, both quantitative and qualitative, and judged with informed perspectives in the light of context.

This chapter showed how that doesn't happen when top-down accountability is narrowly placed on teachers, for performance that may or may not be in their full control, based on weak data and faulty economic assumptions. But it *is* possible when standards and evidence are part of a regime of *mutual* accountability, which the Publicization Project should embrace, as discussed next.

CHAPTER 5

Accountability

> The sea rises, the light fails, lovers cling to each other, and children cling to us. The moment we cease to hold each other, the moment we break faith with one another, the sea engulfs us, and the light goes out.
>
> —James Baldwin, 1964[1]

Accountability's twin is legitimacy. A Publicization Project must embrace accountability that is consistent with its goals and values for its efforts to be credible.

Such credibility must be restored, given that the privatization project has spent the past 40 years delegitimizing the public sector and its professionals, starting with Reagan's inaugural call to arms: "In this present crisis, government is not the solution to our problem, government is the problem."[2] Unaccountable bureaucrats, leading expensive and ineffective programs and protected by public-sector unions, were common attacks. In contrast, the private sector's promised efficiency, its ability to deliver what consumers want via market-based accountability, was the answer. This narrative remains strong today, with the president of the conservative American Enterprise Institute derisively asking: "Is the era of big government back?"[3]

At the start of this book I built a definition of *public* education as schools that produce public goods (democracy, prosperity, comity, and habitability) and that don't exclude (thereby making *themselves* a public good). I've also called for a Publicization Project to strengthen this publicness in how schools are funded, their underlying philosophy, in governance, and the use of standards and tests. All in all, it's a turn away from the individualism of markets toward the community of politics.

To be legitimate among the many stakeholders needed for such an ambitious effort, this new Project must overcome the popular belief that anything other than top-down and market-inspired accountability mechanisms is an avoidance of responsibility, just more of the status quo. As this chapter argues, a Publicization Project can surmount these perceptions, and be understood as a credible alternative to privatization, by demanding *and holding itself to* a regime of *mutual* accountability. I open this section with a brief review of market-based accountability in light of the preceding chapter, before examining what a regime of mutual accountability might entail.

* * *

In the late 1980s, the rising tide of privateness generated renewed interest in vouchers to private schools and outsourced management of tax-funded schools to private companies, and starting in the 1990s, government authorized but privately operated charter schools. With a choice of schools, parents would decide where to send their children, in deference to what they knew best. Placing management companies on terminatable performance contracts would solve the principal-agent problem, incentivizing operators to perform or perish.

Many of these ideas, first introduced by economist Milton Friedman in the 1950s, were given renewed life with the 1990 publication of *Politics, Markets, and America's Schools* by political scientists John Chubb and Terry Moe.[4] In their influential book, Chubb and Moe argued that a government-led approach to school improvement wasn't working and wouldn't, given bureaucrats' self-interest to protect the status quo, agency capture by the teacher unions, and lack of accountability. They extolled the benefits of competition and pointed to freedom from regulation and union contracts as key reasons for student success in private, mostly Catholic, schools.

Their predicted school choice "panacea" concluded with a set of sweeping recommendations to restructure public education according to market principles, with vouchers redeemable at government-operated or private schools in competition with each other for students. The invisible hand of market-based accountability, they argued, would improve school quality and drive poorly performing schools, unable to recruit students, out of business.[5] I worked closely alongside John in the final years of his too-short life, through our education consultancy, and found that his faith in markets and individual liberty was nearly complete.

With Chubb and Moe in mind, one interpretation of the preceding chapter is that teachers are, in fact, unaccountable bureaucrats opposed to performance-based accountability. It follows that the Obama Administration's "craved" use of test data in employment evaluations, to align teachers' self-interest with the state's interest in student achievement, was correct policy. Secretary Duncan's efforts failed, not on the merits, but only because his coalition didn't have enough strength, in a single-round game of pressure politics, to overcome teachers' well-organized pushback.

The opposite view might see it as a rare win for a Publicization Project. Mission-driven teachers already feel intrinsically accountable to students and families. The corporate, privatizing notion of aligning around performance, through a flawed test-and-sanction system of accountability, wouldn't have done anything to raise achievement above current levels. What it did raise was anxiety and unhelpful disruption, and its failure was deserved. Some evidence for this interpretation was provided by the charter school sector: Its leaders, typically champions of test-based accountability, were skeptical of teacher evaluation mandates.[6]

Today, public education advocates may feel emboldened that the political tide is turning, away from free-market neoliberalism toward a belief that government can and has a responsibility to be a force for good.[7] They may be relieved that this turn does not (yet) seem to include a belief, as promulgated by *A Nation at Risk*, that schools are both the problem and solution to the nation's economic, social, racial, and environmental crises. But none of this means that public education has expunged the privatization project. As Elizabeth Popp Berman cautions, the "economic style" has become "thoroughly naturalized" as the "taken for granted approach to policy problems"; it defines "the boundaries of what is seen as politically reasonable."[8] Case in point: the failures of the Obama Administration further delegitimized public-sector solutions and renewed calls for billions in vouchers.[9]

A Publicization Project is left with an obvious question: What *kinds* of evidence and what *uses* of this information, among *whom*, and *to what standard of effort*, will create conditions that legitimize the work of tax-funded schools?

Mutual accountability offers an answer, in which responsibility is vested among stakeholders for what can rightly be considered each's respective obligations. It is what Sonya Douglass Horsford and colleagues call *reciprocal* accountability, envisioned by Cochran-Smith in arrangements with "representation of all stakeholders."[10] Legal scholar Lani Guinier viewed such collaboration, including "students, parents, teachers, and administrators," as necessary to equitably help students cultivate skills, knowledge, and innate talents.[11] This orientation further connects the Project to the roots of the accountability movement, seeded more than 30 years ago at President Bush's convening of governors, with its vision to set goals, measure progress, and, in doing so, create *collective will*. Doing so is more likely to make schools more public, *particularly when done with evidence fit for each purpose*. Here's what obligations in a regime of mutual accountability could entail.

THE PROFESSION'S OBLIGATIONS

What should every teacher know and be able to do, in order to teach well? This is an answerable question that, regrettably, and despite mountains of evidence and national efforts, *the teaching profession* has not yet sufficiently answered to its and others' satisfaction.[12] Hargreaves and Fullan point to "a lot of argument and more than a little aggravation" over disagreements, with only "pockets" of "balkanized" educators teaching well.[13] Advocates of a Publicization Project should demand that this question be answered, so that there is a basis on which to work, to ensure that every student receives a quality education, facilitated by teachers who meet *their own profession's* expectations.

At present, states have different teacher certification requirements. Recent staff shortages have led some to lower job qualifications, as in Florida and Arizona, where a bachelor's degree is no longer required for some positions.[14] The Council for the Accreditation of Educator Preparation (CAEP) claims to assure the quality of K–12 instruction. But its efforts to serve as both "watchdog" and as the "single voice" of the profession have been "fraught with criticism from both within *and* outside of the profession," hindering its legitimacy.[15]

Nor did the recent push by federal policymakers to evaluate teachers by student performance do much to answer the question. Rather than defining good teaching, the effort assumed that good or bad teaching simply gets reflected in test scores. Economist Raj Chetty, a pioneer in value-added modeling, confirmed as much: The data only established that "some teachers are able to raise test scores more effectively than others" and not "whether this is driven by teaching to the test or 'deep learning.'"[16]

Meanwhile, entrepreneurial educators like Bob Marzano, Charlotte Danielson, and Doug Lemov entered the black box and came out with their own answers, respectively *The New Art and Science of Teaching*, Danielson's *Framework for Teaching Evaluation Instrument*, and *Teach Like a Champion*.[17] Their work is detailed, ranges from progressive to baldly instrumental, and is in some cases public-spirited. But they remain private actors, with personal perspectives, commercializing their recommendations.

Perhaps the closest approximation to a collective answer regarding what every teacher should know and be able to do—from the profession itself—is offered by the National Board for Professional Teaching Standards (NBPTS). This nonprofit, private organization was founded in 1987 by prominent educator, labor leader, and American Federation of Teachers president Al Shanker. As its name suggests, NBPTS articulates teaching standards, but at a level of abstraction that gives educators discretion in their practice. This is a good thing in work that's so contingent on content, context, culture, and a learner's prior knowledge.[18] But such generality also risks the persistence of specific teaching approaches that the profession, if asked, would not consider best practice. Nor has NBPTS's impact been as large as one might hope: to date, only 125,000 teachers are NBPTS "board-certified," representing 3.4% of all *current* teachers (and a much smaller percentage of all teachers over NBPTS's 30-year history).[19]

In the absence of widely accepted, profession-endorsed standards of teaching *practice*, it's only a classroom wall that unjustly separates students who get a great education with a teacher who knows her pedagogical stuff, from students who don't have the same opportunity. This state of play invites private interests to assert themselves, as when parents lobby for one teacher over another, or when a school "follows" Marzano or Lamov. It deepens inequity, as when wealthier districts recruit and retain more skillful teachers. It causes national disruption, as when literacy expert Lucy Calkins, whose own approach had "determined how millions of children learn to read," recently made "a major retreat" in the debates over literacy education.[20]

Mutual accountability must begin within the teaching profession, in calls like Hargreaves and Fullan's, for collective professional responsibility to transform teaching in every school, and Cochran-Smith's, for everyone "involved or invested in the larger teacher preparation enterprise to reclaim accountability" in service of "the larger democratic project."[21] How? Imagine a Publicization Project calling for a national teaching summit, not unlike the 1989 gathering that launched the standards movement. Its goal would be simple: define the *specific* teaching practices that every teacher should know and be able to do to teach well, relevant to any learning objective and in particular service to a *public* education's four overarching aims of democracy, prosperity, comity, and habitability.[22]

Here's where the "grain size" matters. General guidance to "facilitate class discussions" allows for everything from aggressive cold calling (which may shut down learning) to wildly branching discourse (cut off from any learning objective). Admittedly, teachers have different *styles*. But within *profession-defined best practice*, all should use a common *substance* like not answering one's own questions, giving students time to meaningfully engage with ideas, facilitating peer-to-peer discussion that requires careful listening, building on preceding ideas and making connections between them, supportively correcting misunderstandings so that incorrect information doesn't take root, following students' own lines of thinking to novel and insightful ends, not yelling, and being patient.

Specificity is key and doesn't mean uniformity. If the profession agrees that context matters, with different students engaging better with different practices, the envisioned range of recommendations would provide enough choice for any one teacher to select the best approach for a particular moment. This rightly honors professional judgment and the nuances of a given situation. This is also the level of detail required if any teacher is to understand, with any clarity, what constitutes effective practice and, by consequence, be accountable to what his profession expects him, minimally, to do.

Such a summit would ask stakeholders to define a multitude of specific and actionable techniques by major domain of practice, from course design and student engagement to the development of assignments and equitable grading. Recommendations would need a basis in research and recent discoveries in neuroscience and the learning sciences, as accessibly described in works like Susan Ambrose and colleagues' *How Learning Works* and Daniel T. Willingham's *Why Don't Students Like School?*[23]

At present, no one body speaks for the teaching profession, as one can find in other professions. Claims of authority by the National Education Association and American Federation of Teachers are challenged by education reformers, and the two sides hardly speak to one another. CEAP has had a troubled history. Other groups that present a big umbrella, like the National Council on Teacher Quality (NCTQ), have engendered more controversy than consensus.

As such, such a summit must broadly invite a diverse group of stakeholders representing competing schools of thought, or risk failing the exclusion test. We'd see experts like Marzano, Danielson, Lemov, and Calkins, along with Carol Dweck on mindset; Deborah Ball on mathematics education; Lisa Delpit, Gloria Ladson-Billings, and Laura Rendón, for their pioneering work in culturally responsive teaching; Linda Darling-Hammond, who for decades has led on issues of teacher quality and, recently, licensure standards through EdTPA; and José Bowen and Flower Darby on teaching with technology, alongside many other leaders in the field. Organizations that champion great teaching, like NBPTS and NCTQ, CAEP, the Interstate Teacher Assessment and Support Consortium (InTASC), and the new Association for Advancing Quality in Educator Preparation (AAQEP), would have a seat at the table. So would disciplinary associations like the Council of Teachers of Mathematics, teacher leaders from their unions, and educators nominated by their schools and districts who exemplify best practice.

But participation, if under the banner of a Publicization Project, is not without preconditions. Contributors must want to make schools more public, as we've defined, and regardless of type—district, charter, or otherwise. They must also commit to our rules of deliberation needed to construct knowledge socially: defending one's knowledge claims on the basis of reliable evidence (the empirical rule) and the pragmatist imperative to consider that one's view might be wrong (the fallibilist rule). If one group, say NBPTS or Lemov's Uncommon Schools, believes its existing teaching approaches already have the answer "right," then let them present their *reasons* to others who may disagree, and *justify* their knowledge claims. Let them *invite* the critique provided by our epistemological rules and embrace the solidarity of believing that one's view can be strengthened by another's. Only under such conditions does space exist for professional consensus.

Even then, it is not the one best set of practices we seek, but the least bad process. Such an approach advances a pedagogy grounded in democratic deliberation. It also protects against authoritarian influences, as in the case of Calkins, and subsequent loss of legitimacy, when those same authorities, however expert, suddenly reverse course or are challenged by other well-organized critics acting on the basis of political power, rather than collaborative persuasion.

A final precondition: once these practices are defined, the organizations and individuals must collectively commit to them. In game parlance, they may not defect. They must hold one another accountable to see their agreement implemented, through whatever direct authority or indirect influence each has, as members of the Publicization Project. To lower the stakes and build trust, they would also commit to regularly revisiting these specific standards of teaching practice in order to keep up with developments in the field, make changes over time, and increase collaboration today through the promise of future rounds of play tomorrow. Self-exile or banishment are not allowed. Like democratic citizenship, this requires sacrifices for the sake of professional legitimacy and educational stability—things that every educator has an incentive to see come about. Otherwise teaching will remain, as famously impugned by the late scholar Richard Elmore, a "profession without a practice."[24]

PREPROFESSIONAL ACCOUNTABILITY

With specific teaching practices in hand, collectively defined and committed to by representatives of the teaching profession, a Publicization Project must hold institutions accountable to meeting them. This begins with colleges of education. Their methods courses, required of aspiring teachers, must prepare teacher candidates in these particular pedagogical approaches. The same would go for alternate certification providers outside of academia. Performance tasks and other demonstrations of skill should be used to determine if such practices have been sufficiently developed. Prior to graduation, teacher candidates should be required to demonstrate both knowledge and skill of the approaches.

Similarly, state agencies should align licensure requirements to these practices, requiring that job-seekers demonstrate their command of these essential approaches. Nor should any school hire a teacher that didn't show these skills as part of the hiring process, through demonstration lessons, video artifacts, and other evidence. Preprofessional training need not be *limited* to these methods, but any graduate must, at a minimum, command them as the prerequisite foundation of profession-defined, evidence-based teaching.

This change won't be easy. Cochran-Smith and colleagues present one of the most affirming versions of this kind of change in *Reclaiming Accountability in Teacher Education.* But they concede that university teacher education has its problems, not the least of which is "markedly uneven quality across programs and institutions."[25] It is conceivable that a floor of practice, endorsed not just by a Lamov or Calkins or Darling-Hammond but by the collective representatives of the profession, could bring a degree of quality control across the sector.

Harder to overcome will be the "failure narrative" describing education schools as "making no discernable difference" in student outcomes, captured by a "liberal bias," and "preoccupied with theory." It is an old critique, as sociologist David Labaree described in *The Trouble with Ed Schools*, stemming from problems intrinsic to preparing a mass workforce in ways "that [do] not cost much money or require much time." Or, as

Hofstadter wrote in 1962, citing research from *1939*, we have sacrificed "quality" of teaching for "quantity" of teachers.[26]

The recent critiques were lobbed by a loosely united group aligned around a neoliberal ideology, notes Cochran-Smith—in other words, the champions of the privatization project. But Cochran-Smith errs in dismissing their "potent concoction of contested empirical assertions" because it was "all wrapped up in politics . . . and political agendas." Rather, ed schools and their champions need to *get political* as part of a Publicization Project. Anything else feels like a surrender to others who are allowed to seize a greater claim to the levers of power, or more of the naïve belief that we can somehow take the politics out of education *schools*.

Hardest to convince may be education school faculty and alternative preparation providers. Both groups consider themselves experts and may take umbrage at an external imposition of the practices to teach in methods courses (and presumably to model themselves). But a professor or instructor's desire to prepare teachers differently, based on what she "knows best," has little defense in light of teaching practices defined by the profession through a process that presumably includes esteemed colleagues.

Rather, this professor should be invited to engage in the next round of play, to present and give reasons that justify her approach and, if persuasive, contribute to revisions that keep the field moving forward. She may point to the complexity of teaching involving culture, language, and identity and seek to ensure that the range of practices are sensitive to these nuances. And nothing stops her from experimenting, in ethical ways, to identify new approaches. The iterative process, as proposed, moves a profession forward in a more orderly way. Need we remember, doctors no longer use leaches, but they *do* practice with their profession's *current* consideration of what's best, in a field that's always innovating.

Otherwise, breakthroughs don't break through as broadly and publicly as they deserve. Deborah Ball's innovations in mathematics education remain reserved to aspiring teachers enrolled at the University of Michigan, where Ball teaches; school districts that choose to work with Ball's consultancy, Teaching Works; and the attendees of her conference sessions.[27] The same can be said of Lucy Calkins's work in literacy education at Teachers College, Columbia University, as informed by the earlier efforts by Donald Graves, now commercialized by Pearson. Or Lamov's *Teach Like a Champion* prescriptions that for a time only circulated among charter schools. If, instead, their ideas enjoy the profession's consensus, as imperfect as its knowledge is at any given movement, the approaches should be brought to life in every classroom, excluded from none, *as long as and until* the next iteration. This approach may be too incremental for some. But it stands the chance of better disseminating best practices to every educator, and overcoming the failure narrative that dogs the field. It also spares us from the policy wars waged over how best to teach reading and math and the abrupt, edu-celebrity driven shifts affecting millions of students. Surely we can do better.[28]

THE POLITY'S RESPONSIBILITIES

With accountability from the teaching profession to define and regularly update standards of specific practices, and a preprofessional commitment from education schools and other teacher preparation providers and from state licensure boards and hiring committees to enforce them, key parts of *mutual* accountability begin to connect. But such standards will likely raise the bar, restricting entry into the teaching profession to only those who demonstrate such skills and dispositions through performance tasks and demonstration lessons, in the eyes of those who know what to look for.

Enter a conundrum facing all professions: Restrictions on entry—as a control on quality—work well in fields with relatively smaller numbers of practitioners, as in medicine with surgeons. But quality-control standards work less well with mass-produced services—like universal free education, which requires millions of teachers. Restrictions risk labor shortages if the bar is set too high. A case in point: Calls for smaller class size, requiring *even more* teachers, are criticized on the ground that instructional quality will suffer. Florida's and Arizona's recent lowering of job qualifications is an attempt to address current shortages.

But this presents a rare scenario where a Publicization Project should enthusiastically embrace a lesson from the private sector: demand more pay to get the talent it seeks. By embracing teaching standards, advocates of a Publicization Project must hold localities, states, and the federal government accountable for providing the resources necessary to attract and retain educators who meet and are held to their own profession's expectation of best practice.

As noted in Chapter 1, this is a level of resourcing that we do not currently achieve, certainly not equitably, in every tax-funded school. Alongside salaries and benefits, resources must also be sufficient to maintain working conditions that allow teachers to perform their craft in profession-expected ways. It is one thing to know *how* to ply one's trade well, quite another to be in situations where one *can*. The best angler cannot catch fish with broken tackle in a river running dry.

Even former Education Secretary Duncan agrees: Teachers "should have better pay, more access to funding for their classrooms, and more respect from political leaders . . . [who have] starved their systems."[29] But Duncan, like so many reformers of his ilk, continues to narrowly construe accountability as top-down. His notion of a "grand bargain" envisions more resources in return for "more accountability" *of teachers,* as if they were solely capable, and should have full responsibility, for student achievement. Mutual accountability is a grander idea, in which a Publicization Project must hold public officials accountable to tax and spend accordingly. Not through competitions that fund some schools and exclude others, but each and all.

Such a *shared* social contract is, at present, broken in many places across the country, as Leo Casey demonstrates in *The Teacher Insurgency*.[30] Public disinvestment has steadily eroded the conditions that would attract and retain talented educators—those most able to meet high standards of teaching practice, in working conditions where they have a reasonable chance to apply their craft well. Such disinvestment prompted a recent wave of teacher strikes and political actions in West Virginia, Arizona, Oklahoma, Kentucky, and elsewhere.

Casey interprets this as teachers re-embracing a necessary political-civic identity. But teachers and their unions alone cannot hold public officials accountable for necessary resources. Their advocacy is too easily dismissed by opponents as material self-interest. A larger coalition, formed by a Publicization Project, is required, one that includes taxpayers who see the value of tax-funded schools and their need for more tax dollars.

Perhaps the most famous example of where this has worked comes from Finland. While the "Global Education Reform Movement" was preoccupied with high-stakes testing and market-driven competition, making "the work of teaching so unappealing that it can't attract the best qualified universities to do it,"[31] Finland invested in the profession and gave it high status. Teaching there is understood as a contributor to "economic prosperity, cultural creativity, and social justice." It is paid well, and schools are well equipped. The larger social-welfare net combats inequity and releases schools, as employers, from meeting teachers' larger health care, family, and retirement needs. As a result, its educators are "superbly qualified, well-trained, and effectively supported," in a system and culture that has generated some of the highest student performance results on international measures.

Hargreaves and Fullan, who studied Finland's experience and led similar efforts in Alberta and Ontario, note that "we tend to dismiss" these examples "too quickly when their politics don't fit our [country's] own ideology." And that's the point of this book. Our politics are what we make them, the result of political projects.

EMPLOYMENT ACCOUNTABILITY

Mutual accountability must extend to employment, if a Publicization Project is to offer a legitimate alternative to the privatization project's well-organized attack on tenure, hiring, and firing. Absent incentive-aligning sticks like performance evaluations based on standardized test data, their argument still goes, America's students won't get the quality of education they deserve.

I got caught up in this thinking, too. But now, out of the crucible, my sense is that the vast majority of teachers are already hardworking, mission-driven, and highly motivated to help their students succeed. Their personal incentives need little aligning to their school's goals. Teachers know *what* they are tasked to do: on-grade-level reading and mathematics, personalized instruction, and closed achievement gaps, among other goals. But I've come to sympathize with the extent to which teachers don't always know *how*. It is a function of the lack of profession-defined standards of practice and solid preparation and support in these approaches, as well as an isolating tradition of individual classroom autonomy making for the "loneliest profession."[32]

For example, how, precisely, should a teacher help a student whose reading ability is more like that of children many years younger catch up to her peers? While teaching a class with two dozen or more other students? Or many sections of a subject with a teaching load of 120 students or more, and only 50 minutes a day with any of them? These are not questions of *motivation* (although such conditions might be *de*motivating). They are questions of technique—the specific pedagogical practices that accelerate learning, as well as of context—the resources and environment that allow a teacher to do what his profession asserts have been shown to work. It is also a function of social and economic inequity, which schools inherit and are expected to redress, an issue I address more deeply in the following chapter.

Profession-accepted teaching practices would answer the "how" question, at least foundationally, for teachers in many situations. They also give a Publicization Project the opportunity to strengthen employment accountability, by providing teachers with clear expectations for their performance on the job. Admittedly, such accountability is politically charged and emotional, as it affects the economic prospects of people and their families. Fortunately, simplifying the issue to only four employment scenarios can guide our thinking.

First, imagine a well-prepared educator who teaches with standards-meeting practices. Her colleagues consistently agree that she's got all the right moves, knows how they relate to her content, and uses exceptional judgment to choose the best depending on the context. On multiple measures of student learning, from colleagues looking together at her students' work with comparisons to exemplary anchor papers to periodic formative and summative assessments, her student outcomes are strong and indistinguishable by race, class, gender, or sexual orientation. This is the easy case: She should keep up the great work and be retained and recognized for her impact. She should also have opportunities to share her expertise with colleagues, through the kind of professional rounds advocated by Elmore,[33] to benefit even more students. Perhaps she even represents teachers in the periodic revisiting of the teaching standards, giving her nationwide impact.

Second, a poorly prepared educator is not using standards-aligned pedagogy, yet his students' outcomes—again across different kinds of evidence—are strong. How do we explain the discrepancy? It's possible that he's innovating. But if on observation it's hard to discern any new methods, and if the standards do, in fact, identify effective practices that promote stronger and more equitable achievement, we can only infer that his students would be learning even more if he were using these profession-endorsed approaches. In this case, he needs to be held accountable to improve his practice. If he doesn't, he should be let go, as odd as it sounds, given his students' strong performance. Just as patients should not have to go under the knife of a freewheeling surgeon—even if the surgery somehow succeeds—students shouldn't either. It's professionally reckless.

In the third scenario, students are doing poorly, and the teacher, by all accounts, is not teaching well. She too must improve her practice. Some in the privatization project have argued that these are sufficient grounds to let her go. Armed with private sector at-will employment, the termination can be made quickly, so that not a single additional student is negatively affected. But such a termination puts all of the accountability on the individual. By comparison, in an arrangement of mutual accountability, the school bears some responsibility, too. It did, after all, hire her.

A school within a Publicization Project should hold *itself* accountable to coach and support the educator. By assigning a co-teacher, students would no longer experience pedagogy that doesn't meet professional standards of practice. Plus, the struggling teacher would have an opportunity to see effective approaches in action. After such efforts are made, if she still fails to improve her pedagogy, the school has done what it can—it has fulfilled its part of the social contract—and she should be let go.

Alternatively, if the teacher improves her practice and student outcomes improve, the school's support was well worth the effort, and may even represent a net benefit, given the cost of recruiting and onboarding a new employee. Such mutual accountability formed the basis of the New Haven, Connecticut, teachers' contract that gained prominence in 2010. In contrast to the era's narrowly construed form of test-based, top-down accountability, the contract was called a "model" by *The New York Times*, showing "what can go right when school districts and unions work together." Its editorial board further noted that "many high-performing charter schools have already adopted similar systems, with measurable success."[34]

The fourth scenario is the bedeviling one. A teacher is using all the best practices identified by his profession. His artistry is admired by peers, who regularly observe his class to learn from his technique. Perhaps he even was the struggling teacher from the previous scenario, who had no prior training, but was coached well and worked hard to master his profession's craft. But his students' outcomes are weak. When his colleagues compare student work, his students' writing is always the weakest. When it comes to mastering a progression of mathematical concepts, his students need more time than their peers in other sections, and they still get a lot of calculations wrong. They are behind and can't seem to catch up. Plus, he feels terrible about it, fully motivated to do right by them. In this case, who is accountable, and for what?

The privatization project puts all the blame on the teacher: there must be something else he should do, that he isn't doing, that would lead to stronger outcomes; clearly, he's not sufficiently incentivized to find the better approach, and he should be replaced, "deselected," before more children are harmed. With its blinkered focus on outcomes instead of inputs, simply executing his profession's standards of practice is insufficient; only student achievement matters.

The argument is deceptively simple and politically effective because of the moral hazard it invites: how can one disagree and still champion the innate ability of every single student? Or not be accused, as George W. Bush famously coined, of having "the soft bigotry of low expectations"?[35] Ultimately, this issue—inputs versus outcomes—became one of the major fault lines separating reformers "on the side of children" from "defenders of the status quo."

But if profession-endorsed teaching standards were to exist, and if this teacher uses them, and if he has been coached and supported by his school, what else can *he* do? Moreover, how much accelerated student learning is possible, cognitively? Are such teaching techniques known and included in the standards? Alternatively, if they are not known, how might they be discovered and developed through ethical forms of trial and error? And in such a case—meaning there is an absence of demonstrable impact or a professional consensus as to what to do about it—for what do we hold the hardworking teacher accountable?

SCHOOL-BASED COMMITMENTS

Within the fourth scenario above, the frustrated teacher should not be let go, as some kind of "students first" expression of tough-love employment accountability. This is where a Publicization Project can distinguish itself by championing *mutual* accountability by holding him and his *school* accountable to keep iterating and to try new approaches within ethical and respectful bounds.

As Hargreaves and Fullan show, the best schools aren't a collection of rugged individualists, with top-down accountability mechanisms that incentivize teachers to isolate themselves in one classroom from the next, keeping the best practices all to themselves, for the private gain it might yield. As Charles Sanders Peirce's 19th-century insight tells us: learning is a social activity. It's among students *and* among teachers, in schools that should be held accountable to foster dialogue among colleagues about what else to try, how else to innovate, within a culture that encourages greater collaboration for continuous improvement. This is how professions improve over time and what is needed for school improvement. It is a networked approach with regular trial, success, error, and refinement, premised on improvement science, as recommended by sociologist Tony Bryk and his colleagues in their provocative *Learning to Improve*.[36] If we're already doing everything we think *should* work, what else might *we* try?

The question becomes, for purposes of *school-based* accountability, what is enough? When has a *school* done everything that is in its control? To the mutual satisfaction of other stakeholders—the polity, parents, and the profession? What is the point at which it is reasonable to conclude that the reasons for students' poor performance legitimately lie with out-of-school factors like poverty, or yet-to-be discovered pedagogical approaches, technologies, and other supports?

For example, DREAM Charter Schools, where I spent a decade on the board, operates schools in Harlem and the Bronx. The students come from low-income families and many—more than the district average—are eligible for special education services. Very few are White. DREAM is led and staffed by extraordinary educators who attend to the development of the whole child, as concerned about academic achievement as social and emotional learning. The network is well resourced, with two teachers in every early-grade class, thanks to generous donors. Schools provide extra tutoring, have small class sizes, conduct home visits, and take family engagement seriously. Expectations are high and the opportunity is open to as many students as their charter allows: DREAM backfills seats, such as when a family moves and a student withdraws, admitting new students no matter the quality of their prior education.

As one might expect, DREAM's academic and social-emotional outcomes are strong. Yet as ideal as these conditions might be, not every student reads or computes on grade level. Only a handful of graduates attend elite private colleges, like Stanford, Skidmore, and Bates, where 90% or more earn their degrees. Most enroll in nonselective public community and baccalaureate colleges, where graduation rates for students of similar demographics range between 30% and 60%. And some go into nondegree certification programs or jobs, which they may find rewarding, but on average are not associated with the social mobility that comes from holding a college degree.[37]

Is DREAM doing enough? Market-based accountability creates little pressure to improve, given long waiting lists for available seats. Government accountability might create an incentive, given that DREAM's schools, as charters, face the threat of closure if state authorities were to shutter them for performance against state tests and middling college placement. Yet had I still been at the NYC Department of Education with oversight of DREAM, I would have strenuously argued for DREAM's continued operation.

On close analysis, the well-established "good faith" standard is at play. This ancient idea, appearing in the Magna Carta and part of Roman jurisprudence, is common in law and employment.[38] It establishes a standard of honesty and diligence, assuming that parties will make sufficient efforts to satisfy their obligations. It is defined in case law as "what a reasonable person would determine is a diligent and honest effort under the same set of facts or circumstances."[39]

DREAM Charter Schools handily meet a good-faith standard, as do many tax-funded schools. In my office's dealings with charter leaders, we shared a *moral* imperative to help *every* student succeed. But our *contractual* accountability metrics did not set a 100% standard and shutter schools that weren't perfect. Rather, city-authorized charters were expected to meet ambitious but achievable goals, relative to other schools in similar situations. Some may call such relativistic accountability a bigotry of low expectations, and from one perspective, perhaps it is. But alongside aspirational language about leaving no child behind, the goals we set more closely matched our day-to-day dealings with committed and well-intentioned educators, working hard and, definitionally, *in good faith*.

Why not make a good-faith accountability standard explicit? It provides a Publicization Project with a defensible alternative to market-defined, "invisible hand," notions of accountability. It gives school leaders a way to dispense with the pretense of real or alleged market forces and instead name the standard that is more typically being enforced. It is also operationalizable when applied to the framework for school improvement developed by Bryk and his colleagues while he led the University of Chicago Consortium on School Research.[40] The Consortium analyzed troves of school data to inductively see what inputs, if any, were meaningfully associated with improved student outcomes.

The research identified five key areas of activity, including a "coherent instructional guidance system," meaning the what and how of teaching and learning—which can be achieved, as I've argued, through clear and mutually-agreed-upon learning expectations and profession-endorsed standards of teaching practice. The second dimension is "professional capacity," given that "schools are only as good as the quality of faculty, the professional development that supports their learning, and the faculty's capacity to work together to improve instruction." Again, this is something that can be achieved by a combination of the profession's preprofessional and employment accountability.

Researchers also found that improved schools had "strong parent-community-school ties." The presence of such connections was "a multifaceted resource for improvement," with direct links to "students' motivation and school participation." Or, as I've characterized, replacing the paternalistic "one best" system of experts, who largely expect parents to leave their children at the schoolhouse door, by putting the politics *back into* education—through deliberative processes of engagement, collaboration, hearing, and heading a school's parents and other stakeholders.

Bryk and colleagues' fourth dimension is a "student-centered learning climate" in which "all adults in a school community forge a climate that enables students to think of themselves as learners." This requires a "safe and orderly environment . . . [with] ambitious academic work coupled with support for each student." In other words, high but achievable expectations in a context that is safe and sufficiently resourced. Finally, effective and improving schools have "leadership" that drives change by executives who can "engage in a dynamic interplay of instructional and inclusive facilitative leadership."

It's hardly a surprising list: thoughtful curriculum and pedagogy, effective teachers, engaged parents and community members, a demanding yet supportive culture, and wise leadership. Notably, the Consortium did not go into its research aiming to prove that these five dimensions mattered. Rather, the domains emerged from the data and first-rate empirical analysis. Plus, here's the kicker: They are interdependent. Schools in Chicago improved when all five characteristics were present. No one dimension alone was sufficient. As Bryk summarized, classroom learning "depends in large measure on how the school *as a social context* supports teaching and sustains student engagement."[41]

In the complex enterprise of education that loves its jargon, there's virtue in the memorability of only five things against which to plan, resource, execute, measure, sustain, or refine, *in good faith*. Plus, this research powerfully endorses educators' work and the very enterprise of education; despite the strong correlation between socioeconomic status and student achievement, the Consortium's findings show that schooling still matters.

These five dimensions give a Publicization Project its best evidence-based framework with which to hold states, districts, and schools mutually accountable to a good-faith standard of effort. The Project must aim to ensure that sufficient resources are in place, that leadership is prudent, that the teachers are good, that parents and community are engaged, that curriculum and pedagogy are coherent, and that school culture is supportive while challenging. Plus, the Project must demand that corrective actions be taken when one party or another is not acting in good faith, in any and all five domains, based on evidence fit for the purpose and in the judgment of other stakeholders with the authority and responsibility to take action.

Good-faith mutual accountability does not have the cinematic, cultural appeal of heroic, "Superman" educators who "stand and deliver" miracles with their students.[42] Lawyers grumble that if not adequately defined, a good-faith standard is too squishy for meaningful enforcement. Nor does it have the political appeal of an uncompromising, no-excuses[43] commitment to children among adults who will "stop at nothing" to see students succeed, as heard in much reform rhetoric.

But "stopping at nothing" is, literally, not operationalizable or even definable, particularly for the purposes of mutual accountability. Such a standard is, by definition, unobtainable. Rather, a good-faith standard actually characterizes the sustained and achievable work of our best educators and their schools. It is a familiar standard that can be broadly operationalized, according to Bryk's five key performance indicators. It can be used to ensure that all stakeholders honor their obligations to one another. It is also sufficiently different from market-based accountability to befit the values of a Publicization Project.

STUDENT PERFORMANCE

Finally, a Publicization Project must resolve the controversy around standardized assessments. Given my friend John Merrow's expletive-emphasized directive to "cancel" the tests, I continue to ask him this chapter's guiding question: *How do we know?* As I've argued, answering this question, in its various meanings, is at the heart of a Publicization Project and necessary for mutual accountability.

Evidence is required in all of the accountabilities described above. The teaching profession can only responsibly set *evidence-based* standards of teaching practice, backed by findings and experience sufficient to believe that a recommended approach will improve learning. Preprofessional accountability of education schools, licensing boards, and hiring committees must require evidence of a candidate's learning and skill, as gathered through performance tasks, demonstration lessons, and the like. The polity can only be held accountable to supply adequate resources in light of measures of student performance relative to desired goals. Each of the four scenarios of employment accountability refers to measures of student achievement—in the opinion of peers, on formative and summative tools, and the like—as a way to gauge a teacher's effectiveness. Similarly, schools can only be accountable to other stakeholders across Bryk's five domains in light of the student outcomes these activities generate and a good-faith effort to achieve them.

The privatization project, drunk on a big-data cocktail and staggering on a high tide of economic reasoning, believed that standardized assessment data could be used for all forms of accountability. Teachers would be hired and fired, schools would remain open or be closed, performance funding would be awarded or withheld, districts would retain autonomy or be taken over by the state, all on the basis of state tests.

But one form of evidence doesn't serve every purpose. For example, quantitative data, such as those gathered through multiple-choice assessments, examined through a randomized treatment-control (RTC) study, is considered a "gold standard" methodology to establish causality.[44] Yet RTCs are less relevant to identifying generalizable outcomes where all else might *not* be equal,[45] such as broadly recommended teaching practices.[46] The limits of RTCs are well explained by Kathryn E. Joyce and Nancy Cartwright in their notable article on the gap between research and practice.[47] As such, a Publicization Project should embrace the principle of "fitness," meaning different forms of evidence, gathered through methods that are best suited for its intended use. Or, as Raj Chetty advised Secretary Duncan, "use [test scores] for what they're worth"[48] and, I'd add, not for what they're not.

In the case of teaching standards, there is not a sufficient body of RTC studies on which to set the practices. But there are decades of quantitative research that employ strong statistical methods alongside carefully constructed case studies and other qualitative research. This collective evidence, responsibly interpreted by the expert and collective voices of the profession, should be considered sufficient to set standards of required specificity.

Within the day-to-day operation of schools, standardized test data are insufficient to create mutual accountability among students and teachers. The once-a-year administration, summative conclusions, and months-long delay in results do not provide teachers with the real-time, formative information needed to determine who is learning what and where to adjust one's teaching. Rather, teachers regularly check for student understanding through discussion questions and quizzes, exit slips on which students indicate what they've learned, tests, papers, projects, group assignments, and other demonstrations of learning. This range of evidence is fit for the purpose: Collectively, it helps teachers know if students are learning what is intended and if teachers need to adjust their instruction to clarify confusions, correct inaccuracies, and revisit skills and knowledge not yet mastered.

Teachers also need evidence fit for the purpose of holding one another mutually accountable, given the progression of students from one teacher to another and across subjects. Such student evidence is collected from common end-of-term exams administered to all students in a subject, regardless of the teacher. Common rubrics, used by all teachers across a grade or subject in a consistent, calibrated way, also generate comparable student performance data about essays, projects, and other nontestable demonstrations of learning. Such information identifies larger achievement trends that need to be addressed across an entire grade or school. Examining these findings in teacher data teams can generate mutual trust and accountability.

Such student evidence, vested with validity through the collective methods by which it is gathered and interpreted, is particularly fit for employment accountability, when considering a teacher's student outcomes vis-à-vis his command of profession-endorsed teaching practices. This employment accountability among teachers and administrators is further strengthened through classroom observations that are themselves standards-based and conducted by peers and supervisors trained in what to look for. Such training ensures that observational data are trusted and fit the purpose of performance evaluation.

None of these are new ideas or practices. Leading scholars like W. James Popham have spent careers developing and advocating for better approaches to assessment. Robert Pondiscio has called to "end the culture of testing" in order to enliven a culture of *learning*. Joe Feldman has demonstrated the real risks of standardized tests to Black, Latinx, and Indigenous students in his important *Grading for Equity: What It Is, Why It Matters, and How It Can Transform Schools and Classrooms*.[49] Having and using a range of tools that collect evidence fit for each purpose is likely to engender more mutual accountability, for the simple reason that modes and methods of assessment feel more authentic.

This *still* does not mean we should "cancel" standardized tests. Such evidence is particularly fit for mutual accountability among schools *and the polity* that a Publicization Project dare not lose. Reliable data about school- and district-level performance allow us to learn how well they are meeting collectively determined goals and standards, an absolute measure, as well as performance relative to other schools. Data indicating strong performance invites conversations about best practices and innovations to be shared. Results suggesting poor performance allows for serious conversations regarding the sufficiency of resources—the polity's accountability—as well as good-faith efforts to improve such outcomes—the school's accountability. None of this is possible absent data fit for the purpose of measuring and comparing schools within communities and from one to the next.

But the need for reliable evidence across states and the nation does not require the current regime of testing every student, every year, in the majority of grades. Rather, sampling can work just as well. Like with NAEP, standardized testing of some students, but not all, gathers enough data fit for plausible inferences about student performance. This approach preempts the use of state test data to evaluate individual teachers, as there wouldn't be enough data gathered from the students of any *one* teacher to make defensible judgments about *that* teacher's particular effect. But little is lost to employment accountability in a regime of mutual accountability with profession-endorsed teaching standards and other reliable evidence.

Nor would sampling generate student-specific data, to know if an *individual* student is meeting learning standards. This requires other assessments, such as the common end-of-term exams, papers, and rubric-assessed projects described above. But sampling *does* allow teachers and administrators to interrogate the generalizability of such findings to other, nontested students, in order to adjust approaches and uphold their good-faith efforts.

Importantly, sampling would provide a Publicization Project with enough data to draw conclusions about the relative performance of students from one school to another, and between neighboring towns, following the widely accepted NAEP model. But whereas NAEP's current sampling generates data fit to draw conclusions at the state level (and some cities), sampling could be extended to generate data required to form conclusions about student performance by towns, districts, schools, and student subgroups.

Random sampling also protects against bias. At present, some states and localities allow parents to opt their children out of state tests. But there are good reasons to believe that such choices are not the same—not normally distributed—across families in different neighborhoods or by race, ethnicity, and class. Although there are methodological techniques to correct this bias, random sampling is a simpler approach. I further suspect that sampling would help to improve the quality of the tests: with fewer students to assess, resources could be redirected to develop much better assessments that require more sophisticated demonstrations of knowledge and skill.

HOW WILL YOU KNOW, JOHN?

Given all of the controversy regarding standardized assessments, it will be difficult for a Publicization Project to bring into its coalition the fiercest opponents of testing. Again, I ask these critics: *How will you know?* How will you know if learning goals are being achieved? Equitably among students by race, class, gender, and sexual orientation, *in every far-flung corner of our country?* How will you know if schools are meeting the long-standing expectations we hold of them—to prepare future citizens, who can live prosperous lives, in greater comity with one another, while being good stewards of the planet? And if you have your doubts, with what evidence will you strengthen your calls for change?

The current circumstances are not unlike the intense methodological debates within the social sciences in the early 1990s. At the time, quantitative methods were ascendant and RTC studies equated "knowing" with statistical methods and methodological precision. This view controversially pushed statistical reasoning onto qualitative research, as famously advanced by Gary King, Robert Keohane, and Sidney Verba in *Designing Social Inquiry.*[50] Rejoinders, including *Rethinking Social Inquiry: Diverse Tools, Shared Standards* by Henry E. Brady and David Collier, *Case Study Research: Principles and Practices* by John Gerring, and *Perestroika!: The Raucous Rebellion in Political Science* by Kristen Monroe,[51] argued for a pluralistic approach, drawing on different research methods and different kinds of evidence to justify what we know.

The difference between the debating schools of thought was captured by Richard Rorty, in his final thoughts on philosophical pragmatism. He spent a career challenging the representational notion that evidence is "something which floats free of human projects," corresponding to some nonhuman reality outside of us, not unlike the confidence placed in RTCs. Instead, he viewed our "demand for evidence as simply a demand from other human beings for cooperation on such projects."[52]

Such cooperation requires more than any one best approach that claims a privileged status in representing reality. It requires the interplay of experience, observation, data, theory, methodology, argument, and interpretation, in order to justify knowledge claims that are persuasive to others, on which to take "successful action," and within an ongoing process of revisiting these claims to confirm, revise, or change our minds. Making school accountability more mutual, excluding none and thereby more public, requires a similarly pluralist approach, with an interplay of evidence fit for each purpose, convincing to one another. It is the approach that a Publicization Project must champion.

CHAPTER 6

Equity

> If we were to select the most intelligent, imaginative, energetic, and emotionally stable third of mankind, all races would be present.
>
> —Franz Boas, 1928[1]

Over a beer, my brother asked for some advice. His daughter's birthday falls in November. She was 3 years old and could start kindergarten next year, but she'd always be one of the youngest in her grade. Alternatively, he and his wife could keep her in preschool. If they wait, he asked, will she be bored, as one of the more mature students in her class? If they go ahead, will she always be behind her classmates, struggling to keep up?

My niece is an extraordinary person, full of curiosity and joy. She's already a great conversationalist, too. She's blessed with two smart, patient, and caring parents. She's surrounded by toys and books and spends days in imaginative play. In the grand scheme of things, she is going to be fine. Actually, she's going to be great, with many of life's opportunities at her feet, no matter when she starts kindergarten.

And yet, this is how we think about schooling: children falling behind or getting ahead, by learning *as much* as they can, *as fast* as they can. It is an inheritance from the Industrial Revolution and the late 19th- and early 20th-century organization of schools as factories. This operating model, what I'll call the "industrial paradigm," became our underlying *mental* model. In our language and assumptions about schooling, we construe children as products moving along assembly lines. It's accepted as simply the way schools work, an assumption so pervasive as to be invisible.

This chapter argues that the industrial paradigm doesn't work for anyone and is a particularly pernicious cause of inequity. Following a discussion to define equity, I present the failures of the industrial paradigm and how contenders to succeed it, like an "*innovation* paradigm," are based on the same, and inequitable, *how much, how fast* assumption. I then propose an Intellectual-Emotional Paradigm as a worthy successor, which imagines educational outcomes based less on *academic* competencies that privilege advantaged groups over others, and more on *human* competencies, which all can develop and the future needs. Only by changing what we value in an education, from things easily measured by *how much, how fast* metrics, to gifts and talents measured by *depth and quality*, can a Publicization Project replace a 100-year-old system designed to sort, rank, and *exclude* opportunity, with one that helps everyone flourish.

DEFINING EQUITY

We can think in two ways about equity that makes schools more public. The first pertains to *inputs* sufficient to educate each and every student, without exclusion. Yet, as I've shown in preceding chapters, resource inequity is deeply ingrained in America's tax-funded schools in service of private interests. Funding and the governance that controls it advantage children of the well-off, in affluent suburbs or neighborhoods, creating class-based inequity. Given the strong relationship between class and race, this disproportionately and negatively affects Black, Latinx, and Indigenous children. Where equal or greater resources could make the most difference, they are least present.

Equity advocates continue to fight for fairer opportunities, including efforts to reduce segregation that excludes better-resourced schools from one group or another. For example, the Bridges Collaborative works across 20 states, major cities, charter school networks, and housing organizations to "promote racial and economic integration."[2] Another prominent case includes changes to middle school enrollment in New York City's Community School District 15, where my sons attended school.[3]

But these well-intentioned initiatives are unlikely to root out *input* inequity, given the pervasiveness of private interests of which school segregation is merely a symptom. Recall how Greenwich, Connecticut—with its access to extraordinary wealth—has been under a state order to racially balance its schools *for over a decade*. Boston in the 1970s remains a harrowing cautionary tale, too. Its busses, carrying African American students into White neighborhoods, were "pelted with eggs, bricks, and bottles," as "police in combat gear fought to control angry white protesters besieging the schools."[4] Bolder approaches, as previously discussed, are required to address the *causes* of input inequity.

The second dimension relates to equity of *outcomes*, our long-standing belief that education is a great equalizer. Imagine student achievement, particularly what's needed for citizenship, prosperity, comity, and habitability, that is indistinguishable by students' race, ethnicity, class, gender, sexual orientation, or region of the country. Outcomes still *vary* from child to child, based on innate talents and interests. The law of large numbers leads us to expect a normal distribution—the famous bell curve—of students' work. But an *equitable* curve would see nearly every student achieving at or above some minimum set of expectations and, importantly, a mix of students, with no discernable demographic patterns, plotted under the curve.

This too is not the case, with the outcomes of poor students predictably clustered on one side of the distribution and the affluent on the other; White and Asian students over here and most Black, Latinx, and Indigenous students over there (with students of Middle Eastern descent not even categorized[5]).

The pattern starts early. In one of the first comprehensive analyses of the U.S. Department of Education's Early Childhood Longitudinal Study, researchers Valerie E. Lee and David T. Burkham found that "inequalities of children's cognitive ability are substantial right from the 'starting gate.'" Even before entering kindergarten, the average cognitive reading scores of the highest socioeconomic status (SES) children were 60% above the lowest. Math achievement was 21% lower for Black children than White, and 19% lower for Latinx children.[6]

Lee and Burkham, equity champions both, provide a variety of policy recommendations to narrow these gaps, from the impact of child care and preschool to the implications of having a home computer. But such catch-up strategies are unlikely to advance equity, as they still accept the industrial paradigm's mental model. Betrayed by their title, students are at "starting gates," racing to learn *as much*, *as fast*, as they can, and focused, given the limits of the data set, on academic rather than human competencies.

But here's the thing: Children at the front of the line don't slow down, as much as they might like to or even should for their own developmental health. Today's cultural and educational pressures only force them to run faster, as far ahead of their peers as they can. It's a rational response to an industrial paradigm we need to better understand if it's to be replaced.

STRUCTURAL INEQUITY FROM "THE CULT OF EFFICIENCY": THE INDUSTRIAL PARADIGM OF SCHOOLING

The industrial paradigm was constructed by the "cult of efficiency," a term coined by historian Raymond E. Callahan in his classic study of schools during the first half of the 20th century.[7] In eloquent prose, Callahan showed how the hallmarks of industrial production—assembly lines, division of labor, timed tasks, graded performance, factory bells—were enthusiastically adopted by education leaders to create industrialized schools for an industrialized age. Reformers were inspired by the famed (and ultimately flawed) efficiency studies of Frederick Winslow Taylor. They coordinated their efforts nationally—an industrializing *project*—through annual, invite-only gatherings like the Cleveland Conference.[8] John Dewey and others objected to the "inappropriate application of business and industrial values and procedures." But in the heyday of American industrial might, such dissents were "lost in the wilderness."[9]

This 100-year-old industrial paradigm is plain to see for anyone who visits a typical school today. Like my niece, students are sorted by age, assigned to classes, and set on an educational assembly line. They will be taught, tested, and graded on material they are expected to acquire, rolling along at roughly the same pace, year by year. As a student advances, teachers will specialize by subject, compartmentalizing knowledge. Such parts—classes in history separate from English, biology, or math—are more efficiently assessed by teachers responsible for their place on the line. Learning itself is construed as the installation of more and more parts on the brain's chassis. This approach is reinforced by the physical architecture with the familiar egg crate school design: rows of classrooms lining both sides of long halls, each room a "shop" for different subjects.

Within subjects, content is similarly ordered and sequenced for students to acquire as efficiently as possible, *moving on* from one topic to the next, week after week. These sequences may be driven by a field's internal logic, such as mathematics, where number sense must be learned before arithmetic, or chronologically, as in history. But the clock still governs; teachers keep students *moving along*, to make sure everything required in a year is "covered." Yet it's common for June to arrive with some classes not getting to everything they were supposed to learn. It calls to mind the famous bit of absurd comedy on *I Love Lucy*: like teachers with their students, Lucille Ball and Vivian Vance couldn't wrap the passing chocolates quickly enough.

Meanwhile, teachers serve as factory line managers, grading to efficiently sort students. They fill up grade books with points for homework, quizzes, tests, exams, extra credit, respectful behavior, punctuality, handwriting, listening skills, and the like, categorizing and tracking academic competencies. The approach, another industrial and economic inheritance, is premised on the presumed benefits of extrinsic motivators, from behaviorist thinking developed by Ivan Pavlov (who conditioned dogs) and B. F. Skinner (who trained rats). To this day, it remains a "full-blown economic system of incentives and penalties," teaching students to care more about points and less about learning, as Joe Feldman powerfully critiques in *Grading for Equity*.[10]

From time to time, students might be taken "off the line" for special, project-based learning. Others may receive academic interventions, to "catch up" to peers. If this doesn't work, students might be "held back" to repeat a grade, which has about the same stigma as a recalled car. Yet all throughout, the efficiency assumption reigns, with textbooks to "get through," days measured in seat time, and learning assessed in points on one test or another.

This industrial paradigm goes largely unquestioned in all but the most experimental or alternative of schools. In America, it's simply what it means to go to school. Or in the cardinal sin of historians,[11] it is a mistaken, teleological view of public education evolving over time toward some ideal, *intended*, end. It leaves young parents, like my brother and sister-in-law, with only a decision on *when* to place their daughter at the starting gate. Anything else feels risky, like a kit car made in one's garage—not something we'd ask a child to test-drive.

It is possible that the industrial paradigm holds such power over our imaginations because of its *seeming* sense of fairness. All students are treated the same, expected to learn the same body of grade-level knowledge each year, tested and scored against the same criteria. They learn it and advance all together. When some don't, they may still advance and receive extra support to stay "on track." But *equal* treatment is not a guarantor of *equitable outcomes*, given that we know from Lee, Burkham, and others that America's children start school with different advantages that are discriminately sorted by race, ethnicity, and class.

And once in school, some lines move faster than others, *by design*. There are tracks for the "talented" and others for those merely performing "on grade level." Those "off-grade" may be lucky enough to get on an "accelerated" path,[12] or diverted to a slower-moving assembly. Affluent communities may accelerate schooling for *everyone* by offering algebra as early as middle school, to keep students "on their way" to AP Calculus. Other districts may be satisfied if students just meet their state's graduation requirements.

The tests and grades used to set the pace are rife with inequity, too. Feldman, building on work by Doug Reeves, Thomas Gusky, Ken O'Connor, and others, shows how implicit biases affect assessment of activities and participation.[13] Teachers subjectively "hack grades" when a computed score doesn't match what they think a student *actually* deserves. This is compounded by a history of lower expectations among non-Black teachers of Black students. These and related problems lead to grading that "disproportionately favors students with privilege and harms . . . students of color, from low-income families, who receive special education services, and [are] English learners."[14]

As with so much of the inequitable privateness found throughout tax-funded schools, the industrial paradigm unfairly rewards the affluent. Like luxury car models, the "top" students have all the extra features, like SAT tutoring and Advanced Placement courses. If these differentiators become too ubiquitous, "those with the greatest resources merely redefine excellence" to their advantage, notes historian Jack Schneider.[15] Normed to "White upper-middle-class performance," the SAT is a reliable "proxy for wealth" more than anything else, showed Lani Guinier in *The Tyranny of the Meritocracy*.[16]

Paulo Freire, in *Pedagogy of the Oppressed*, called it a "banking concept of education," in which some students start with more in the bank—metaphorically and literally—and keep depositing even more as they go along.[17] It is to these students, who have deposited *as many* academic competencies *as fast* as they can, that society bestows its greatest educational rewards: admission to our most selective colleges, with all of the lifelong advantages that they confer. Guinier made it plain: The current paradigm does nothing less than the "sieving" of young Americans in the "production and reproduction of privilege."[18]

Let me note, these students are hugely accomplished young people. They should be commended for their academic and extracurricular achievements. They and their families are responding with perfect rationality to the powerful incentives of the industrial paradigm. But as long as educational success is defined as the assembly of knowledge and achievement onto a person—as quickly as possible by age 18—schools will remain complicit in sustaining inequity. The problem is not merely that schools were perfectly designed "to prepare the bulk of kids for assembly-line jobs," as Arne Duncan's chief of staff Joann Weiss once observed;[19] schools *are* assembly lines.

* * *

As I write, "learning loss" is an issue of national concern, given the extraordinary disruption of the COVID-19 pandemic.[20] Without question, students spent less time in intentional learning situations with teachers and peers. Unsurprisingly, it shows in NAEP data. As *The New York Times* headlined: "The pandemic erased two decades of progress in math and reading." The effects were "devastating" for already low-performing students. Black students lost 13 points in math as compared with 5 points among White students, with other "profound" impacts on low-income and Hispanic students.[21]

Meanwhile, more affluent families drew on their private resources to hire tutors or enroll their children in a private school that sustained in-person instruction when tax-funded schools went remote or hybrid. Others formed learning "pods," with small groups of students and a hired instructor or a parent volunteer "to remake learning based on *their own* visions" (emphasis added).[22] As the Center on Reinventing Public Education characterized it, they devised "solutions to supplement or replace" traditional schooling.[23]

Equity advocates rightly called out this unfair expression of privateness. They demanded supplemental services, paid for by federal COVID-relief packages, for less affluent students to catch back up. But if we listen carefully to the language, their well-intentioned advocacy still accepts the underlying logic, with its built-in inequity, of the industrial paradigm.

Perhaps, tragically, the one aspect of this paradigm that equitably affects students of all backgrounds is its negative impact on mental health and wellness. The imperative to learn as much as fast as one can, in competition with peers, has students overworked, overburdened, and stressed-out. In 2021, the Centers for Disease Control reported that 44% of high school students were feeling sad or hopeless, up from 40% in 2019 and 26% in 2009. Suicide is now the second-leading cause of death among children 10 to 14 years old.[24] The American Council on Education finds that mental health issues are at an all-time high on college campuses, and Healthy Minds, a research and advocacy group, reports the same. Bill Deresiewicz's *Excellent Sheep: The Miseducation of the American Elite* powerfully portrays the industrial paradigm's soul- and imagination-crushing effects as ambitious students, from every race and class, put *themselves* under extraordinary pressure. Case in point: Yale undergrads now need to *apply* for *clubs*, with hundreds rejected. Feldman adds: it's "as if we wanted to create for our students the most stressful, disempowering, and least desirable work environments imaginable."[25]

A BRIEF HISTORY OF PROGRESSIVE ALTERNATIVES TO THE INDUSTRIAL PARADIGM

Enough is enough. A Publicization Project cannot succeed equitably for all students if it tries to fix the assembly line. It must replace that paradigm's underlying assumptions about schooling, learning, and student achievement. The Project must throw its wooden shoes into the gears—and advance a new vision, based on powerful precedents.

It won't be easy. John Dewey and Ella Flagg Young tried to buck the industrial trend at their Laboratory School. Founded in 1896 in conjunction with the University of Chicago, it emphasized experiential learning and the development of new pedagogical approaches. But the constant experimentation proved too hard (and serves as a cautionary tale to advocates, such as Bryk, of continuous improvement via networked learning). When Dewey left the school in 1904, teachers resumed more traditional practices.[26]

By midcentury, another famous challenge to the status quo was A. S. Neill's Summerhill School. Premised on self-governance, students and teachers would collectively make decisions in an effort to eliminate the coercive power of adults over children. Students' emotional well-being was prized.[27] Although Neill's school inspired a generation of progressive educators, few schools look like this today.

Decades later, Deborah Meier and Ted Sizer also attempted to bring a new paradigm to schooling.[28] Through their Coalition of Essential Schools, they emphasized performance tasks and authentic demonstrations of student learning through portfolios of work and PhD-like "defenses" before a committee of teachers and experts. A similar effort was launched by their colleague Dennis Littky in his Big Picture Schools, with a focus on project-based learning.[29] Imagine a student taking a year to build a boat while learning the required geometry and physics and reading *Moby-Dick*. But the impact of these alternative models was limited and short-lived, in part because their ideas were so out of step with test-and-sanction notions of accountability. The coalition formally disbanded after a respectable run of 32 years.[30] Only remnants of progressive schooling can be found nationwide.[31]

THE INDUSTRIAL PARADIGM REWRAPPED: THE "CULT OF INNOVATION"

Another contender advocated by education reformers seeks to replace the Industrial Age model with something more befitting our Information Age. Call it an innovation paradigm, with adherents a cult of innovation. Raised in Silicon Valley, they have an unquestioned faith in virtual learning, artificial intelligence (AI), and the wondrous algorithmic insights of Big Data.

In the near future, they argue, much of a student's education will be delivered online. Students will be able to move at their own pace as quickly or slowly as they need, to demonstrate mastery of a subject or skill. In such a scenario, teachers will play more of a facilitator role—assisting students in online or blended formats, based on where each student is and the support she needs. But even such facilitation is temporary; as AI becomes exponentially better—ultimately achieving the "singularity" of self-awareness—computers will provide student-specific guidance, too.[32]

Despite its futuristic allure, these predictions still accept the same efficiency assumptions as the industrial model: self-paced students acquiring knowledge *as rapidly as each can*. It risks exacerbating inequality, as affluent students possess all the latest gadgets and " gifted and talented" students move ahead online, at their own *swift* pace, ahead of their peers.

An innovation paradigm further risks a reductionist view of learning limited to individual academic competencies versus social human competencies. Demonstrating to a computer that I've mastered facts and can perform mathematical procedures narrows curriculum to what a computer can assess. Learning ceases to be a social enterprise in which we construct knowledge and skill together, giving reasons to justify our knowledge claims, to develop and appreciate epistemological norms.

The cult of innovation's likely retort is, "Just wait! Soon enough, computers will be able to do this, too. Programs are in the works to simulate these collaborative experiences. We're training AI on more pedagogical techniques than a human could ever master, or call on in the right moment, at such lightning speed!" Perhaps. But truly astonishing AI technologies like ChatGPT present an obvious question: If computers can create the assignments, teach the lesson, complete the homework, and grade it, what is left, and essential, that humans can only learn together?[33]

FOR CONSIDERATION: AN INTELLECTUAL-EMOTIONAL PARADIGM

Given that the industrial paradigm's inequitable assumptions are just as present in an innovation paradigm, what else could take its place? If I am true to my previous chapters on governance and standards, a Publicization Project must put the question to parents, educators, experts, employers, elected officials, and citizens. What *kind* of schooling will best advance our common goals of democracy, prosperity, comity, and habitability?

Caveat noted, some stakeholders may be unfamiliar with alternatives, given the industrial paradigm's century-long grip on our thinking about schooling. So in an effort to give the conversation some shape, a Publicization Project should strongly consider what can be summarized as an *Intellectual-Emotional Paradigm*.

Its very name positions *human* competencies at the center of schooling. Imagine an education organized to develop—and celebrate—students' curiosity and creativity, their ability to think carefully and deeply, that is joyful, cultivates a love of learning, and helps students grow as kind and considerate people. It would be one that helps students learn how to collaborate, build self-managing "executive" functioning, and how to persist in the face of adversity or ambiguity.

Such an approach reconnects us to the oldest goal of Western education: the good life. It's what Aristotle called eudaimonia, understood as an individual's happiness and humanity's flourishing. We surely could use more of both, and helping students cultivate these qualities requires the judgment that only a human can bring to a situation, in social settings, whether in person or online. Such judgment is particularly necessary when addressing opinions and managing the tricky "demarcation problem" between facts and beliefs.[34]

My intuition is that this approach will also give us more equitable outcomes. By valuing human competencies that can't be learned and measured *as fast as possible*, but rather take time to develop and demonstrate in authentic, social ways, the Intellectual and Emotional Paradigm disrupts the industrial paradigm's controlling assumption. Rather than schooling that rewards those who master the most facts the most quickly, à la Dickens's Superintendent Gradgrind, this approach prizes the cognitive skills and emotional capabilities innate to us all. They can therefore be equitably developed, as captured in the opening statement of this chapter by anthropology pioneer Franz Boas, regardless of race, ethnicity, class, gender, or sexual orientation and anywhere in the world.

INTELLECTUAL CAPACITIES

A persuasive statement of the *intellectual* elements of such a paradigm was developed through decades of experience by noted educator Deborah Meier.[35] In her 2002 book *The Power of Their Ideas,* Meier presents five habits of mind that connote quality, critical thinking. Specifically, she advocates an education that helps students make sense of the *significance* of something—why it's important or isn't. The second is schooling that cultivates an appreciation for the point of view, or *perspective*, of a person, a reading, analytical approach, or historical interpretation, as well as what alternate perspectives might teach us.

The third habit of mind focuses on the quality of *evidence*, posing to students the very same question before every responsible educator: *How do we know?* The fourth habit looks at *connections* one can make, to intentionally apply learning from one situation to another. Finally, Meier's fifth habit asks the all-important counterfactual of *supposition*, to fire our power of imagination, by contemplating if and how the matter at hand might be different, and if so, what implications follow.

These five habits apply as much to educators' work as they do to student learning. How can teachers best convey the *significance* of what students are expected to learn—in lesson plans, curricula, and learning objectives? Based on what *evidence*, strong or weak? *Connected* to what, and from whose *perspective*? And might we make different educational choices, on readings, homework, and assignments, if we *suppose* different ends? Meier herself taught by this creed. When she and I co-taught at Wesleyan University, our students always needed to be ready for her penetrating intellect.

Meier and colleagues developed and refined these habits at her famed Central Park East Elementary School, other affiliated schools in East Harlem, and the Mission Hill Pilot School in Boston. I visited with Meier at Mission Hill in 2004 with a group of leaders from New York City's teachers' union, the United Federation of Teachers, as part of our planning for new, union-operated charter schools. It was noisy, full of conversation, with students enjoying a level of freedom that many of us found chaotic. It was, perhaps, also full of intellectual curiosity connected to the excitement, joy, and other emotions of learning. What we saw didn't seem like what school was *supposed* to be like, revealing just how deeply I had come to accept the rows-of-desks assumptions of the industrial paradigm.

Helpfully, the Habits of Mind align well with growing insights from the field of cognitive science. Its burgeoning research finds that learning happens most deeply when ideas are intentionally connected to prior knowledge and skill. When such prior knowledge is activated, it creates relevance. When significance is clear, students appreciate why they are learning what is expected of them, which is motivating.[36] Plus, as much as Meier's recommendations are part of an older progressive tradition dating back to Dewey and Montessori, they serve the needs of today's information age. Data are at our fingertips in nanoseconds; what we need are contributing citizens, productive workers, good neighbors, and stewards of the planet who can make meaning of it all, together with others.

Moreover, employers are consistent. As trade associations like the National Association of Colleges and Employers make clear, organizations want employees who can think and collaborate, with command of ideas; who can creatively think of new ones; and who are able to take initiative based on good judgment.[37] They do *not* want assembly-line workers prepared by an assembly-line education.

EMOTIONAL CAPACITIES

Within an Intellectual-Emotional Paradigm, such cognitive capacities must be paired with schooling that appreciates and activates the *emotional* dimensions of learning. Think about how it feels when you encounter a new idea or unfamiliar task, from hearing about Critical Race Theory for the first time to trying to assemble furniture from Ikea. Even such different moments can provoke emotions from excitement and joy to fear and insecurity; more than once an Allen wrench has slipped out of my nervous hand.

Plato separated thinking from feeling; we now know there is no such distinction. To state the obvious: Children and adolescents are full of emotions, like us all. Brain science shows that they are still developing the apparatus to manage their emotions, make sense of feelings, and form coping strategies to be less governed by them.

This presents educators with a choice: We can either embrace and direct students' feelings to allay fears and ignite curiosity, in service of the goals of schooling, or we can ignore feelings or ask students to repress emotions by forcing them to sit still at their desks and pass through halls in silence—effectively dousing learning with an unhelpful emotional response: boredom. Or worse, driving students to places of anxiety, fear, and defensiveness that may harden pre-existing beliefs, opinions, factual inaccuracies, and prejudices.

The educational concept of imposter syndrome is a helpful illustration. This occurs when a learner doesn't feel as if she's good enough to be in a certain school or class, perhaps surrounded by peers she views as more capable. If the feeling is left unaddressed by a teacher who may not be attuned to the emotional dimensions of learning, such insecurity impedes progress. The emotions may even drive this student to switch classes, take something easier, change schools, or drop out—despite having every innate cognitive ability to do well.

In response, some of the best guidance on the emotional dimensions of learning has been produced by the Aspen Institute through its National Commission on Social, Emotional, and Academic Development. Acknowledging that schools have overemphasized academic skills, the Commission points to "overwhelming evidence [that] demands we complement the focus on academics with the development of the social and emotional skills and competencies that are equally essential for students to thrive in school, career, and life."[38] Its work includes a research agenda, policy recommendations, and specific practices that attend to students' emotional well-being.

Another resource is Lisa Damour's particularly insightful research and practical recommendations. A clinical psychologist affiliated with Case Western Reserve, Damour also served as a fellow at Yale's respected Zigler Center in Child Development and Social Policy. Her *The Emotional Lives of Teenagers* positions the strong emotions of adolescents as developmentally appropriate and shares strategies to help teens who feel at the mercy of these feelings. Practical approaches address friction at home, spiking anxiety, risky behavior, the ups and downs of relationships, and the pull of social media. Her *Untangled* focuses on girls, explaining seven distinct "and absolutely normal" developmental transitions. She notes that when parents and educators know what makes a girl "tick, they can embrace and enjoy the challenge of raising [and educating] a healthy, happy young woman."[39]

Shifting to an Intellectual-Emotional Paradigm will require meaningful changes to school staffing. It redefines the role of teacher, from conveyer of cognitive capacities to developer of human ones. It will require many more social workers and guidance providers, too. At present, the American School Counselor Association reports only one counselor for every 408 students, on average.[40] In a six-hour, 180-day school year, this translates to only two and a half hours with each student annually. The Association recommends no more than a 250 to 1 ratio, but even this is likely conservative.

Curricular approaches will need to change, too. An Intellectual-Emotional Paradigm likely will require much more interdisciplinary learning, with more flexible schedules for the time required of any given task. Ideally, students would have greater opportunity to learn, reflect, discuss, refine, and revise, together with their peers and for independent work. Age-based and grade-level teaching tasks that are timed by the class period, term, or year would likely become irrelevant. Progression from one set of material to more challenging tasks would be based on demonstrated mastery of prerequisite material, skills, dispositions, and habits of mind, through performance tasks and work portfolios.

I saw this approach in action at the Francis W. Parker Charter Essential School in Massachusetts, which Ted Sizer founded with his collaborator and wife Nancy in the late 1990s and named after a contemporary of Dewey's.[41] The school is located on the grounds of a decommissioned army base. Ted acknowledged the double irony of, first, it being housed in the nearly windowless intelligence building, given that the school prized intellect, and second, acerbically, so that their unconventional methods didn't leak out.

As with my visit to Meier's Mission Hill, I was admittedly thrown when a team of educators explained student promotion to more demanding work based on demonstrations of learning before a committee of teachers, so discordant was it from my age- and time-based assumptions. I would see the approach again at a small consortium of New York City high schools. To graduate, students had to decide, in consultation with their teachers, when to defend their accumulated work and readiness for college before a panel of educators and professionals. To be done well, such defense committees need to be highly trained in what to look for and why. I served on one, and felt wholly unfit to judge students' work, such as whether a piece of writing reflected an appropriate level of sophistication. But I did come to appreciate the approach's humanity—empowering students with the agency to decide, with their mentors, when they were ready for more challenging work, and expecting them to show the evidence and justify, why, with good reasons.

Such an approach to evaluation, as part of a new Intellectual-Emotional Paradigm, answers the all-important question, "How do we know?" that a student has met the expectations we seek for her. It also fits a Publicization Project's call for mutual accountability with evidence fit for each purpose, accelerating changes in assessment toward greater use of portfolios and performance tasks with rubrics and other calibration tools to ensure that students' work is being judged equitably across a school, a district, and beyond. Schools would also need meaningful ways to conclude that a student is kind and tolerant and emotionally well integrated, and evaluate the extent to which he is curious and can think clearly, write persuasively, and compute well.

We'd also expect the profession's standards of practice to be aligned to an Intellectual-Emotional paradigm and be enforced through preprofessional and employment accountability, appropriate to what is reasonably in a teacher's, guidance counselor's, and social worker's control.

Mutual accountability between the polity—holding schools accountable to a good-faith standard of effort—and schools—holding the polity accountable for sufficient resources—would similarly need new evaluation tools to sample and aggregate the outcomes of the Intellectual-Emotional paradigm. For example, DREAM Charter School takes its students' social– emotional learning seriously. Its work is informed by the Aspen Institute's resources. As a DREAM board member, I regularly got reports about our progress in this area and was relieved (and in retrospect not surprised) that our students had strong emotional *gains* in persistence and resilience during the pandemic.

But at present, measures of emotional development are not a term and condition of DREAM's charter renewal. State officials largely focus only on academic competencies, as measured on standardized tests. This incentivizes a narrow focus on academics and disincentivizes a wider lens on "the whole child." DREAM attends to the emotional life of our students because of our mission. But it should not be left to choice. For an Intellectual *and* Emotional Paradigm to flourish, a Publicization Project must demand accountability for both.

Nor does shifting to an Intellectual-Emotional Paradigm, premised on human capacities, rule out excellence at the highest levels of academic competencies. Take calculus. It is one of humanity's greatest intellectual achievements. As such, how could it not be available to students with a passion for mathematics? The difference, though, is that we would not have an entire and inequitable paradigm of schooling built for the winners who take calculus and the losers who don't.

Further imagine integrated curriculum across traditional subjects and aligned to the overarching goals of a public education. For example, themes of learning, over months and years, might address "The Other," in pursuit of greater social cohesion (good neighbors) and a healthy democracy (engaged citizens). Any meaningful engagement with this broad topic would necessarily draw on great works of literature, history, the social sciences, and current events to examine its full complexity. It would be *more* intellectually and emotionally demanding, and relevant, than our present approach.

THE INTRINSIC EQUITY OF AN INTELLECTUAL-EMOTIONAL PARADIGM

Returning to the focus of this chapter, my instinct is that an Intellectual-Emotional Paradigm is necessary to fully achieve equitable student outcomes indistinguishable by race, ethnicity, class, gender, sexual orientation, or place of birth. It rejects the "as much, as fast" assumption at the cold mechanical heart of the industrial paradigm. It centers *human* competencies innate to us all and that take time to develop. It advances human flourishing.

Consider the recurring effort necessary to develop intellectual aptitudes to *habitually* understand the significance of something, from different perspectives, based on the quality of evidence, in connection to what else we know, while supposing how it might be different. I'm about as well educated as one can formally get, and I can't say that I think in these ways as much as I should. Take a further moment to consider the introspection and ongoing interpersonal efforts required for emotional maturity. People spend lifetimes "doing the work." I don't underestimate the damaging early effects of poverty on intellectual development and mental health. But I suspect that the time required to develop *human* competencies is more similar among students who are poor or rich, White or Black, gay or straight, than the time needed for academic competencies that allow some students to race ahead of their peers.

This hope is premised on my belief that children's innate intellectual and emotional endowments, which the Intellectual-Emotional Paradigm would further develop, are similar enough at birth such that educational inequities would not be exacerbated by the privileges held by one group or another. Such faith was deepened by my drama students at Tiger Kloof School in South Africa. They were phenomenally creative. Our many multilingual productions were extraordinary vehicles for their intellectual and language development, to experience respectful gender relations to expand cultural awareness, and for personal growth. And we had *fun*. We set Shakespeare in

Soweto, staged scenes by Athol Fugard, performed students' original works, and discovered *Where the Wild Things Are* in their children's theater.

The fact that we were in a poor and rural province of South Africa, or that the majority of our students were Black and came to Tiger Kloof from resource-starved Apartheid-era elementary schools, posed no limit to their artistic, intellectual, and emotional capabilities. Their performances—these demonstrations of learning—stages in churches, the town hall, and circles drawn in chalk at the center of school courtyards—were spaces of human flourishing.

Not coincidentally, an Intellectual-Emotional Paradigm is also what the affluent often seek for their children. They do *not* want their children sitting, isolated, in front of a computer all day, or stuck in overcrowded classrooms with rows of seats facing a knowledge-dispensing teacher. Rather, the most fortunate pay tens of thousands of dollars for their children to spend days in play-based learning, as at Montessori Schools, or around tables in dialogue with peers and teachers, as in Exeter Academy's Harkness approach, or with hands-on tasks, at the Putney School with its working farm, led for years by noted progressive educator Emily Jones.[42] Recall Rawls's test of fairness: If a private, progressive education is what the rich would seek if their children were to be randomly assigned to a school, why then not an Intellectual-Emotional Paradigm available to all?

A POLITICAL, NOT AN EDUCATIONAL, PROBLEM

There is no shortage of Intellectual-Emotional exemplars, from Parker, Dewey, Neill, and Montessori to Deborah Meier, Ted Sizer, David Matthews, Emily Jones, and many others. My friend Ted Swartz, founder of the Bronx Charter School for Better Learning and a protégé of progressive educator Caleb Gattegno, has been at it for years, albeit within the test-and-sanction constraints of New York's charter school law.[43] So have the Hyde Schools, with their emphasis on character education, founded in Bath, Maine, by Joe Gauld and replicated elsewhere.[44] There are more. They prove an alternate way of organizing students' work to promote a different kind of learning. As Horsford and colleagues believe, these are "the building blocks of a new paradigm."[45]

Why name it something as pretentious as an "Intellectual-Emotional Paradigm"? Because we can't change what we can't name—the thesis of this book. We need new language that readily captures what equity, as part of a Publicization Project, entails. As the political adage goes, you can't beat something with nothing.

Who will go for it? Every student and family who has felt on the losing end of the industrial paradigm race is a natural ally. So is every family on the winning end, if they wish to avoid the emotional toll that the assembly line exacts. Selective colleges and universities would need to upend their admissions processes, no longer able to rely on inequitable proxies for achievement, but wouldn't they want to admit students prepared as more than Deresiewicz's "excellent sheep"? Employers should be in for it, too. They're already not getting the kinds of creative and collaborative employees they seek for a world of AI productivity, to do what only humans can do.

The stakeholders exist. They need organizing, which a Publicization Project can coalesce into a coalition that's broad, durable, and powerful enough to bring about a more equitable paradigm. It will require a campaign that outlives any one administration or superintendency. It must expect many rounds of play, to build trust and collaboration over time, and to show that the new paradigm solves as many—and more—of the problems "solved" by the old one.

Doing so will be our best chance, in words that Callahan wrote in 1962, for America to "break with its traditional practice, strengthened so much in the age of efficiency, of asking how our schools can be operated most economically, and begin asking what steps need to be taken to provide an excellent education for our children." It will force us to "face the fact that there is no cheap, easy way to educate a human being . . . that a free society cannot endure without."[46]

Part II

CASES

No action without research; no research without action.

—Kurt Lewin, 1946[1]

At the start of this book, I posed the question: What is "public education"? and offered a two-part definition: schools that produce public goods and that don't exclude. Yet as the preceding chapters show, when we apply our definition with the aid of the exclusion test, through the lens of various criteria, we find that tax-funded schools have long been rife with privateness, amplified in recent decades by the privatization project. It leaves me with the unsettling thought that our public schools aren't all that public.

Yet we can take heart that the characteristics of publicness are in our control. As I have argued, a Publicization Project can make schools *more* public by:

1. Ensuring that free, tax-funded schools have the resources necessary to meet expectations of them, for all children, with resources fairly distributed and comparable from one school to the next;
2. Basing what is taught on facts and knowledge-making norms, so that schools help to sustain our democratic form of government, equitably expand prosperity, bring society more closely together, and preserve our planet;
3. Bringing stakeholders into dialogue regarding what is taught and how, through decision-making processes that hear and heed different views, in light of expertise and responsibility when one voice deserves more weight than others;
4. Articulating the results of this deliberative and participatory governance into expectations that represent what it means to be an educated American and, as such, what schools will address, with evaluation processes that answer the all-important question "How do we know?";

5. Enforcing mutual accountability, with evidence fit for each purpose, holding every stakeholder to a good-faith standard of effort and, in doing so, deepening schools' legitimacy; and
6. Expanding equity, through the effects of the first five criteria and by replacing the industrial paradigm with an Intellectual-Emotional Paradigm that prepares students in ways that families should welcome, that society needs, and that employers want, by developing human competencies more likely to be indistinguishable by race, ethnicity, class, gender, sexual orientation, or place of birth.

In Part II I show how a Publicization Project, guided by this definition and equipped with these criteria, can make education more public in two necessary cases: charter schools and the teacher unions. Each is entrenched on either side of the major divide in American education politics. One is the dominant front of the privatization project, the other the most politically influential advocate for district-run schools. But since tax-funded schools are not nearly as public as they need to be for sake of the common good, the unions have work to do. Similarly, the charter sector faces a fundamental choice: It can lean into its privateness and concern itself less with the common good, or join—and in some areas lead—a Publicization Project. Purely by the size and influence of both camps, a Publicization Project needs to bring both into its coalition if it is to succeed. These two chapters show how.

The first draws on my years as a leader in the charter school movement, in a form of action research, to explore what the future might hold for charter schools as part of a Publicization Project. Today they are the most well-established manifestation of the privatization project's market-based philosophy of choice and competition. As such, they are the obvious, most present target of self-described defenders of public education. But as I will show, charters are not nearly the force for privatization that the overheated rhetoric would have one believe. Without question, there are clear ways that charters should strengthen their publicness. But these schools also hold lessons that can make *district* schools more public, too.

The second case draws on my years with the teachers' union, to examine their influence on the publicness and privateness of tax-funded schools. For a long time now, the privatization project placed nearly all the blame for the shortcomings of tax-funded schools at the unions' feet. But that attack is as hyperbolic as the one against charter schools. By applying the six criteria, we find that unions have sustained the publicness of tax-funded schools in many important ways. But this contribution remains constrained, in its own fundamental way, by the unions' fealty to the industrial paradigm. This too can change, strengthening unions' ability to make tax-funded schools more public and be the ally that a Publicization Project needs.

CHAPTER 7

Charter Schools

... this sturdy old precedent has had a rebirth.

—Ted Sizer, *Chartered Schools: Two Hundred Years of Independent Academies in the United States, 1727-1925*[1]

In the spring of 2021, the Network for Public Education (NPE) sent an "urgent" message to "Stop Federal Funding for New Charter Schools." Because of "waste and abuse," NPE implored subscribers to let Congress know that "enough is enough." It further warned that "right-wing Libertarians . . . are committed to destroying public education . . . [and] charter schools are certainly part of their plan."[2]

Meanwhile, the schools are classified as "public" by the U.S. Department of Education. The Education Commission of the States, another well-respected authority, adds the caveat "semi-autonomous," but still otherwise public.[3] The National Alliance for Public Charter Schools (NAPCS) asserts that "charter schools are innovative public schools," although its position has changed depending on the issue—be it funding, school uniforms, or labor rights—defining charters as either public or private in legal briefs.[4]

For some of us who worked in the charter school sector for decades, this fight—over whether charter schools are public—is old and tiresome. It's like watching two Rock 'Em Sock 'Em robots duke it out, and about as boring. So which is it?

It's worth establishing some facts. Today, 3.4 million students attend 7,700 charter schools across 44 states and in Washington, DC. Each school is a creature of its state or territory's unique charter law, with 58% in urban areas, 26% in the suburbs, and 16% in rural areas. Nationwide, charter school students are 35% Hispanic, 30% White, 25% Black, and 10% of Asian or other descent. The majority come from low-income households, with 59% eligible for free or reduced-priced lunches. Most charter schools are nonprofit organizations governed by a board of trustees. Nationwide, about 12% are managed by for-profit companies. The majority, 65%, are unaffiliated with any networks, be it a nonprofit "charter management organization" like KIPP Schools, or a for-profit manager like National

Heritage Academies. Regardless of their tax status or management affiliations, all are tax-funded and free to attend.[5]

Such geographic, demographic, and operational diversity belies any simple answer of what's "public," *unless one simply defines charter schools out of the answer*, by arguing that only district schools, operated by a local board or state authority, can be considered public. Over the years, this has largely been the fighting line, with charter defenders and detractors trying to win their point of view with better marketing and stronger pressure politics.

But when we apply the six criteria of publicness, and better understand the history and practice of *chartering* new tax-funded schools, we find that the issue is dynamic. A charter school's publicness or privateness—just like a district school's—depends on how the school is created, operated, and regulated by government authorities. Such dynamism is an opportunity for a Publicization Project, which should not simply oppose charter schools, as demanded by groups like NPE. Doing so can harm the education of the millions of students that charters enroll, children, notably, who are disproportionately Black, Latinx, poor, and living in underresourced urban neighborhoods. Rather than turn its back and exacerbate inequity, a Publicization Project should reclaim some of the founding ideas behind the charter sector and put these schools to even greater common purpose.

THE PUBLICNESS OF CHARTER SCHOOL FUNDING

The first criterion of any school's publicness is its funding: tax-supported, free, and excluded to none. Charter schools are tuition-free, supported by tax dollars, and open to any child via lottery. On this most reductive measure, they are public schools.

But are they also *fairly* funded—a key characteristic of this first domain? Putting aside the larger question of whether resources are sufficient to achieve their chartered goals, do these schools receive, at a minimum, a bundle of tax-supported resources comparable to the resources provided to district schools educating similar students?

This question has long been a cause of debate. Charter school opponents point to huge gifts from benefactors and claim that the schools are overfunded, particularly when they enroll fewer students requiring additional support. Detractors further argue that no amount of tax dollars should be "drained away" from already underresourced district schools. Meanwhile, charter advocates maintain that the schools unfairly receive less funding per pupil than the district-operated school around the corner. They propose that funding should "follow the student" to whatever school the family picks, making it "lost" to no one school or another.

The question's answer doesn't fit on a bumper sticker. It requires careful analysis, sensitive to local context and students enrolled, accounting for publicly provided dollars *and* services, for both day-to-day operations and facility expenses. This question of equitable charter funding (and thereby publicness) was also my first trial-by-fire as director of New York City's office of charter schools more than 20 years ago.

Advocates for Children, a powerful champion for students at risk of school-based discrimination, threatened to sue the city's Board of Education. They argued that the city had ultimate responsibility to educate students with disabilities and therefore had to meet this obligation to students enrolled in charter schools by increasing funding or deploying staff and services. The effort was backed by charter leaders, including Joe and Carol Reich, of the influential Beginning with Children Foundation, who founded one of New York's first charter schools.[6]

My office studied the issue with NYU's Institute for Education and Social Policy, led by the respected progressive activist Norm Fruchter.[7] On close study, we found that New York's charter schools received *federal* funding to educate students with disabilities that was *identical* to district schools. Charters also received comparable state and local funding, on average per pupil, for *general education* expenses. But a likely unintended glitch in state funding formulas led to *underfunding* for special education—a difference of about 50 cents less per dollar, totaling thousands of dollars per eligible student.

The empirical finding provided the basis needed by New York City to increase funding and close the gap. The addition made the bundle of federal, state, and local resources provided to city charters comparable, on average, to what the city's district schools received for their *operating* expenses. But for many years, New York's charter schools did not receive any state or local tax funding for school facilities and did not have access to government-owned buildings—a clear instance of resource inequity.

The absence of adequate capital resulted in low-cost solutions nationwide, as in Florida, where charters can be found in "strip malls, old grocery stores, and industrial parks."[8] In the Bronx, I admired the pluck of a charter located in a renovated sausage factory, but always felt that we could do better for its students. It was a far cry from the 19th- and early 20th-century conception of schools as palaces of learning, replete with marble trim and Corinthian columns.

The federal government's Charter Schools Program—the object of NPS's ire—fills some of the void. But insufficient public capital made the charter sector increasingly reliant on private donors.[9] The Walton Family Foundation has provided over $400 million since 1997 through its Public Charter Startup Grants.[10] The Charter School Growth Fund has supported over 1,200 schools that enroll over 530,000 students across 31 states.[11] In Brooklyn, the Reichs's charter school is housed in a former Pfizer plant, remodeled at their own expense. DREAM Charter School gut-renovated a crumbling ice factory on the Harlem River into a "spectacular" new school, designed by the celebrated architect of the National Museum of African American History and Culture, David Adjaye. Public officials praised this new civic landmark as a place of "hope and opportunity." But the $50 million price tag was paid privately.[12]

In effect, state and local fiscal policies pushed charter schools along the spectrum toward privateness. This unaddressed basic need—a roof over students' heads—allowed districts to benefit from an infusion of federal and private capital. Buildings were constructed and others renovated without local tax or bond revenue. The situation improved the overall capital stock in places where buildings were aging—dramatically by DREAM—and expanded the number of school seats in overcrowded districts. However, such forced reliance on private benefactors, making charter *funding* more private than public, gave charter opponents an all-too-easy line of political attack: The schools *must* be beholden to the private interests of donors. It was also a missed opportunity to influence charter operations through the terms and conditions of publicly provided space.

Recall that another aspect of fair funding pertains to the exclusion of students from resource-rich schools due to attendance zones and district boundaries. In this regard, charter schools likely fare better on this measure of publicness than their district counterparts, given that most charters are open to any student who is accepted by lottery.[13] In theory, districtwide charter lotteries are blind to students' race, ability, and socioeconomic status, although the mechanics of such lotteries matter. If families have to seek them out, must meet deadlines, face language barriers, or are homeless, it is the parents with more free time and who prioritize schooling who are better able to incur these "transaction costs." They have a private advantage.

Are charter schools "public" on this first measure? A Publicization Project has work to do, which I will discuss at the end of this chapter, if funding is to be sufficient for students in any tax-supported school, district *and* charter. What we know is that operating funding comparable to tax-funded district schools requires nuanced analysis and well calibrated funding formulas. Capital funding requires a better solution than private largesse. And lotteries need to pass the exclusion test.

THE PUBLICNESS OF CHARTER SCHOOL CURRICULUM

The second measure of a school's publicness asks: To what extent is its curriculum based on socially determined facts and knowledge-making norms, subject to the anti-authoritarian empirical rule and test of fallibility? Posed in the negative, to what extent is a school *not* advancing private or ideological points of view that may undermine the civic, economic, social, and environmental goals of tax-funded schools and, in doing so, that school's publicness?

A preemptory way to answer this question is by the goals to which charter schools are held accountable. Their performance is typically measured by students' achievement on state tests. A charter school risks closure if it does not align its curriculum to the standards being assessed. Logic dictates that a charter school's curriculum is only as fact-based—and therefore only as public or private—as the district school around the corner, assuming that both are held to the same state expectations.

Yet within state standards there is room to maneuver. For example, the Michigan-based National Heritage Academies made headlines, in the early days of the charter movement, for its back-to-basics approach "with a religious tinge."[14] Teachers came from Bible colleges, mothers prayed in the building, and students learned in science class about Adam and Eve. New York's Hebrew Language Academy Charter School caused similar controversy,[15] and I had a close call to make when an application for the Hellenic Classical Charter School landed on my desk in 2004. The proposal was from leaders of the recently closed Greek Orthodox school in Brooklyn. It planned to use the same building. Its curriculum included classes in Greek culture and language. After a lengthy review, my office concluded that it was not a "converted" private school, as prohibited by state law, and narrowly satisfied the law's secular requirements. Our preliminary approval was then delivered to the state's publicly appointed Board of Regents, which granted the charter.[16]

Schools like Hellenic and Hebrew Language have had to meet federal guidelines applicable to charter schools that demand, "as public schools," that they must be "non-religious in their programs, admissions policies, governance, employment practices and all other operations, and the charter school's curriculum must be completely secular."[17] Yet former Secretary of Education Betsy DeVos expressed her desire for charters affiliated with religious organizations to also be eligible for such funding,[18] and Oklahoma heeded the call.

In June 2023, Sooner State officials approved the St. Isidore of Seville Catholic Virtual School, the nation's first religious charter. NAPCS president Nina Rees said it "runs afoul of state law and the U.S. Constitution," adding that "all charter schools are public schools, and as such must be nonsectarian."[19] Longtime charter gadfly Michael J. Petrilli noted that whether religious *affiliation* also allows for religious *instruction* remains to be seen, and the charter's legality will likely be appealed to the Supreme Court. But given its conservative turn, SCOTUS may disagree with Rees's legal interpretation.[20]

In some respects, it's not surprising that private interests, like water, find a way into a charter school's curriculum, given the long-standing pervasiveness of private interests in America's other tax-funded district schools. Nor should we be surprised that public leaders like DeVos use the policy instruments at their disposal to advance their priorities. As Senator Mitch McConnell famously said on the confirmation of Amy Coney Barrett to the Supreme Court, which secured its 6 to 3 conversative majority, "elections have consequences."[21]

If the Oklahoma school is found to be constitutional, does that make charters, by definition, more private than public, given their newfound ability to mix fact with belief? Not necessarily. It is important to remember that the Catholic Church did not give *itself* a charter to run a tax-funded school. Nor did charter advocates and lobbyists grant the charter. In Oklahoma, as elsewhere, charters are awarded by state authorities who allow its founders to incorporate, usually as a nonprofit corporation, separate from the local school districts, governed by their own boards of directors. The government-awarded charter gives certain autonomies from state and local regulations for the school to manage its own finances, set its own policies, and implement the curriculum described in its charter application. In return, the school is expected to be accountable to that government authority. If performance is poor (however defined), the authority can revoke the charter or leave it to expire. If achievement is strong, the charter is typically renewed. The school must also be accountable for good governance, sound fiscal management, and the health and safety of its students and employees.[22]

Within this arrangement, the publicness or privateness of what a charter school teaches *is not the school's to decide*. It is the governmental chartering authority that holds such power. Oklahoma's Statewide Virtual Charter School Board authorized St. Isidore of Seville, albeit in a controversial split decision. In New York, my office and New York's Board of Regents could have interpreted the state's charter law to hold Hellenic Classical charter schools to a stricter standard of publicness, concluding that it was little more than a reinvented parochial school. We did not.

Here again we see that a Publicization Project has work to do. How state authorities use their publicly vested power to charter new schools is up for grabs. It is a function of the political processes and interests of the electorate. In McConnell's vernacular, this power is a democratic "consequence." It's also an opportunity for the Project to make charter school curriculum more public, by influencing and holding charter schools' governmental authorizers accountable, as discussed more in the closing recommendations.

THE CHARTER SCHOOL "COMPACT" AND ITS COMPLICITY IN THE INDUSTRIAL PARADIGM

These first two criteria, fair funding and schooling that's premised on facts, suggest that charter schools *are about as public* as their neighboring district schools. Funding varies from state to state, but in New York's example, charters receive about a comparable bundle of public operating resources.

Their lottery-based method of enrollment, open to all, makes some charters even more public than district schools with exclusionary attendance zones. The extent to which charters deliver a fact-based curriculum is determined by the same state learning standards against which they and district schools are measured; when facts slip into beliefs, it is with the ostensible approval of duly elected authorities. So what's all the fuss?

To begin, the charter movement's core "compact"—autonomy in return for accountability—legitimized the sector. As the argument still goes, these schools will outperform their district counterparts or be shuttered. Freedom from state regulations, district bureaucracies, and collective bargaining agreements is necessary for leaders and teachers to deliver the caliber of education that raises achievement and closes equity gaps.

Charter enthusiasts, me included, embraced the compact. It gave us a plausible theory of change about an overly regulated system of education. We were dismantling the "one best" system (which proved to not be) and were part of a new national movement advancing social justice. The work had integrity, too. A charter school would shutter if it didn't outperform its district counterparts. We didn't want to see children and parents disrupted, but that was the deal, to ensure that no child would be left behind in a failing school.[23]

But the sector's compact legitimized the privatization project's economic mode and the inequitable assumptions of the industrial paradigm. A charter is itself a time-limited performance contract, designed to "align incentives" through the threat of closure. Stringent top-down accountability for performance on state tests precludes a broader notion of mutual accountability with evidence fit for each purpose. Charter leaders' legal obligation to outperform district schools can only be conceptualized in a competitive industrial mode; *their* students must move faster, farther along the educational assembly line than those in district schools.

Alternative models of schooling, in the vein of the Intellectual-Emotional Paradigm, did not succeed as charters. For example, Middle College and International High Schools at LaGuardia Community College in Queens, New York, struggled to demonstrate their impact as charters. Both use, to this day, portfolio assessments with students defending their work to committees, like the one on which I served. They are among 38 members of the New York Performance Standards Consortium that don't measure students' achievements by the tests prized by state chartering authorities. So counterculture was the approach that both schools ultimately converted back into district schools within the New York City system.[24]

The charter sector's commitment to test-based accountability further limits schools' ability to bring stakeholders into dialogue, through deliberative governance structures, regarding what to teach and how, another criterion of publicness. One might think that a charter school's autonomy from state and local bureaucracies would be ideal for this kind of stakeholder collaboration. But they are constrained to stick to what's being tested, in the manner they were authorized to achieve it, or risk closure. In the presence of a vocal parent seeking change, and given these constraints, all that a charter school may feel free to do is suggest that the child go elsewhere.

In New York, charter autonomy also allows schools to cap class and grade sizes and choose not to backfill seats as they become available. None are a luxury afforded to a typical district school, which must educate every student who resides within its attendance zone and shows up on the first, or any, day of school. It makes for a competition between district and charter schools that truly isn't fair. Plus, turning students away when an enrollment cap is hit, or leaving coveted seats empty, fails the exclusion test. It makes charter school enrollment more of a private good for those fortunate enough to be selected, via lottery, at a very young age.[25]

COMPETITION AND THE CONSERVATIVE AGENDA

Private advantages, like controlled enrollment and the presence (or perception) of rich benefactors, are leading causes of charter schools' controversy. Interestingly, the charter sector could have emphasized both as models of what every student deserves in any tax-funded school—reasonable class sizes small enough for personalized learning, supported with sufficient resources. Instead, sector advocates emphasized the schools' superiority, in direct competition with district schools for students and funding, à la Chubb and Moe's "panacea."[26]

Such overt competition left little room for these nonprofit chartered organizations to be seen as anything more than a force for privatization. They were not offering civil society's helping hand, only the cold, invisible back of the market's. Charters *aim* to undermine public education, as opponents still argue, by putting district schools out of business. Aggressive student recruitment campaigns confirmed perceptions, with smiling students in prep school jackets and ties in highly produced commercials, mailings, and signage at bus stops. Against such marketing, district alternatives seem like a poor man's second choice.

Perceptions of privatizing competition were reinforced by *actual* private-sector involvement. The late 1990s saw the rapid emergence of for-profit educational management companies like Chris Whittle's Edison Schools, Steven Wilson's Advantage Schools, Steve Klinsky's Victory Schools, and others. Hired to manage charter schools' day-to-day operations, the companies further privatized what were legally constituted as nonprofit educational corporations. Although NAPCS reports that only 12% of the sector's schools are managed by for-profit companies, the idea of profiting off children still dominates the discourse.

In some charter circles, the disruptive competition was a source of pride. When I took my post in New York City, charter advocates were quick to educate me: District and charter interests were fundamentally opposed; when the charters succeed (as of course they would, given their freedom), district schools will shutter (as they should, to finally give students the education they deserve). The founding president and CEO of NAPCS, Nelson Smith, was grateful for my competent administration of the city's obligations to charter schools, including on-time funding, busing services, food deliveries, and other district-provided supports. But there was little way, he said confidently, that district leaders would ever truly embrace charter schools, given the competition for students and resources. At an invitation-only charter leadership conference that Smith organized in 2006, Margaret Raymond, the founding director of Stanford University's Center for Research on Education Outcomes (CREDO), baldly described this conflict in terms of well-established, predictable stages of war.[27]

CHARTER SCHOOLS AND THE TEACHER UNIONS

A final cause of charter school controversy, indirectly related to the six criteria of publicness but pertinent to a Publicization Project, is the sector's relationship with the teacher unions. First, some context.

In a unionized school district, all teachers are represented in employment matters by their union's chapter, the "local." In labor parlance, this is a "closed shop." Every employee, no matter their individual employment wishes, is covered by employment terms and conditions negotiated by district officials and union representatives. Terms are memorialized in a collective bargaining agreement, or CBA. The approach is considered efficient, so that management doesn't have to negotiate every person's contract individually. It also intends to create some esprit de corps by removing potential favoritism, with an egalitarian sense that everyone has a right to, and gets, comparable treatment and pay. There may be some variation in CBA terms within a district from school to school. But by and large, these agreements set wages, working conditions, and due process requirements for every teacher. Teachers are not obliged to be union members (although many are). Nor are nonmembers obliged to pay an "agency fee" to the union to help cover the cost of representation, as the Supreme Court recently ruled.[28]

So imagine a new nonprofit education corporation called a charter school, authorized by the state, setting up operations within a school district, funded in part by local tax dollars, and free to students. Its teachers aren't automatically union members. Nor does the existing CBA apply to this new school, as that is a contract between two different legal entities, the union and the district; the newly chartered corporation is not party to the existing agreement.

Exemption from such CBAs became a hallmark of charter school autonomy; charter school management sets wages, benefits, and working conditions. CBAs also include terms generated over decades of negotiations, resulting from issues that a new charter school may never encounter. This clean slate is, in theory, an opportunity to reimagine human resources in education. For example, the Equity Project Charter School caught the attention of *60 Minutes* for its $125,000 teacher salaries.[29] Today, there are over 200,000 charter school teachers, most of whom are not represented by a union and are hired as "at-will" employees without due process protections other than the nondiscrimination requirements set in state and federal law.

Unions, meanwhile, depend on the number and activism of their members and the density of their presence in an industry, making this large unrepresented segment of the education force a threat to their influence. Members' dues pay for political activity to elect officials sympathetic to their interests. Legal funds pay for representation and other member services. Union activism shifts agendas, as when members mobilize to support one cause or another or provide leverage for the bargaining table. As Terry Moe has written, when their political influence is strong, public-sector unions turn the principal-agent problem on its head, given that teachers can influence the election of public officials who are supposed to hold districts, schools, and their teachers accountable.[30] (Although, in fairness, this is no different from corporations influencing elections through campaign donations to elect leaders sympathetic to *their* interests.)

The simple *effect* of a nonunion bloc of tax-funded schools, diluting a union's strength and influence, was enough to draw ire. Further inflaming the situation was the *intent* of the privatization project to grow this nonunion segment for political purposes. Groups like the Atlantic Legal Foundation published guides "to educate charter school leaders [on how] to deal with efforts by public employee unions to burden charter schools with intrusive union work rules that stifle innovation." Its authors hailed from the conservative Mackinac Center on Public Policy and Jackson Lewis, LLP, a notoriously anti-union law firm whose workshops include "Remaining Union Free: A Counter Organizing Simulation."[31]

Some charter advocates note that charter teachers are always free to unionize if they wish. Factually, the statement is accurate, in states that allow collective bargaining. But the comment knowingly ignores the time, expense, and risks. To unionize, a majority of teachers first need to express their intent to form or join a union through a secret ballot election or signed authorization cards, known as Card Check. Such representation must then be recognized by the school and state or the National Labor Relations Board. All this must occur before any collective bargaining can begin. In that period, school management has every opportunity to run Atlantic Legal's playbook of tactics to intimidate teachers, fire union activists for permitted reasons, and defeat the effort.

Plus, for a long time, I didn't encounter many young and idealistic charter school teachers who wanted formal representation and collective influence.

They were born and raised within the era of the privatization project. At-will employment seemed the norm, with self-representation even empowering. Plus, the risk of losing one's job from speaking up could be high. I saw too many good educators lose their jobs during union organizing drives at places like Merrick Academy in Queens. Today, this may be changing, given the progressive turn in American politics and more positive attitudes about organized labor. But at the time, reform rhetoric successfully painted teacher unions as part of the problem, protecting bad teachers and harming students. Who would want to join *that*?

MAKING CHARTER SCHOOLS MORE PUBLIC

Charter schools remain controversial. But controversy is not, in and of itself, a measure of privateness. Are they public? If not funded fairly, they are reliant on private largesse. If authorized to stray from facts into ideology, they may undermine long-standing common purposes of schooling. If they cap enrollment, they risk failing the exclusion test. If they counsel parents to find a better fit, unwilling to heed their and other stakeholders' voices, they're not engaging in deliberative governance. The strong degree to which they've embraced test-based accountability impedes mutual accountability with evidence fit for each purpose and legitimizes the "as much, as fast" assumption of the industrial paradigm. Some may advance equity for the Black, Latinx, and poor students they enroll and help to "get ahead," but doing so unwittingly impedes the more equitable Intellectual-Emotional Paradigm.

Lest we forget, many of these same private interests are present in tax-funded district schools and have been for far longer than charter schools ever existed. Yet these attributes lead self-described champions of public education, like NPE, to conclude that charter schools are, for all intents and purposes, publicly funded private schools. Accordingly, NPE calls for an end to federal charter school funding, in an effort to contain or shrink the sector. Some district activists go further, stating that "every charter school must be closed down—Every. Single. One."[32]

But the charter sector is now too large to shutter, wish as they might. Its 7,700 schools have a well-established ecosystem of advocates, funders, researchers, and supporters who protect their interests—including billions of dollars in annual state, local, and federal funding.[33] Millions of parents are invested in the charter schools to which they send their children and are organized into a powerful political bloc. Combined, it's a strong set of protective "sustaining politics."[34] Case in point: charter enrollments *grew* during the COVID-19 pandemic.[35]

Where, then, given this reality, might charter schools fit within a Publicization Project? There are two scenarios: First, the growth of charter schools tapers off, as the Project focuses resources and support to district schools. District and charter schools find a political détente and mutually coexist, with periodic and localized political skirmishes over funding, facilities, performance, and accountability. The teacher unions come to accept their representation of a smaller share of the workforce, because of the high cost of union-organizing drives, and work with school boards to make district employment more attractive.

Alternatively, the number of charter schools continues to increase. Their advocates and constituents champion their efforts. Private philanthropy continues to fuel new buildings, marketing campaigns, and two teachers in every class. In places with a growing population, these schools help to keep up with demand. Elsewhere, they may continue to gain a larger share of the local student enrollment.

In *either* scenario, champions of a Publicization Project must come to terms with the fact that charter schools are here to stay. They currently educate one out of every 15 of the country's elementary and secondary school students. These students are disproportionately Black, Latinx, and poor. Who are these future citizens? How well will they be prepared to enjoy and share in the nation's prosperity? To what extent do they value social cohesion from being good neighbors? And will they be responsible stewards of the environment?

A Publicization Project dare not leave these questions to chance. Nor can it in good conscience turn its back on students who will most benefit from a quality education, by treating equity as an imperative only in district schools. Charter schools, if left to their own devices, may well still serve public purposes and interests, as many already do, in a parallel universe of tax-funded schools. Alternatively, the charter sector may lean into its privateness; the events in Oklahoma, when blessed by the Supreme Court, may be a precursor of much more to come.

Given this risk, the years of controversy, and the degree to which charters have been used by the privatization project to advance its neoliberal vision, a Publicization Project's only real choice is to embrace charter schools and sector leaders who seek to make these schools, and all of American tax-funded education, more public. How might this look?

"INVISIBLE" VERSUS "HELPING" HANDS: COMMUNITY-BASED CHARTER SCHOOLS

In 2013 I helped organize a coalition of about 30 community-based charter schools in New York City, which later evolved into the national Coalition of Public Independent Charter Schools, led by Steve Zimmerman.[36] These were largely stand-alone schools like the Math and Science Academy founded by Arthur Samuels, Amber Charter School led by Vasthi Reyes Acosta, Steve Barr's Green Dot New York Charter School, and, at the time, DREAM's single founding site led by Eve Colavito and Rich Berlin. Notably, the schools were unaffiliated with networks and management organizations like Success Academy, KIPP, Achievement First, and Uncommon Schools, whose aggressive growth strategies—backed by tens of millions in private philanthropy—were a source of controversy. These networks' well-funded advocacy usually represented the voice of the city's charter sector. Although interests were typically aligned, the other small and unaffiliated schools wanted to speak with their own voice.

Bill de Blasio had just been elected mayor with support from the city's teachers' union, the United Federation of Teachers.[37] He campaigned hard against the education reforms of his predecessor, Michael Bloomberg, who enthusiastically supported charters (and continues to, recently pledging $750 million to expand the sector).[38] In his victory speech, de Blasio declared, "We have to be willing to reverse so many mistakes of the Bloomberg years." Scholar Pedro Noguera noted this to mean "charters, choice, and school closures," a strategy that Bloomberg executed "more effectively than any other mayor." Ravitch, a champion-turned-opponent of the privatization project, predicted that de Blasio could be "the most important national leader against the movement to close down and privatize public education."[39]

De Blasio called for a moratorium on new charter schools and threatened to charge rent to those in public buildings. In response, outspoken charter leaders like Eva Moskowitz of Success Academy and her affiliated lobbyist Jeremiah Kitteridge of Families for Excellent Schools organized impressive protests in Albany and New York City that made national headlines.[40] Across the country, charter leaders watched closely, as the election of this anti-reform, self-described progressive was a potential bellwether in national education politics.[41]

Amidst such hostilities, our coalition thought that some quiet diplomacy might have a positive effect. The facts were undeniable: Here was a mayor who ran—and won—by repeatedly attacking charter schools. Politicians don't keep saying things that lose them votes, and with de Blasio, it didn't. The city's political mood was shifting, and we believed that the charter sector would be well served to find a new footing, more in step with the progressive politics emerging nationwide and in line with the noncompetitive, community-based values that our group already embraced.

So we reached out to the new administration, a move not appreciated by the city's charter school power brokers. At the time and later in print, they attacked the coalition as naïve and divisive to much-needed unity.[42] Over drinks, Nelson Smith explained that NAPCS preferred to keep such "rump" disagreements private, strongly suggesting that we should stop. Another coalition leader received a call from a major donor, heavy on implications that grants might get pulled. I even received a call one weekend from longtime charter school attorney Eric Grannis, who incredulously asked what we thought we were doing.

I explained that our coalition's message to de Blasio was simple: Chartering was used by the previous administration as part and parcel of the privatization project, with an emphasis on competition. But de Blasio could embrace chartering in ways that emphasized the schools' publicness. Rather than charters as neoliberal creatures of the *market*, de Blasio could use city policies and his bully pulpit to reshape the sector's *character*, positioning the schools as part of *civil society*. This new approach would expect charters to complement the work of district schools. Schools could be chartered to meet educational needs identified by the city, in essence, a Publicization vision of chartering as a collaborative *helping hand* instead of a competitive *invisible* one.

In numerous meetings with administration officials, we further emphasized that a third-way approach to chartering was in keeping with de Blasio's stated commitment to the city's most underserved residents, evoked ad nauseum in his "tale of two cities" rhetoric.[43] We also stressed that de Blasio would find ready allies among our coalition of community-based charter schools. These schools were already operating in a civil society tradition and perceived as trusted members of their communities. Practically, they were already serving the low-income communities he claimed to champion. Plus, political opportunism was at play: Rather than remain slavishly anti-reform, the new mayor could redefine what chartering should be and do. It would be a Nixon-in-China moment, complicate pat narratives, and reappropriate policies and practices for his preferred use.

We also gave it a shot because many in our coalition were uncomfortable with an aggressive public fight. We were aligned with the mayor's rhetorical commitment to equity—one reason why these charters chose to locate in some of the city's poorest communities. We wanted to put a different face on the sector, one that more accurately depicted our values. In New York and nationwide, I've found that many charter school leaders have little interest in the competition narrative fueled at the national level by the privatization project. More often than not, they simply want some freedom to try their hand at things to do better by children. This motivation is similar to what inspired founders of new small district schools pioneered in East Harlem in the 1980s, of which Meier's Central Park East was one. These more pragmatic intentions have been documented in books like *A Smarter Charter: Finding What Works for Charter Schools and Public Education* by Rick Kahlenberg and Halley Potter and the earlier *Emancipatory Promise of Charter Schools: Toward a Progressive Politics of School Choice*, edited by New York University's Lisa M. Stulberg and the late activist-scholar Eric Rofes, which notably has an introduction by Marxian scholar Herbert Gintis.[44]

* * *

De Blasio did soften his stance on charters a few months into his term, in what observers considered a *mea culpa* speech.[45] He called on public officials and educators to join forces and improve education for all children, an odd phrasing given his own divisive campaign rhetoric. He "had not properly explained his decision to limit the expansion of charters," he said, and that "mistake had inflamed the conflict." It was arguably the first of many deBlasian reversals on many issues to come.[46]

Our small coalition held no illusions that our diplomacy caused the pivot, as compared to the tremendous show of political force by Moskowitz and her allies, including an intense negative-advertising campaign against the new mayor. But we were encouraged. Our hopes were sustained by the appointment of a prominent social welfare and charter school leader, Richard Buery, as deputy mayor for strategic initiatives—including education.[47] Following de Blasio's retreat, we met on and off with Buery and administration leaders for about a year. I got tapped to serve on a "shared space" working group, charged with easing tensions between schools co-located in the same building.[48] But ultimately, our efforts did prove to be a fool's errand. De Blasio showed no desire to repurpose the charter sector to greater public effect. Rather than a mayor for all of the city's students regardless of the type of tax-funded school they attended, he was a partisan on the side of district schools.

But to what end? The city's charter sector continued to grow during his 8 years in office, albeit at a slower pace, given pro-charter state authorities and parent demand. Charter schools continued to serve the poorest communities that his progressive administration claimed to support, albeit without any coordination with City Hall. Meanwhile, de Blasio's benign neglect left chartering—one of the policy tools at his disposal—unused in the largest public school system in the United States, where every hand is needed to make the tremendous work a little lighter.

CHARTER SCHOOLS AND THE PROGRESSIVE AGENDA

In retrospect, de Blasio is the poster child for why the country, and particularly progressive Democrats, need a Publicization Project writ large, and that includes charter schools.[49] My sense is that de Blasio thought that simply opposing the privatization project would be enough. By *not* making charters, choice, competition, top-down accountability, and test-based teacher evaluation part of his agenda, he could restore public education to the way it "should be." How wrong he was.

Pundits across the political spectrum agree that his education record was a failure. *City Journal* wrote that the mayor's education department was "characterized by its effective abandonment of issues as basic as the importance of compulsory education, the primacy of achievement, and the need to provide feedback to students on their performance and to the public on the results of their investment in the schools." The American Civil Liberties Union charged that "de Blasio never successfully addressed the disparities between who gets punished in City schools and who gets a second chance. Black, and Latinx students, as well as those with disabilities, still continue to bear a disproportionate burden of school suspensions and arrests." His schools chancellor, Richard Carranza, quit over efforts to advance equity in education within the mayor's own district schools, which a senior schools official told me de Blasio "stymied." Teacher activists poetically characterized his 8 years as "sound and fury, signifying nothing."[50]

You can't beat something with nothing. De Blasio could not have been more vocal in his desire to beat back the privatization project. But he had no alternative, no coherent set of guiding ideas attractive to a growable coalition. If self-described progressives are to make schools—district *and charter*—more public, they need their own Publicization Project. De Blasio missed his chance to lead such a movement, in general and by reimagining the charter sector. But hope springs eternal, and doing so requires a number of things.

Equitable Funding

To begin, if champions of public education believe in equitable resources for all students enrolled in free, tax-funded schools—the first and most fundamental criterion of a school's publicness—this must extend to students who attend charter schools. If resource inequity is unacceptable from one town and state to the next—and it should be—this inequity must be just as odious from one tax-funded school to the next. For public authorities and a Publicization Project to defensibly hold charter schools to the same expectations as other tax-funded schools, charters must have comparable and requisite resources. Private interests will always find a way, like the $1 million raised *annually* at my sons' elementary school, PS 321, and in gifts, like Bloomberg's to charter schools. But a minimum and sufficient public commitment shouldn't rely on private largesse.

Resource equity must include capital needs, too. A 2014 change to New York's charter law provided an imperfect fix, with rent assistance for new and expanding charter schools. But a bolder approach is necessary, and New York City's School Construction Authority (SCA) provides a useful example. Although regularly criticized for its bureaucracy and cost of construction, the Authority separates capital planning from schooling. It takes a long-term view on demographic trends and the age of infrastructure to decide where to invest new public dollars for construction and renovation.

Why not include both district and charter schools in the SCA's mandate, in New York and similar authorities nationwide? Its technocratic approach aims for more prudent capital planning than if facilities funding simply "follows the child." With a charter, this approach would also simplify the school's autonomy-for-accountability compact: If it loses its charter, the event is not complicated by the lease or ownership of a building. Rather, the facility would remain in public hands for public use, eliminating the risk of a private asset built at public expense.

Would the SCA have spent $50 million to renovate an ice factory into "one of the most spectacular school buildings in the city"?[51] It's unlikely. The Bronx saw higher-than-expected population growth over the past decade, but its total population has declined by 80,000 residents since 2020. Its population is aging, too, with a total census 12% less than when most of its school buildings were constructed.[52] Asked another way, might it not have been in the interest of DREAM's donors to have had the SCA pay *all* of the cost to renovate an *existing* school building? And might the lobbying and policy development for charters to receive comparable treatment by the SCA—with its long-term charter sector-wide benefits—have cost less than $50 million? It's in charter donors' interest to find out.

Charter opponents will likely invoke their frequent objection that such resource equity merely drains even *more* funding away from district schools. But a Publicization Project cannot sustain, in any principled way, a two-tier commitment to tax-funded education—one that has a responsibility to put a roof over some students' heads but not others. Moreover, by including charter school leaders in the fight for funding sufficient to meet educational goals, a Publicization Project can gain new allies. It would present an even more powerful and united front to officials who control the purse strings.

Charter School Tax-Status: The Question of "For-Profit"

Second, there are strong, but not universal, reasons why a Publicization Project should demand that charter schools and their management companies operate exclusively on a not-for-profit basis. As noted above, some states allow these schools to subcontract operations to a for-profit manager, an arrangement that works against a school's publicness. For-profit companies have a fiduciary obligation to their owners and shareholders, in most cases to maximize profits. This is not a mutual obligation among many stakeholders to maximize performance. The profit motive invites conflicts of interest, as when less expensive services, less likely to strengthen the quality of education, are provided over costlier ones. It introduces a moral hazard, as when merely *meeting* chartered goals is sufficient, rather than the extra spend to *exceed* goals.

Moreover, funding provided to charter and district schools is typically determined through some kind of political process. It represents the level of financial support that approximates the priority that a town or state places on education—its "policy preference." Fiscal adequacy lawsuits argue that these levels are already insufficient for schools to meet expected outcomes. Such funding is made further insufficient if reduced by an operator's profit.

Defenders of private enterprise argue that the profit motive incentivizes greater efficiency and, in the process, point to examples of public-sector waste. It's plausible that a company could make its profit on the hypothesized difference between the two. But the actual cost of a quality education is hard to define. Affluent families pay tens of thousands of dollars to send their children to well-appointed private schools. Their willingness to spend more argues that any public-sector "waste" should be redeployed into the student experience, not redirected to shareholders. Plus, cost saving measures in the name of efficiency, like lower salaries and 401(k) retirement plans instead of defined-benefit pensions, ultimately cut against a school's ability to recruit and retain talented educators.

For-profit is certainly part of the American way of life, and we can point to very mission-driven organizations that also generate profit and pay taxes.[53] The capital markets are willing to take more risks to back promising innovations than are government and private philanthropy. Can we square this with a Publicization Project? I think we must.

One option is for school districts to hire a for-profit management company on a cost-plus basis, meaning whatever the cost would have been to run a school plus a percentage that is, presumably, the company's profit. This is common practice in large government contracts, particularly the defense industry, where the marginal cost of production is not immediately clear and where only a few firms have the requisite expertise. A school district might want to learn from a firm that has spent private capital to develop innovations that the district did not have the funding or entrepreneurial drive to develop on its own. Or a school may wish to hire the company because of its track record of success with particular students.

Admittedly, these are special circumstances. They require a careful examination of the for-profit activity and negotiation of terms. Although it would be simpler for a Publicization Project to draw a bright line excluding for-profit activity from its movement, doing so foreswears capital that can drive innovation. Plus, the proposed project is not about drawing lines that separate, but rather creating more space for different stakeholders to come together and make their contribution to the collective good. This coalition will need investors and businesspeople. Under the right circumstances, the project can, and should, be *for* profit.

Charter Lotteries and Enrollment

Last summer my wife and sons saw *Hamlet* by the New York Public Theater, for free in Central Park. They got to the Delacorte Theater at 7:00 in the morning. A hundred people were already ahead of them in line, for distribution that started at noon, to see an 8:00 P.M. show. House managers repeatedly announced that they could not leave the line and come back, could not save a place for someone else, and would only be allowed two tickets each. In our privatized age of block purchases by resellers and preferred front-of-line access, such are the lengths that the aptly named Public Theater takes to ensure that the free seats are filled as fairly as possible, excluded from no one who can wait in line.

Such is also the allure of charter school lotteries, similarly open to anyone in a district or town. But as noted above, they may not be as nonexclusive as theorized. The application process may intimidate some families, particularly if language or other cultural barriers exist, or privilege those who value education more. The children of families who are homeless are particularly vulnerable. Deadlines may come and go. Plus, who has the time and energy to do all the paperwork for multiple schools? Who has the luxury—and patience—to stand in line at the Delacorte for 5 hours?

Charter lotteries can be made even more equitable if conducted centrally, by a school district or organizing body, and universally, for all students in a district. Rather than waiting to see who applies, every student gets a random assignment. The initial, *default* position is universal participation—driving nonexclusionary, common benefits—rather than among only who seek to participate.[54]

District schools are just learning lessons that charter schools have known for decades about the equity-promoting benefits, as well as the unintended consequences, of such lotteries. For example, lottery admission now places every middle school student in New York City's Community School District 15, which adopted the policy to advance greater racial and economic integration. In the past, parents jockeyed to get their children into only two or three schools. The process has forced them to consider more alternatives, and they're finding a wider range of interesting options. At present, a similar approach is rolling out for admission to most of New York City's district high schools, too.

Under such circumstances, real estate is less of a structural force for inequitable schooling. Families can no longer buy their way into a preferred attendance zone, aggregating class interests just as much as school choice can for group interests. Universal lotteries stand a chance of building a broader coalition for the resourcing of all tax-funded schools, by putting Rawls's thought experiment into practice: Not knowing where my child will be assigned, I have an interest in the quality of them all. A Publicization Project should put the idea to the test.

Strengthening the publicness of admissions via lottery, across charter *and district* schools, is easier than the publicness of enrollment. If a school's lottery is oversubscribed, at what size student body does it draw the line? If a districtwide, universal-participation lottery does not have enough overall seats to assign every person to a school, what does it do? If student and family preferences are expressed, what happens when a student doesn't get a top choice?

All of these scenarios fail, to some extent, the exclusion test of what makes something more of a public good. There are ways to address them, such as expanding the size of a popular school, replicating its model at a second location, adjusting class sizes, staggering schedules, and other fixes. But one thing that every charter school can do—and that a Publicization Project should demand—is backfill seats as they become available, as when a family moves and their child enrolls elsewhere. This is one of the simplest actions that a charter can take to exclude less and be more of a public good.

Deliberative Decision-Making

Regrettably, I've attended one too many charter board meetings as a member or authorizer held in corporate office buildings, high in a skyscraper, through carefully guarded doors. During the pandemic, board business was conducted via Zoom. The locations and optics could hardly be less conducive to attendance by others, let alone participation. These exclusionary settings emphasize a school's privateness. Such venues also give charter opponents an easy target, inviting suspicion of unknown board members, talking behind closed doors, about hidden agendas.

But this, too, is an easy fix. Charter boards should insist on meeting at the school, or in a public forum, at times when parents, community members, and other stakeholders can join, and encouraging them to do so. Doing so passes the exclusion test. Board agendas should include time for parent and public comment and discussion, to hear and heed these voices. Authorizers should require and enforce it. It embraces mutual accountability and shows that these schools have nothing to hide, no privatizing agenda. It may make meetings messier and a little less predictable. But that's life in a free and open society, of which tax-funded schools, in service of democracy, are a part.

Protecting the Public Interest: Charter School Authorizers

Fifth, a Publicization Project should seek to strengthen the oversight capabilities of charter school authorizers. At the same time, the Project must acknowledge the fundamental—and potentially instructive—differences in the ways that charter and district schools are held accountable.

As discussed above, governance of district schools evolved over 200 years, originating in parental and then local control by elected boards. Progressive reforms bureaucratized many of these functions through curricular and fiscal controls. Oversight was standardized through regulations. But there was nothing preordained in this arrangement, and well-founded doubts about the failings of this "one best system" eroded trust in experts.[55] It led some educators to seek alternate approaches based less on compliance and more on outcomes via professional discretion. Chartering provided the mechanism.

Although considered something new, recall that education beyond grammar school in the 19th century was provided by thousands of state-chartered academies. Governments recognized a public *interest* in secondary education. But rather than taxing and spending to control and operate such schools, states *deputized civil society* to fill the gap between primary education and the nation's colleges. Like today's charters, these academies were governed by private boards, not elected bodies.

A Publicization Project should take note. Today's district system of governance has no more intrinsic publicness than this alternate form of school governance and accountability that is fully in keeping with the country's political traditions. It's possible to see *chartering* as being as American as little red schoolhouses and urban school systems. It is perhaps even preferable to the rule-based systems of control in which district schools operate.

Today, charter school authorizers are the public officials who guard the public trust. They are themselves accountable to elected representatives and government bodies. Authorizers review school proposals and approve charters (or recommend approvals to a governmental body). They oversee charter school finances and operations to ensure responsible use of public dollars. They monitor academic performance. Critically, they have the power to revoke charters or let them expire, enforcing the core compact of autonomy for accountability.

Amidst much of the heated rhetoric about charter schools, one can be forgiven for believing that the schools are self-created and free of any kind of government oversight. They are not. It is true that authorizing was developed on the fly in the early years of the charter movement.[56] I was on that plane, developing policies just as educators were applying for charters and opening schools. But over the decades, a sound body of authorizing principles has been established, thanks to steady leadership from the National Association of Charter School Authorizers and its founding President and CEO, Greg Richmond.[57]

A Publicization Project must ensure that charter school authorizers have the resources and clout to implement these best practices. It must watch these watchers, to ensure that authorizers don't allow private interests to displace public purposes. Short of authorizers being directly elected like school board members, the Project must work to get leaders elected who seek to make all tax-funded schools more public and appoint authorizers accordingly.

The Publicness of Charter School Governance

Next, champions of a Publicization Project should welcome charter school board members into the Project. Many are respected leaders in positions of great influence, not unlike the prominent citizens who led the 19th-century academies. At least in New York City, it's not uncommon for charter boards to include leaders of finance, industry, culture, and civil society. For the Project to succeed, it needs what they can do, sometimes with a single phone call.

But today it's unclear if these board members believe that their responsibilities include a broader commitment to public education. It's plausible that they feel as if their charter service "does their part," through the considerable time and resources they give. But what about the students in the district school around the corner? Or across the country? What risks to our polity, society, economy, and ecology do charter school trustees let go unaddressed, because it's the responsibility of *other* schools?

Advocates of a Publicization Project must show why it's in these board members' interest to join the effort. The above example regarding the private expense of DREAM's new school, with the hypothetical and less costly alternative, is one. Similarly, DREAM's donors support 33% of the network's annual operating expenses. If we assume that these added resources get the network's total budget closer to what it actually takes to deliver a quality education in *any* tax-funded school, might not DREAM's donors prefer that government pick up the full bill? And throw their considerable weight behind fiscal equity campaigns that benefit both district and charter schools?

Another example comes from a recent DREAM board meeting where we celebrated the college acceptances of our first-ever class of high school seniors. The school's management team sought approval for gap grants, to close the difference between the cost of college attendance and financial aid packages. But a fellow board member, doing the calculations in his head, asked, "How expensive is this gap grant program going to get? As we grow larger, and over our students' four years of college? How much money will we have to raise?"

His skepticism was well placed even if his solution—privately raised scholarships—wasn't. He saw the issue through charter schools' lens of privateness—a problem for our *own* school to solve, drawing on private resources, to the private benefit of only our *own* students. But, in fact, this particular problem exists because of decades of government divestment from higher education.[58] It would be better—and in my former fellow board member's financial self-interest—to advocate for collective solutions, excluded from none, like doubling the size of Pell Grants for our *and other* low-income college-bound graduates.

Moreover, the ideas in this book may cause charter school board members to reevaluate their personal politics in light of the charter movement's, leading them to *want* to join and help lead a Publicization Project. By understanding the work of schools through the lens of publicness and privateness, it's harder to claim that their board service is apolitical, merely focused on fiduciary obligations to their *own* school. Collectively, the charter sector is a central player in the nation's education politics and the most prominent front of the privatization project. If charter board members feel more allied with the aims of a Publicization Project, how will they advance them? What changes will they make to strengthen the publicness of the charter schools they serve and across all tax-funded schools? How will they direct the sector's advocates who, in theory, represent the interests of the sector's schools? Do charter school board members even know who these lobbyists are?

Charter Schools, Innovation, and the Intellectual-Emotional Paradigm

Finally, charter schools can be powerful allies in a Publicization Project's embrace of mutual accountability and equity through an Intellectual-Emotional Paradigm. To understand why, it's helpful to briefly revisit the modern history of the charter school idea.

In 1988, amidst the birth of the standards movement, American Federation of Teachers president Al Shanker took to the podium at the National Press Club.[59] The country was still grappling with *A Nation at Risk*. But in Shanker's estimation, the flurry of reforms were still only benefiting "kids who are able to learn in a traditional system, who are able to sit still, who are able to keep quiet, who are able to remember after they listen to someone else talk for five hours, who are able to pick up a book and learn from it—who've got all these things going for them."[60] In other words, kids who succeed within the strictures of the industrial paradigm. Shanker estimated that this was a small number, with reforms still "bypassing about 80 percent of the students in this country."

In response, Shanker called for a "second reform movement" and introduced, to a national audience, ideas developed by educator Ray Budde. Shanker advocated for groups of teachers to be given authority by their local school district to experiment for a period of time with new methods of teaching and approaches to schooling. They'd have autonomy from district and state rules and regulations that got in the way of their ideas—freedom to try something different. This profession-driven view of improvement assumed that teachers—those closest to the work—are best positioned to innovate in ethical ways. If things were going well, their autonomy would extend for another period of time and their practices shared with colleagues. If not, their experiment would end. In essence, this would be in-house R&D, by small networks of educators, with permission to operate outside of the rules and routines.

The word "charter" didn't appear in his speech, but Shanker's promotion made Budde's ideas the sector's intellectual foundation. The notions were picked up by founding fathers and mothers, including Ember Reichgott Junge, Joe Nathan, and Ted Kolderie, who led the passage, in 1991, of the nation's first charter school law in Minnesota.[61] And in a consequential choice, the Minnesota law established charter schools as independent nonprofit corporations, outside the legal jurisdiction of school districts. As noted above, such institutional autonomy made teachers the employees of the nonprofit organization. It placed them *outside* of any existing collective bargaining agreements and union membership.

This, to put it mildly, was not what Shanker intended. As a founder of the modern teacher union movement, Shanker knew better than anyone the importance of a union's size and strength. Losing potential members to new tax-funded schools undermined the solidarity that any union needs to pursue its members' interests. Despite his initial support, Shanker turned against the idea. The charter sector's subsequent embrace by the privatization project, with its emphasis on choice, competition, standardized test-based accountability, and at-will employment, further justified his volte-face.[62]

The turn of events also wedded the charter sector to the industrial paradigm. Without question, there is pedagogical diversity across the nation's many charter schools. But the most prominent charters—those that dominated the sector's politics—embraced a back-to-basics, no excuses approach.[63] Charter incubators like Building Excellent Schools gave generous grants to school founders allied to this thinking. School leaders were determined to excel in a regime of test-based accountability, endeavoring to run the most efficient assembly lines of all. I well remember visiting one nationally celebrated charter school whose founder would walk the halls with a stopwatch, timing students as they passed from class to class. Somewhere, Frederick Winslow Taylor was smiling.

Autonomy to innovate is an empty promise if a charter's underlying "as much, as fast" assumption constrains educators to think of their students as widgets on an assembly line, limited to test-based demonstrations of *academic* competencies. But if given the chance, with an openness to different kinds of evidence and ways of knowing fit for different aspects of accountability, I suspect there are many charter school educators who would embrace an Intellectual-Emotional Paradigm. They could use their autonomy to help students cultivate *human* competencies. This is, after all, how Meier developed her Habits of Mind at Central Park East Elementary School. It was a charter in spirit, as she pushed against the constraints of her district to get some freedom to innovate.

Chartering gives a Publicization Project a ready set of policy tools to create the autonomous conditions necessary to prove the virtues of an Intellectual-Emotional Paradigm. Interestingly, Budde's notion of small groups of teachers working together is eerily similar to the "networked learning communities" promoted by Bryk and colleagues' *Learning to Improve*. This envisions rapid prototyping and revision of new approaches, within the guardrails of improvement science. Bryk and colleagues' recommendations can find a natural home in the charter sector, given the schools' autonomy, and if its school leaders are truly freed by their authorizers to pursue a new, more equitable paradigm.[64]

FINDING COMMON GROUND IN THE COMMON GOOD

Ultimately, charter and district schools must find common ground. A Publicization Project cannot succeed for *all* students in *every* tax-funded school if political hostilities persist. The Project cannot fight thousands of charter schools, with their well-organized advocates, in some futile hope of seeing them go away. Nor should the Project seek to harm these schools with funding cuts. Doing so only exacerbates resource inequity for millions of young Americans enrolled in these schools, most of whom are poor, Black, and Latinx. Alternatively, hoping for some steady state of charter-district relations, based on mutually assured political destruction, risks sustaining the privateness that is rife across the charter *and* district sectors.

As I've shown, there are many ways to strengthen the charter sector's publicness and for the sector to join a Publicization Project. Fair funding, better authorizing, a reimagined role of charter board members, expanded use of lotteries, and freedom to innovate are just a few ideas that spring from the criteria of what makes schools more public. The bright and imaginative leaders of the charter sector will no doubt think of many more.

To do so, it will be necessary to forgive past injuries from what was nothing less than an education civil war. As a combatant in those battles, I know it won't be easy. Nor will everyone join; there are still educational and political ideologues in our midst. But my hope is that there are enough of us who want to make amends and move forward to make schools more public.

But what, ultimately, about the teacher unions? Can their existential fight with charter schools find some peace? Or are differences irreconcilable, on the fundamental fact that lost membership is lost influence? And what role must they play in a Publicization Project?

CHAPTER 8

Teacher Unions

> Doubtful it stood,
> As two spent swimmers, that do cling together
> And choke their art.
>
> —William Shakespeare, *Macbeth,* Act 1, Scene 2[1]

In recent decades the teacher unions have been the most outspoken opponents of the privatization project. But if the tide is turning, with privatization going out to sea, the unions cannot sail back to familiar harbors. A Publicization coalition needs the union's political strength on key areas of common interest. But for the Project to make schools more public, it also needs the unions to change in fundamental ways. Hargreaves and Fullan write that the unions and federations will have to "follow their most avant-garde leaders to share or even lead [this] responsibility."[2] To understand why, the foil of charter schools provides more insights.

EDUCATION PORTFOLIOS AND COMPETITION AT THE APEX OF EDUCATION POLICY

By 2004, major school districts were competing to have the most charter schools. Newark aimed to be the nation's charter "capital." In New York City, Mayor Michael R. Bloomberg and Schools Chancellor Joel I. Klein imagined a charter school "Silicon Valley." Oakland, California, was a charter "boomtown." A year later, Hurricane Katrina decimated New Orleans. Charter proponents used the tragedy to eliminate the system of district schools, void the teachers' union contract, and establish an all-charter district.[3]

Competition, the privatization project's article of faith, found its way to the marketplace of school *districts.* Superintendents outdid one another to retain and import charter school operators. Private philanthropy from the Robin Hood and Pisces foundations, Silicon Valley's New Schools Venture Fund, and others bankrolled charter replications in Houston with Yes Prep, across New York with Uncommon Schools, and nationwide with KIPP.

Viewing the education bureaucracy as a giant monopoly, Klein brought to his job the trust-busting skills he honed at the U.S. Justice Department.[4] Also, any lingering doubts among charter advocates about the "incompatibility" of a district's and charter school's interests, as Nelson Smith had believed, were decidedly put to rest.

The embrace was based on more economic reasoning, a supply-side diagnosis of the problems facing districts. Superintendents including Klein, for whom I served as director of charter schools, became "unalloyed"[5] charter champions as a way to bring new talent into the school system. Chartering gave entrepreneurial teachers, many of whom were Teach for America alumni, a way to run their own schools. Doing so addressed the "supply problem" of not having enough good schools for every student. Plus, charters brought highly influential people into the work of fixing the "broken" public education system, leading Diane Ravitch to quip that "the wealthy used to collect racehorses and yachts; now they start their own charter school."[6] (In fairness, wealthy Americans also created hospitals, libraries, parks, settlement houses, universities, and museums.)

Furthermore, the theory of an education "portfolio" provided a market-based underpinning for the co-existence of district and charter schools.[7] Like an investor who manages a portfolio of investments, selling off poor performers and expanding one's "position" among investments with great "returns," superintendents similarly were to manage their own portfolio of high- and low-performing schools. Developed by Paul Hill of the Center on Reinventing Public Education, the theory asked district leaders to open new schools, replicate high achievers, and shutter poor performers. The unapologetic disruption was intentional, operationalizing economist Joseph Schumpeter's (and, later, businessman Clay Christensen's) ideas about the creative upheaval needed to innovate. The approach turbocharged charter school-style authorizing, now in the hands of district leaders serving as authorizers of their own *district* schools—as Klein once said, "charterizing" the entire system.

At the time, it was hard to not be inspired by Hill's enthusiasm for his theory, which he zealously promoted. But as with most theories, it proved complicated in practice. Measuring school performance within a high-stakes context of potential closure proved challenging. It had none of the ease of watching stock prices go up or down, the result of millions of trades, to make decisions.

In New York City, central office staff responsible for the city's school portfolio took an otherwise hands-off approach to school management. Leaders defined the role of HQ as the opening, measuring, and closing of schools. The approach was in contrast to previous administrations' chronic improvement initiatives, such as the city's Chancellor's District, with its extra resources and prescriptive instructional models that aimed to turn around struggling schools. Rather, the absence of central office support was intended to free principals from bureaucratic meddling; school leaders were expected to run their schools as they saw fit, with a focus on outcomes rather than compliance, and would be held accountable for results.[8]

Here was the charter sector's core compact of autonomy for accountability applied, writ large, to the management of entire districts. But at times HQ's calculations of "good" and "bad" schools were viewed as simply heartless. Parents nearly always rallied to their "failing" school's defense. Community groups and the teachers union organized opposition to keep schools open, regardless of student performance on state tests, with demands that HQ make the schools better. Demonstrations were held outside of schools. When closures were on the agenda, board meetings regularly ran into the early morning hours. Invariably these were schools in communities with high rates of poverty. This top-down, "incentive aligning" closure avoided mutual accountability to figure out *how* to educate students with the greatest needs. As one anonymous observer who was very close to the work noted, the city never really figured out how to educate these children, it just shipped them around.

Alongside this district turmoil, Klein's championing of charter schools was seen as preferential treatment.[9] As district schools closed, my office revived the city's role in creating new charter schools.[10] While the city's new Fair Student Funding formula threatened budget cuts to district schools,[11] we increased charter school funding for greater financial parity. When city start-up grants were made available to new district schools, we extended the support to new charters, too, over objections from district advocates. When the department adopted a new capital plan, it included $100 million in matching funds exclusively for charter school construction.[12]

Most controversial was the co-location of charter and district schools in underutilized city buildings. No longer were charter schools relegated to what space they could renovate or build in the city's expensive real estate market, like that old sausage factory in the Bronx. And in many ways, co-location was a symbolic moment of arrival for the charter movement, as these schools entered buildings that represented a community's public school. But co-location forced district and charter school leaders to be in constant, and usually testy, negotiations over shared use of the gym, cafeteria, hallways, and entryways. Invoking the charter sector's more martial mentality, Eva Moskovitz likened co-location to a "Middle East War."[13] Overall, the city's collection of pro-charter policies and rhetoric raised charter–district tensions to new heights.

OUT-REFORMING THE REFORMERS: THE UNITED FEDERATION OF TEACHERS

At the time, Randi Weingarten was president of New York City's union local, the United Federation of Teachers (UFT). It was and remains a position of significance to education policy and politics nationwide. The UFT is the single largest teachers' union local in the United States, with over 200,000 members. It represents educators and staff in the nation's largest school district, which enrolls 1.1 million students.[14] The UFT was formed in the early 1960s as an amalgam of smaller associations by a number of prominent teacher-activists, including Al Shanker, who would go on to become a nationally recognized figure in education, civil rights, and Democratic party politics. It pioneered the modern teacher union movement through precedent-setting public-sector collective bargaining. The UFT won many of the employment terms and conditions that New York City teachers enjoy today through hard-charging pressure politics, including a number of consequential, and controversial, strikes in the 1960s.[15]

The UFT has also been the proving ground of three of the past four presidents of the American Federation of Teachers (AFT), the national organization founded in 1916, which Weingarten has led since 2008. With 1.7 million members, the AFT is smaller than its counterpart, the older National Education Association (NEA), founded in 1857, with three million members.[16] Both AFT and NEA advocate nationally on education policy, run political action campaigns, and support their local affiliates on district and state issues. The NEA's source of power is largely from suburban areas, as I saw in Connecticut, with the state-affiliate Connecticut Education Association's (CEA) considerable strength from bedroom communities. The AFT's 3,000 local affiliates include New York City's union local, Chicago's, Los Angeles', and other major cities'. This puts the AFT on the front lines of urban school reform, where three out of five charter schools are located, and in direct conflict with the privatization project.

Weingarten and the UFT initiated a positive relationship with Mayor Bloomberg when he was elected in November 2001, just a few difficult weeks after the 9/11 attack. Bloomberg had a city to rebuild, and the UFT moved its headquarters a few blocks from the World Trade Center site "as a symbolic gesture of support."[17] Bloomberg also inherited an expired teachers' contract, which he quickly settled. Subsequent contracts raised the top teacher salary to $100,000, in an effort to attract and retain teachers and be competitive with the suburbs.[18]

But, notably, Bloomberg did not make any pronouncements on his education policies until he won control of city schools, turning the Board of Education into his own "Department" of Education. This was soon followed by Klein's appointment as Schools Chancellor and months of a leave-no-stone-unturned planning process dubbed Children First. Committees of staff and management consultants examined every aspect of school operation to develop new ways forward. I was on the "choice" working group, reporting to then-Deputy Chancellor and longtime civil servant Tony Shorris, alongside venerable colleagues, including Beverly Donohue, chief financial officer of the then $13 billion system.

The UFT participated in Children First, but relations soured when it became clear that Klein intended to disrupt long-standing organizational structures that gave the UFT, politicians, and other interests ready access to school and system decisions. First, the city centralized 32 districts into 10 regional offices, led by superintendents reporting directly to Klein. This structure was itself later disrupted, as schools self-affiliated through a marketplace of support providers held accountable through portfolio management.[19] Tensions also got personal. In the spring of 2003, the UFT sued Klein for racial discrimination over the city's plan to lay off 1,000 paraprofessionals who were disproportionately Black and Hispanic.[20]

Amidst constant disruption and personal enmity, continued privatization project attacks on the teacher unions, and growing competition from nonunion charter schools, Weingarten made a bold move. She announced that the UFT wanted to run its own charter schools, in a way that "the late Al Shanker . . . promoted and popularized."[21] Few in education reform circles thought that Weingarten's announcement was more than a publicity stunt. In New York and nationwide, teacher union opposition to charter schools was felt from statehouses to community board meetings and throughout the halls of co-located charter and district schools.[22] Surely she wasn't serious.

Hostilities were mutual, given that union animus was among the articles of faith of the privatization project. Its argument is still that restrictive collective bargaining agreements tie school leaders' hands from making necessary decisions that would improve student achievement; the "just cause" standard embedded in state tenure laws creates a level of due process so high as to, in effect, guarantee a job for life, giving teachers no incentive to work hard; union-negotiated step-and-lane teacher salary schedules, with pay based on years of experience and level of education—and no other performance pay incentives—gives teachers little reason to go the extra mile for their students.[23] Only solutions like nonunion charters, vouchers to nonunion private schools, reconstituted nonunion and all-choice districts such as in New Orleans, performance pay, at-will employment, and outcome-based performance evaluations will free schools of union shackles. Only then will students get the quality of education they deserve. Anything else is too incremental, too "collaborative—[the] elixir of the status quo crowd."[24]

The teacher unions rightly understood this as an existential threat from a well-connected and -funded adversary that had quickly moved from the periphery of public education to the core of the nation's largest districts. They were well aware of the decades-long decline in union strength in the private sector. Although public-sector unions have a distinct difference (and as Terry Moe argues, an advantage) in their ability to elect sympathetic public officials,[25] the teacher unions were no less concerned about their future. Why, then, would Weingarten show any sign of accommodation? Why legitimize any of the privatization project's ideas, particularly its most prominent front—charter schools?

First, she was responding to the city's portrayal of the teachers' contract as an overly restrictive, rule-filled barrier to student achievement. Weingarten could have pointed to many successful NYC district schools, like my sons' PS 321, which employ and manage teachers through this agreement, to cast shade on Klein's critique. But she went further, arguing that the success of the UFT's *own* charter schools, operating by this *same* contract, would "dispel the misguided and simplistic notion that the union contract is an impediment to success."[26]

Second, I believe that Weingarten wanted to out-reform the reformers and, in doing so, take the wind out of their anti-union sails.[27] A successful, *unionized* charter school would refocus attention on why some charters (or *any* tax-funded schools) succeed or fail, due to the quality of curriculum, the ability to attract and retain good teachers and leaders, the level of family and community engagement, and the availability of sufficient resources—all against compounding issues of poverty or wealth.

Again, Weingarten could have pointed to existing, successful, and *unionized* charters, such as Renaissance Charter School in Queens, which followed the citywide agreement as a district school that converted to charter status. Amber Charter School in Harlem has its own collective bargaining agreement. Even the KIPP network's flagship charter school in the Bronx observed the citywide agreement, particularly for salaries and benefits (albeit mostly in the breach for other working conditions). But a bold stroke—a money-where-your-mouth-is moment of UFT accountability—would be more powerful than a handful of instances that don't necessarily disprove the ruling belief.[28]

The idea of UFT-run charters was also a candid admission that the teacher unions needed a new approach to the growing charter sector. As Weingarten explained to her membership just a few years later, charter schools were "now a part of the education landscape," and "no one should ever forget that charter schools are public schools." Nor should charter and district schools "be pitted against one another," because "education is not a game where we can afford winners and losers."[29]

The proposed UFT charter schools would embody her union's changing stance toward charters and provide a proof point for AFT and NEA locals across the country. They would be an innovative, "avant-garde" accomplishment she'd take with her to the AFT as its expected next president. The UFT's schools would also blur the distinction between charter and district, a small step in a then-yet-to-be-named Publicization Project. Plus, what better recruitment tactic to the teachers of nonunion charters?

THE CREATIVE ENTANGLEMENTS OF UNION-RUN CHARTER SCHOOLS

I was intrigued by Weingarten's announcement, which came while I was still leading the city's charter schools office. By that time, Bloomberg and Klein had leveled the operational and financial playing field between charter and district schools. We were authorizing new schools and putting teeth in the charter compact—revoking the first charter in New York State from the troubled REACH Charter School[30] and turning around another, Clearpool School, through a carefully managed probation.[31] The mayor and chancellor's leadership culminated with the launch of the New York City Charter School Center, an advocacy and support group founded with $41 million from the Robin Hood, Tiger, Clark and Beginning with Children foundations and led ably for many years by James Merriman, a nationally respected figure.

Yet because of the city's full-throated support, charter schools were increasingly in the political crosshairs. If Weingarten was serious, I calculated that her UFT schools would challenge the pat political antagonisms in all the right ways. No longer could teacher unions oppose *chartering* writ large; they'd have to debate the character of the sector—in other words, its publicness or privateness. If located in public buildings, her schools would change the conversation about shared space. UFT-run charter schools might also encourage union allies, like small schools operator New Visions for Public Schools, to consider chartering (which it ultimately did).

If successful, union opponents would no longer be able to point to collective bargaining and union contracts as the de facto reason for school failure. They'd have to find different answers and perhaps look more closely at the educational, economic, and social effects on students. If the UFT's schools failed, it would force some soul searching. I also wondered about the possible, constructive influence of the UFT having more charter school members, as well as the sector having more unionized schools. Such entanglements could, perhaps, get partisans out of their comfortable sides into the muddling middle and, once there, search for common ground. I remember talking through these implications with Merriman, who was then still serving as authorizer for the State University of New York. His Cheshire cat smile let me know that he was game to see what would fly.

So I quietly reached out to Weingarten through a trusted colleague, New York City's legendary school fixer, Burt Sacks. She sized me up over dinner in a dim basement restaurant. If she was serious, I was willing to help. By our second drink it was clear that Weingarten was very serious, and we came to employment terms a few days later. Only in time would I realize the courage it took her to move the idea forward. She took great lengths to socialize the idea with skeptical colleagues and her outspoken membership, which ultimately voted to move forward.[32] Weingarten also secured a $1 million start-up grant from charter booster Eli Broad, in another counterintuitive move that aimed to change the narrative.

The UFT's elementary charter school opened first, in the fall of 2005, in East New York, Brooklyn,[33] a low-income community with great educational need.[34] The neighborhood had symbolic meaning, too, just next door to Ocean Hill-Brownsville, where in 1968 a racially charged citywide teachers strike originated over the firing of white and Jewish teachers by an all-Black community school board. Mindful of this history, we first met with the area's City Council member, Charles Barron. A former Black Panther, Barron did not hide his delight that the UFT was asking for his permission. "So if I say 'no,' you'll go somewhere else?" he asked. "Yes," we assured, and proceeded with his blessing.

The next spring we threw the new school a splashy gala at the Tribeca Film Festival. The night included a UFT-commissioned documentary about the school's founding, at a premiere attended by then-Senator Hilary Clinton.[35] Chancellor Klein gave the opening remarks, further legitimizing the UFT's effort and raising already high expectations. Here was no modest pilot with the risk of failure kept out of public view. It was a very public statement of the UFT's evolving position on charter schools and education reform—literally screened for a future presidential candidate.

The UFT Charter High School opened in 2006 a few blocks away, and both shared undercapacity buildings with district schools. Then, in 2007, Weingarten convinced Green Dot Schools, the Los Angeles operator of unionized charters, to open a school in the South Bronx—its first outside of California. Green Dot was led by its charismatic founder, Steve Barr. A longtime Democratic Party activist, Barr co-founded Rock the Vote in 1990, helped pass the Motor Voter Act, and was dubbed "The Instigator" by *The New Yorker* for his hard-charging approach and shoot-from-the-lip candor.[36] Along with Sandy Blazer, Green Dot's talented chief academic officer, Barr's schools had a reputation for quality and strong community connections in Inglewood, South Central, Watts, and other LA neighborhoods.

Nationally, Green Dot was best known for its pro-labor stance and "thin" union contract that was silent on many issues that were instead delegated to teachers and administrators to decide. Green Dot's teachers were represented by the statewide California Teachers Association (CTA)—not the local United Teachers of Los Angeles—through their own collective bargaining agreement. The novel arrangement was similar to other school-based and network-wide contracts being negotiated at places like UNO charter schools in Chicago.[37]

In New York City, the UFT and Green Dot came to terms on a 28-page contract specific to the South Bronx school and separate from the citywide agreement that runs hundreds of pages.[38] Weingarten enthusiastically characterized the new arrangement as "a model for connecting teacher professionalism and student achievement [and] labor relations" before thousands of union leaders at the AFT's annual convention.[39] At about the same time, AFT locals in Illinois, Pennsylvania, and elsewhere were ramping up efforts to organize charter teachers. The Service Employees International Union (SEIU), then led by Andy Stern, was also getting into the action in Chicago and Los Angeles.[40] The flurry of activity, suggesting a turn toward unionization, was noticeable enough to make the pages of the *New York Times*.[41]

Union-run charters, thin contracts, organizing drives, and charter teachers among the union rank and file horrified both dyed-in-the-wool unionists as well as charter advocates wedded to the privatization project.[42] Personally, I found it fascinating and generative of new ideas, approaches, and complexities to solve. These moves were full of risks and uncertainty, but much more interesting than predictable, Whack-A-Mole fights between reformers and the status quo crowd. And as we'll see, these disruptive innovations provide valuable insights and examples that should inform a Publicization Project.

A MIXED RESULT

The UFT's charter schools were not the smashing successes that Weingarten predicted, nor the "Potemkin villages" that opponents warned against.[43] The UFT Elementary Charter School struggled under a well-intentioned but inexperienced principal. A die-hard union loyalist from the UFT's professional development division, she was constrained by teachers' direct access to Weingarten, who was both their union president and—as demanded by the school's authorizer—chair of the school's board.[44] Day-to-day challenges of any start-up were compounded by a steady stream of curiosity seekers, a film crew, and well-intentioned "help" from a small army of UFT assistants (including yours truly). In retrospect, it was an unfair position for any leader and a miscalculation by Weingarten to not appoint a proven leader. The school's initial 5-year charter was renewed for a second term and changes were made to leadership, but it ultimately closed in 2015.[45]

The UFT Charter High School was similarly led by a team of untested administrators. Its founding principal had a short tenure, despite on-site mentoring from noted New York City educator and principal coach Mary Butz.[46] From 2009 to 2012 the high school had four different principals and supervision from a former state official hired by the UFT, all in an effort to turn around an "ambiguous or mixed record of achievement."[47] After 15 "rocky" years, it was reabsorbed by the city as a district school at the UFT's request.[48]

Only the Green Dot New York Charter School, renamed "University Prep," found success, regularly graduating nearly all of its students, earning charter renewals, and winning a 2016 National Blue Ribbon Award.[49] Of the three, this one did not follow the citywide teachers' contract and was not managed by the UFT, but rather by Green Dot. These three schools weren't the city's best or worst. And failure is celebrated in improvement science and by innovators as necessary for learning and change. But the mixed record was nonetheless embarrassing, given the exceedingly high expectations.

A CRASH COURSE IN LABOR HISTORY, POLITICS, AND PRACTICE

The UFT's short-lived experience as a charter school operator holds valuable lessons for a Publicization Project, elaborated on in this chapter's closing recommendations. These include particular insights from the Green Dot school and its school-based teachers' contract, which I will examine in depth. But to fully appreciate these lessons, it's helpful to first establish some context about teacher unionism and collective bargaining.

When I started with the UFT, I had no idea what to expect. I do not come from a family of teachers or trade unionists. Growing up, I'd hear complaints about union demands driving another factory out of town. As a child amidst the Reagan Revolution, I was inclined to think that unions had passed their prime, reinforced by headlines about corruption and late-night TV jokes about Jimmy Hoffa.

My education was swift. I learned about the UFT's proud history of achievements on behalf of teachers in combating workplace discrimination. Within the living memory of the UFT's most senior members, teaching positions had been gained and lost through political patronage. Pregnant women were not allowed to teach because of the perceived corrupting influence on children. Suspected Communists were driven from classrooms. Low pay was acceptable because teaching was "women's work."[50]

By banding teachers together in the 1960s the UFT, like any union, gained strength in numbers. It first campaigned for teachers' *right* to unionize—a novelty in the public sector. Then the UFT was elected by city educators to be their sole representative on matters of employment. Although not the nation's first teachers union local to win the right to bargain collectively—precedents existed in Montana, Minnesota, Illinois, and Rhode Island—events in New York City were "a watershed."[51] Teacher collective bargaining rapidly spread across the country. The AFT's growing success forced the NEA—historically dominated by administrators—to compete for members by fully embracing a labor identity. Within a dozen years, teaching was "among the most unionized occupations in the nation."

In the decades since, NEA and AFT state and local affiliates have negotiated pay raises, improved benefits, put limits on the workday and year, gained due process protections, made workplaces safer, achieved professional autonomies over things such as lesson plans, and gained a voice for teachers in professional development and school decision-making. The set of topics varies by location but collectively represents the "scope of bargaining," meaning the issues about which labor and management are *obliged* to negotiate.

In addition to collective *bargaining*, the NEA and AFT organize collective *action*. Both national organizations and their affiliates endorse candidates for local, state, and national offices. They mobilize teachers to vote. Come budget season, the unions are outspoken advocates for tax-funded schools. In these and other regards, the teacher unions are like any other organized interest in American civic life—from right-wing and corporate PACs to nonpartisan issue advocates and progressive or left-wing lobbyists—fighting for its group's interests, bringing to bear what power they have, to see their interests achieved.

The teacher unions have also been the strongest and most successful opponent of the privatization project. They stopped or delayed passage of charter school laws in many states. They fought against merit pay. They defended due process protections amidst proposals to replace tenure with at-will employment. They campaigned against the interlocking regime of standards, tests, and job evaluations. They continue to oppose vouchers to private schools. As such, it's no surprise that the privatization project portrays the teacher unions as Enemy Number One. Were it not for this opposition, and the legal obligation of unionized districts to negotiate with teachers' formal representatives, the privatization project could have flourished unchecked.

In these regards, a Publicization Project owes the teacher unions a debt of gratitude. When few other defenders of public education had the resources or infrastructure to fight privatization, the teachers' union did. But it was not easy. I remember days at the UFT when some colleagues felt as if the fight was unwinnable. They would lament that the wealth and influence behind the privatization project was too strong to overcome, particularly given popular faith in the private sector. During Friday morning staff meetings, Weingarten would bolster their confidence, reminding colleagues that political seasons come and go, and that we were in this fight for the long haul. And long it was: Five presidencies and 40 years would pass after Reagan described government as "the problem" until President Joe Biden described Reagan's economic and political orthodoxy as having "never worked," to a 2021 joint session of Congress and again in his 2022 State of the Union address.[52]

MISSION ACCOMPLISHED? THE ROLE OF TEACHER UNIONS IN MAKING SCHOOLS MORE PUBLIC

Where does all this leave the teacher unions vis-à-vis a Publicization Project? I suspect that union leaders can embrace the definition of a public school as one that produces public goods and doesn't exclude. Plus, they likely agree with the six criteria proposed in these pages, through which schools can be more open and public and less exclusionary and private. For example, the unions have long advocated for increases in school budgets to ensure that free, tax-funded schools have resources sufficient to meet expectations. They have also been strong supporters of fiscal equity campaigns and lawsuits. This advocacy advances the principle of fiscal fairness, our most basic measure of publicness.

The second criterion of publicness pertains to an educational philosophy based on facts, in order to advance civic, economic, social, and environmental common goods. These, too, likely find union support, particularly in regard to schools' role in sustaining democracy. The American Federation of Teachers has a long history of advocating for the importance of education in strengthening our form of government, under its founding motto "democracy in education, education for democracy."[53] The position was inspired by philosopher John Dewey's career-long explication of the relationship between education and democracy and his support of collective action. Notably, Dewey co-founded the AFT in 1916 and was the New York local's first official member.[54]

Unions, the UFT and AFT included, also have internal commitments to democratic decision-making. As documented in texts like *Union Democracy* by sociologists Seymour Lipset, Martin Trow, and James S. Coleman,[55] unions have their own political parties that caucus, advance position papers, and nominate competing candidates for union leadership positions. In New York City, Shanker's founding Unity Caucus regularly faces opposition from the Movement of Rank and File Educators (MORE), one of four opposition groups. Monthly assemblies of teacher union delegates from schools across the city are often raucous affairs. Debate from the floor on controversial matters can be more like Question Time with the United Kingdom's prime minister—who gets peppered and jeered by members of Parliament—than sleepy C-SPAN coverage of a United States senator addressing an empty chamber.

The result, as imperfect as it may be, are union positions, decisions, and contract ratifications that reflect the democratic will of its members. At times, I observed processes as slow and messy as our polity's democracy. Plus, the unions get criticized when they take positions on social and global affairs outside of their educational "lane." But these statements are part of their commitment to a free and open society. It adds another organized voice to our body politic. By organizing members through representative and participatory decision-making, the union also ensures a level of commitment to whatever decisions are made or actions taken. All things considered, a Publicization Project has a strong ally in its efforts to ensure that tax-funded schools have the fact-based philosophy necessary to sustain our democracy and produce other public goods.

* * *

Beyond funding and facts, the remaining measures of publicness may prove more challenging for the teacher unions to fully embrace. In this closing section I address them, with examples that show how the unions can draw on their own values and past efforts to be full contributors to a Publicization Project.

Joining the Conversation as Equals

Recall that the criterion on governance examines the degree to which stakeholders are brought together into dialogue, regarding what is taught and how, to collectively decide what it means to be an educated American. Schooling passes the exclusion test—is more of a public good—when more voices are brought into the conversation. The teacher unions' commitment to democracy would suggest a natural affinity for such shared decision-making. But in my reading of the relevant history, the teacher unions became comfortable with having an *outsized* voice in education policy and politics and accustomed to being the *only* other voice at the bargaining table across from management. Only within the past 2 decades has the privatization project mobilized stakeholders and used private influence as effectively as the unions, to challenge the degree to which the union's voice was heard above all others.

Moreover, teacher unions operate in the mode of industrial labor relations. This approach assumes competing interests necessitating demands—not dialogue—to achieve one's interests. To be fair, it takes two to tango. Sometimes only a demand will be heard by tone-deaf management. Yet I am reminded of my efforts to find common ground in Connecticut. The state's AFT and NEA affiliates already had the loudest voice in every conversation. State leaders, like Commissioner Pryor, were committed to dialogue. But even with this willing partner, the two unions stoked fears among teachers that their voices weren't being heard, organized protests outside the capital, and filled town halls with teachers shouting down a Democratic governor they helped to elect. It was pressure politics to gain leverage, and pursuing one's goals in this way—by *any* interest group—is not deliberative decision-making.

A Publicization Project needs the teacher unions to come into its conversation as an equal to other stakeholders, even when their political power exceeds that wielded by others. I am not suggesting that the union unilaterally "disarm" to other interests. It is not *any* conversation I'm proposing, in which interests may be irreconcilable. It is a conversation in which all of the stakeholders are trying to make schools more public and are committed to their common purposes. If this is in the union's core interest—and I believe it is—they need to be at this table with others. Together, they must agree to turn their swords into plowshares and commit to decisions, however compromised, knowing that they are temporary, to be revisited again. Otherwise, pressure tactics are a defection from the democratic game, an authoritarian use of political force.

Teacher Unions and Mutual Accountability: The Profession's Obligations

The preceding pages argue that a Publicization Project should replace top-down accountability with mutual accountability, upheld with evidence fit for each purpose and used with good judgment by stakeholders who hold one another to a good-faith standard of effort. There are clear ways in which the unions can support this goal, particularly in regard to professional and employment accountability.

For example, the AFT champions the National Board for Professional Teaching Standards (NBPTS), and Weingarten serves on its board.[56] To become nationally board-certified, teachers must "prove their effectiveness" through a portfolio of accumulated teaching artifacts and evidence. Such board certification is intended to provide "a public assurance that teachers have met the profession's highest standards for accomplished practice."[57] Yet to date, only 125,000 teachers have earned this distinction. What does that say about the millions of others? Plus, not everyone agrees that NBPTS certification is the guarantor of quality it claims to be.

For the teacher unions to fully embrace professional accountability as part of a Publicization Project, they must become more robust advocates for national teaching standards. As described above, the unions should be among the stakeholders setting such expectations. If there is skepticism about NBPTS, they should justify their knowledge claims with reasons aimed to persuade others and learn from critiques on an assumption of fallibility. Ideally, this leads to more broad acceptance of NBPTS or its successor, which the unions and others would then commit to, perhaps through a national, entry-level "bar exam" for teachers. It's one of the few ideas on which Weingarten and Klein agreed.[58]

The existence of nationwide evidence-based and practical teaching standards for the entire profession would no doubt force some out of teaching. This is another consequence of a Publicization Project that the unions may find difficult to accept, given their fiduciary obligation to protect a member's employment. But this is the self-regulating obligation of any profession and the justification of their relative autonomy from government oversight. To honor this trust, the unions must better ensure the quality of the rank and file by enforcing the standards by which a person becomes and remains a practitioner. Otherwise, a Publicization Project's goal of mutual accountability will be hamstrung.

Teacher Unions and Mutual Accountability: Employment Practices

Third, a fully realized embrace of mutual accountability—including civic accountability to adequately resource schools—opens a window for unions to embrace employment accountability in ways that they struggle to today. At present, they have a legal obligation to defend teachers from termination and other disciplinary actions to the best of their ability. These legal proceedings often turn on the quality of evidence that management brings to bear, challenged by the union, in the eyes of an arbitrator. Mitigating circumstances, including underresourced schools, poorly trained evaluators, and lack of managerial feedback, serve to strengthen the union's defense. It creates plausible doubt as to who bears responsibility.

The result is that school systems don't take disciplinary action against many teachers, and the two sides talk past one another about why: unions arguing that the processes for employment accountability exist but go underused; management arguing that the burden of proof is too high to make the process a practical option. But within a context of adequate resources and prestige, as found in international exemplars like Finland, South Korea, and Canada, teaching is an attractive career and there is no shortage of talented people seeking to join the profession. Well-supported evaluation processes would allow teachers and administrators to review job performance with evidence and observations that are trusted for the purpose, against profession-defined expectations of practice. When the process identifies a struggling teacher, she is made aware of problems and given a coach, professional development, and other opportunities to improve. If she doesn't, by all accounts she shouldn't remain in the profession.

Such a process was memorialized in New Haven's collective bargaining agreement in 2010. The contract included a streamlined process for dismissal if no improvement was made after a period of corrective action and support.[59] The improvement period was key to the agreement: If the teacher was ultimately terminated, the union had satisfied its legal obligations of adequate representation. Although New Haven's contract remains an outlier, it is a prominent example of how the teacher unions have, and can, within their obligations to both individuals and the profession, strengthen employment accountability.

The Future of Due Process?

Due process is at the heart of these debates. Specifically, how much consideration is an employee due before being terminated? Unionized teachers typically start their employment within a probationary period. During this time, a school need not invite the teacher back for the next year. The educator is, effectively, an at-will employee.

Following probation, a "permanent" or "tenured" teacher is typically employed on the basis of a "just cause" due process standard. This term of art has been defined over years of practice and case law. This standard is met when a disciplinary action satisfies seven tests: First, that a rule or work directive is reasonably related to the operation of the business or enterprise; second, that the employee had notice of the rule, directive, or performance standard and that she could face consequences if it isn't met; third, that management investigated the matter before taking disciplinary action; fourth, that the investigation was fair and objective; fifth, that the investigation found sufficient evidence of misconduct or discrepancies in performance; sixth, that the employee was treated fairly, with the rules and expectations consistently applied to her and her colleagues; and seventh, that any discipline was proportionate to the seriousness of the problem.[60]

privatization project reformers object to the just cause standard as too onerous; as noted, they call for at-will employment to give school leaders authority to manage their workforce and deliver student outcomes. Unions defend the just cause standard as necessary to create the employment conditions necessary to attract and retain talented educators; such due process, they argue, provides the predictable employment that people need to make a career in education and long-term financial commitments, like taking on a mortgage or having a family; it prevents patronage and favoritism, and allows dissenting views on educational matters.

Such diametrically opposed conceptions have given us all-or-nothing fights; it's tenure or at-will, take it or leave it, with victories and setbacks for both sides. Instead, a Publicization Project should reconceptualize the issue. It must engage union leaders, reformers, and the best legal minds to reexamine *the constituent parts* of due process, in order to identify changes that advance both fairness to an employee and professional excellence for the sake of students.

For example, what does it mean, precisely, to be at the "end" of one's probationary period, moving from one level of due process to another? What does an early-career teacher need to know and be able to do at this moment of transition, and to whose satisfaction? Surely a teacher would have to demonstrate skills and knowledge that meet the collectively defined, profession-set teaching standards. But perhaps at an intermediate, rather than beginner level of mastery. And in whose eyes? Likely one's peers and administrators. But what about other stakeholders, including students and parents? The more seriously this process is taken at key stages in one's career—beginner, intermediate, and expert—the better the profession can assure quality. Doing so also rebuts the unproductive criticism that "the only thing you have to do" to get tenure "is show up" for one's first few years of employment.[61]

Just as earning tenure can be made more meaningful, what must a teacher do to *retain* this level of due process? The New Haven contract shows how an educator could move from a stronger to a weaker level of due process if performance is weak and corrective support has little effect. A related concept is the professional ladder, with movement up—but perhaps also down—based on a variety of factors. Such arrangements make due process more dynamic and contingent on professional skill, student impact, and stage of career. I do not know if New Haven's teaching force has grown in quality since 2010, and the contract is just one of many factors that influence hiring, retention, and turnover. But the agreement itself is evidence that due process reforms are possible and mutually agreeable.

A dynamic conception of due process designed to support the quality of educators' work is likely better suited to attracting and retaining those who will excel at teaching, as in top-performing countries that recruit teachers from the top 30 percent of university graduates, compared to the United States, which "at best recruit[s] mostly from the bottom 40 percent."[62] So here's a question to reformers: Which of the seven tests of just cause need modification and why? And to the unions: What evidentiary standard is sufficient and not overly burdensome, such that the process does not go unused when needed? And questions for both: What levels of turnover from other professions, other countries, and under what circumstances can serve as helpful benchmarks to estimate if teacher turnover is too much or too little? And in whose judgment? An arbitrator? A committee of colleagues? Might a school board get the final say? Who will give all parties confidence in a final decision?

These are not easy questions to answer. But they are smaller in scope, and therefore more answerable, than large-scale fights to end or defend tenure once and for all, in a single round of high-stakes play. Working in good faith through the smaller component questions can help each party understand what the major disagreements are really about. It is classic problem-solving: deconstructing something complex into constitutive parts and working through each one. It allows for testing and innovating on different aspects, to build the trust necessary to tackle thornier questions. A Publicization Project should facilitate this sincere engagement and thoughtful deliberation, not stylized pressure politics among warring tribes.

The Complicity of Industrial Labor Relations in the Industrial Paradigm's Inequity

I fear that equity, the sixth criterion of publicness, will be the hardest for the NEA, AFT, and its local affiliates to embrace, but not for obvious reasons. Over their histories, these organizations have been committed to economic, social, and racial justice. They are rightly proud of their contributions to the Civil Rights Movement. The AFT had a close working relationship with Bayard Rustin and a prominent role in the 1963 March on Washington for Jobs and Freedom.[63] Through to the present, the unions continue to fight for civil liberties and voting rights, against racism and income inequality, and for LGBTQ dignity and equal treatment, with Weingarten recently denouncing Florida's "Don't Say Gay Bill" as "heinous."[64]

But the unions' commitment to equitable *educational outcomes*, defined as student achievements indistinguishable by race, ethnicity, class, gender, sexual orientation, or place of birth, is compromised by the legal and operational context in which they operate: *industrial* labor relations. This mode of bargaining often involves stylized presentation of demands by district and union negotiators that are well in excess of what both parties expect in a final outcome. The two sides negotiate away, over days and months, until an agreement is met or "fact-finders" are called in to advise on a settlement, which may be forced by third-party arbitrators. While working for the UFT and following our first successful unionization drive at a charter school, I was stunned when the bargaining department told me not to expect a first contract "for months, maybe years."

Within an industrial approach, union leaders often speak *for* their members. I was in bargaining sessions where teacher representatives were at the table but not expected to talk. Nor was the school principal or other representatives of management. The attorneys talked to the attorneys. Only when both sides separately caucused did teachers share their views. We would privately talk through pros and cons before bringing a unified front back to the bargaining table, often based on what the union rep advised.

My union friends will cry foul, that this is an overly combative and disenfranchising mischaracterization of collective bargaining. That the process is, in most places, more collaborative and that teachers participate in large committees and complete surveys and other mechanisms to ensure that their voice is heard and heeded by their representatives. That collective bargaining is closer to an "interest-based" or "reform bargaining" paradigm, which identifies common interests, builds trust, and achieves some quick wins before collaboratively tackling thornier topics.[65] But the civility and level of member participation are only part of my point.

The inequitable industrial paradigm of *schooling* could not have a better friend than industrial *bargaining*. With schools organized like factories, the terms and conditions of teachers' work are more easily specified in collectively bargained contracts. Just as students are shuttled from class to class in 50-minute periods, teachers' work is almost always defined in such agreements by the number of teaching periods, prep time, and breaks. Teacher workdays start and end at set times. Professional development, rather than negotiated as an ongoing professional responsibility, happens on a handful of inservice days. Contracts state whether lesson plans may or may not be reviewed by management. The mechanistic examples go on, as industrial *bargaining* accepts and legitimizes industrial *assumptions*. It conceptualizes teachers as workers on a shop floor, with set tasks to be performed, within set periods of time, and within set work rules.

As I've argued, equitable outcomes will not be achieved as long as schools operate within the assumptions of the industrial paradigm. Schools cannot be construed as factories, and students cannot be seen as products moving along an assembly line, if we are to equitably educate students in the human competencies that they and society need for human flourishing. Meaning that for unions to fully embrace greater equity through an Intellectual-Emotional Paradigm, they must abandon industrial bargaining.

This won't be easy, given that industrial bargaining on behalf of all union members is a key source of strength in numbers. It is also the method of negotiation by which unions achieved decades of gains. It is what they are designed to do, and they are unlikely to disrupt themselves. Plus, management's *obligation* to negotiate issues within the scope of bargaining has been the only legally enforced check on the worst excesses of the privatization project. Moreover, today there isn't an external force strong enough to move the unions away from their industrial ways: Recall that the privatization project, for all of the political power it has amassed, fully embraces the "as much, as fast" industrial assumption, albeit in nonunion "shops" where school management is decidedly the boss.

Teacher Professionalism as a Countervailing Force

So here is another puzzle: The unions, based on their history and public statements, support greater equity in education. But they are incentivized by past success and present risks to sustain the inequitable assumptions of the industrial paradigm via industrial labor relations. The task for a Publicization Project is to help unions move to a new approach, one more conducive to an Intellectual-Emotional paradigm with its more equitable assumptions about students and schooling.

Teacher professionalism may be the answer. Inasmuch as union leaders are disincentivized to relinquish the power that comes along with negotiating industrywide contracts, they face competing pressures from members to professionalize the work. Such pressure challenges the school-as-factory assumptions that limit teachers' ability to exercise their own judgment on important questions of the structure and operation of the particular schools in which they teach, how best to use their own and students' time, pedagogical approaches, and other professional matters.[66]

These contradictions between trade unionism and teacher professionalism have been carefully examined by Charles Taylor Kerchner, Julia Koppich, and Joseph Weeres in their important *United Mind Workers*, which includes proposals for greater professional agency in service of educational quality.[67] Adam Urbanski, the longtime head of the Rochester (NY) Teachers Association, co-founded the Teacher Union Reform Network (TURN)[68] with a similar desire to change what unions do. Ted Kolderie, a founder of the charter movement, proposed "teacher professional partnerships," modeled after medical and legal practices, in which teachers "co-own" their schools and make decisions as "partners."[69] A germ of the same idea can be seen in the networked-learning among small groups of educators advocated by Bryk.[70] Research on professional development by Linda Darling-Hammond, Andy Hargreaves, Michael Fullan, and others provides ample evidence of the value of educator empowerment.[71]

These approaches, toward more professional models of labor relations, can be the justification that unions need to *bargain their own way* out of the industrial paradigm. A Publicization Project should support this change in the name of equity. It is possible, of course, that Bryk's networks or Kolderie's partnerships use their agency to create the next generation of factory-inspired schools. If we're being honest, many charter schools used their freedom in just this way, creating "no excuse" models and timing students with stopwatches. This means that movement away from industrial labor relations doesn't guarantee movement toward an Intellectual-Emotional Paradigm. But it is a necessary, if not sufficient, change.

School-Based Bargaining

Industrial bargaining, as the name suggests, aims to represent and negotiate on behalf of workers across an entire *industry.* This approach, strengthening leverage through representation of an entire workforce, was pioneered in the early 20th century by John L. Lewis, president of the United Mine Workers of America. Amidst the Great Depression, with support from pro-labor New Deal policies and through an "all-out organizing drive," Lewis's union organized 92% of all coal miners by 1933. It changed the face of organized labor in America, and in 1938, Lewis became the first president of the Congress of Industrial Organizations (CIO).[72]

One can see this industrywide approach in teacher union contracts—representing every teacher, paraprofessional, and other staff member—"wall to wall"—and across an entire district, applicable to every school. It stands in contrast to an earlier tradition of trade, or "craft," unionism, in which different groups of skilled workers each have their own association. Organized labor in America was founded on this model by the American Federation of Labor (AF of L), which was formed in 1886 and was led for nearly 40 years by Samuel Gompers.[73]

The distinction between industrial and craft unionism is relevant, as it connotes different ways in which workers can organize to achieve the benefits that come from collective action while still attending to their professional interests and identities. And like with chartering, the unions can draw inspiration from their own precedents in the history of American political development to move beyond industrial to more professional arrangements. School-based bargaining is one possibility. But it's benefits are by no means certain, as the following events attest.

* * *

In my final years with the UFT, I grew weary of the city and UFT's constant political battles and fruitless negotiations over a contract that set employment terms and conditions for 100,000 teachers and staff in 1,600 schools. Inspired by the professionalizing ideas within *United Mind Workers*, Kolderie's thought experiments, and Shanker's original promotion of charter schools, I thought that new and different kinds of labor agreements within the city's five boroughs might create constructive precedents to influence the much more consequential citywide talks and, perhaps, collective bargaining nationwide.

Others shared this view, including attorney Chad Vignola, who served as general counsel to three city school chancellors. He drafted Klein's "signature proposal," an eight-page "thin" contract that devolved many decisions to schools and included "a few key protections for teachers."[74] But the proposal went nowhere, largely because of the acrimony between the two sides; Weingarten ridiculed it as "no contract."

Proof points of more professional labor-management arrangements were still needed, and the charter sector, full of nonunion charter schools, was a tabula rasa on which to negotiate something new. Inasmuch as an original argument for chartering was to develop innovations to share across public education, why not innovations in labor relations, too?

So I threw myself into organizing charter school teachers and negotiating employment agreements at places like Amber Charter School, Merrick Academy in Laurelton, Queens, and elsewhere. Having no experience or training in union organizing or contract negotiations came, needless to say, with its pros and cons. I could speak to charter teachers candidly about their interests, the process of joining the UFT, and what to expect (or so I thought) when negotiating their own school-based employment agreement. I wasn't a typical union organizer, had been a teacher, and brought charter sector credibility as a former authorizer. I was also able to ease concerns among some teachers nervous about joining an organization that had opposed charter schools and was labeled part of the problematic status quo.

But I was also ignorant of what little power any union has to protect teachers *in the process* of unionizing. I underestimated the trust necessary for successful negotiations, naïve to the lengths that charter school leaders would go to stop organizing drives. Two cases are instructive, the first with teachers from a KIPP charter school in Crown Heights, Brooklyn, and the second with Green Dot's school in the South Bronx.

In 2008 a group of KIPP teachers approached the UFT with a story as earnest as it was true.[75] They were unhappy with how the school was being run by an unseasoned leader. They had gone to him individually, suggesting changes that fell on deaf ears. They went in groups, but the response was the same. So they weighed their options. À la Hirschman's typology, they could have exited, to work somewhere else. But they were loyal to the school's students, parents, and community. They didn't want to leave, but didn't want to get fired by continuing to challenge management. Yet remaining in loyal silence, when in their professional opinion things needed to change, wasn't an option either. They wanted some power behind their voice and asked the UFT for help.

We were surprised by the outreach. One of our organizers, Alan Cage, had met with KIPP teachers at its flagship in the Bronx. He dog-eared many pages in Jay Mathews's hagiographic *Work Hard. Be Nice.: How Two Inspired Teachers Created the Most Promising Schools in America.*[76] Cage concluded that KIPP was run with the loyalties of a family business and, he explained, family-run businesses don't unionize. But KIPP Crown Heights didn't have that family feel, and the initial group of teachers led the organizing drive, guided by UFT staff. Together we spoke to their colleagues and collected union Card Check authorization forms from a majority of teachers. These cards expressed their desire to be represented by the UFT in a school-specific bargaining unit, the first step toward a school-based contract. A petition was then delivered to KIPP leadership, requesting union recognition.

Weingarten called KIPP founder Dave Levin to explain the situation and encourage him to honor his teachers' wishes. A collaboration, albeit one forced by KIPP's own teachers, could have explored the next generation of professional, thin contracts, à la Green Dot, which Weingarten had recently signed and publicly commended. The moment was a potential hinge in the history of American education politics: on either end of the line was the president-elect of the national American Federation of Teachers, with its 1.7 million members and thousands of union locals, and the co-founder of the nation's largest charter school network and a de facto leader of the country's charter movement.[77]

But it was not meant to be. KIPP leaders chose to not recognize its teachers' petition. In the following months, KIPP deployed a predictable set of union-busting tactics and fired a teacher leading the effort. Although dismissed for stated reasons unrelated to the organizing drive, there was reasonable disagreement as to whether the termination was proportionate, or a known consequence, of the offense. But in the precarious period between going public with a union petition and its recognition by management, she was still a vulnerable, at-will employee. I was astonished by what little the UFT could do to protect her, and the firing had a chilling effect on other teachers' resolve.

Following KIPP's refusal of union recognition, the teachers' petition went to the New York's Public Employment Relations Board (PERB). Its review took a number of months. Only following PERB's approval did negotiations start. The UFT surveyed KIPP Crown Heights teachers regarding their interests and demands, but in an unforced error, we let bargaining proceed along predictable, industrial lines.

The first meeting was held at the midtown offices of KIPP's attorneys. The UFT's negotiator, an independent counsel from a New York labor law firm, formally presented written demands. These were officiously received across the table by KIPP's counsel, who immediately asked to caucus privately with his client, KIPP's management representatives. Each side retired to separate conference rooms for about 15 minutes. When we reconvened, KIPP's attorneys asked for time to consider the demands and develop their response—a typical reaction in such stylized bargaining. Calendars came out and the next meeting was booked, *weeks* into the future, all while the teachers and school managers sat in silence.

In the succeeding months, KIPP's dilatory tactics made it abundantly clear that this nationally celebrated charter management organization was opposed to employee representation and collective power backed by the force of law.[78] Bargaining dragged on. Teachers who signed the union authorization cards left the school. KIPP forced a revote, and only a minority of teachers were still supportive of the effort. KIPP brought the new tally back to PERB, and the bargaining unit was "decertified."[79]

In retrospect, the UFT was too wedded to the way it usually did things—industrial labor relations—with its stylized approach and assumption of competing interests. Had negotiations been approached differently by labor *and* management, as interest-based bargaining or facilitated mediation, the outcome might have been different. But the UFT believed that its tried-and-true process would prevail and win accolades from its newest members; nor did KIPP give us much of a choice, given its intransigence. The effort to create a new national model for charter–labor relations was stillborn.

By comparison, our experience with the Green Dot New York Charter School could not have been more different. Green Dot's founder, Steve Barr, believed that charter-union and district-union political fights weren't getting anybody anywhere. A shrewd politician, Barr encouraged his Green Dot teachers in Los Angeles to unionize with the California Teachers Association. The move sidestepped local disagreements with the United Teachers Los Angeles and its president, A. J. Duffy. The contract gave Barr labor peace and a phenomenal, maverick talking point in national education debates: great, *unionized* charter schools.[80]

Barr was just the kind of ally that Weingarten needed in her effort to change the charter-union conversation. Following a quick courtship, Green Dot opened its South Bronx charter in fall 2008. Per New York labor law, the teachers were not automatically union members. But once employed, they quickly voted to join the UFT. Their decision was immediately recognized by the school's board of trustees, on which Barr and Weingarten still serve. With the benefit of a trusting management partner, my UFT colleague Leo Casey and I were able to facilitate a collaborative, interest-based process to negotiate the teachers' first contract.

We began a conversation with the school's teachers about what they'd like to see in their employment agreement. Meetings at the school coalesced a teacher leadership group that had their colleagues' trust. Together we discussed some of the design features on which Green Dot schools were built and that were already memorialized in the school's legally binding charter, such as a "professional day" that expected teachers to fulfill their teaching and other responsibilities, but otherwise did not have work-to-rule start and end times. The teachers reviewed the contract then in effect at Green Dot's Los Angeles schools, to learn what their New York agreement might contain. We also took teacher leaders to see Barr's West Coast schools in action.

Together we talked at length about the appropriate role of teacher voice in school decision-making, the need for effective management to get things done, and the responsibilities—and accountabilities—that come with greater authority. Nor did we shy away from challenging topics, such as processes for involuntary termination and conflict mediation. Over time, the group developed points of view that felt in keeping with their professional identities and the norms of Green Dot schools. They shared proposals with colleagues, who also found them reasonable.

Then, over a weekend the following spring, the teacher leaders sat with the school principal and representatives from Green Dot's management team. The teachers explained various points, with Casey and me in a supporting role. Some differences of opinion were discussed, alternate views considered and amicably worked out, without teacher rallies and pressure politics or fact-finding and binding arbitration. By Sunday night there were handshakes over dinner and drinks.

Developed through trust and mutual respect, the result was a contract that Weingarten would describe only a few weeks later to her AFT membership as a national model. Notably, the contract did not include an at-will probation period: Teachers enjoyed a meaningful level of due process from their first day on the job. But also of note, involuntary dismissals could only be appealed to the school's board, not an external arbitrator (as is required by New York's state tenure law for district-school teachers). It named staff committees responsible for major school decisions, including curriculum and budget, meaning, for example, that teachers' own salaries were considered by teachers in light of other resource choices, trade-offs, and student needs. The annual budget deliberations replaced industrial paradigm rules and regulations with educator voice in a professional practice.

Negotiating the contract felt like a model *process*, too. Casey and I weren't speaking *for* the Green Dot teachers. Rather, we helped them speak *for themselves* with informed points of view. Some union friends say that this is a difference without a distinction: Teachers are the union, and the union is the teachers. Perhaps this is more the case in smaller school districts, with only part-time union staff, more teacher leadership, and more personal relationships with administrators. But this is less likely the case in large cities and their school districts, where the industrial paradigm dominates and inequity persists.

Can school-based bargaining, with its professionalizing benefits, happen at scale? Across a city with 1,600 schools? I think it can, and I will say more about this a moment. But first I think it necessary to address some of the more philosophical objections to collective bargaining.

* * *

The privatization project is premised on control. We see this in the controlling power of parents to choose, in their *own* estimation, a school for their child. The push for at-will employment seeks to put control over employment *exclusively* in the hands of management. Similarly, opposition to collective bargaining seeks to give school leaders ultimate control over decisions, unbound by any legal requirement to negotiate terms and conditions of employment with teachers. Absent "final say," leaders of nonunion school believe that decisions won't be made in students' best interests. They argue that formally empowered teachers may act from their own self-interest, or have less information than management, and therefore be less able to put students first. In some cases, teachers may find some decisions just too hard to make, like the involuntary termination of a beloved, but otherwise ineffectual, colleague. Or teachers will use such power to reinforce industrial structures that exacerbate inequity.

This line of thinking leads to the undemocratic conclusion that some school stakeholders must have more power than others, because they know more, know better, or are less conflicted. It's an authoritarian argument and unconvincing. Take, for example, early work by influential scholar Frederick M. Hess, who found that administrators can be just as susceptible to self-interest and short term-thinking.[81] The management-championed follies of recent years—aggressive adoption of the Common Core, misuse of standardized test data, finance-inspired "school portfolios"—further suggest that management's "better angels" are, at times, no better or worse than anyone else's.

Acknowledging that *both* administrators and teachers only ever see through the glass darkly evokes the philosophical debates around "representation." Over much of the history of Western thought, philosophers have pursued some intrinsic objective reality that exists outside of us, that can serve as the foundation of our beliefs, the "truth." If we look closely, we can detect this line of thinking in efforts to achieve "one best" systems of schooling—be they perfected industrial models or AI-powered panaceas. The privatization project lives in this intellectual tradition, too: Markets are the *best* way to organize social projects. By getting the power arrangements "right," schools will operate the way they're *supposed* to—and test data will prove it.

But as readers should know by now, I'm with the pragmatists. John Dewey, in Richard Rorty's estimation, spent his career campaigning "against the view that human beings needed to measure themselves against something non-human," some reality "out there."[82] Dewey's anti-authoritarianism asserts that it is "impossible to strip the human element" out of our thinking. Rorty asks us to "set aside *any* authority save that of a consensus of our fellow humans" to find "unforced agreement . . . about what beliefs will sustain and facilitate projects of social cooperation."

For pragmatists, "believing is inherently a public project." We all "have a responsibility to each other not to believe anything which cannot be justified to the rest of us." This should include our beliefs about schooling in a democracy, with an obligation to present our reasons for one educational approach over another. As it pertains to democratic politics—and I'd add schools preparing future citizens for these politics—Rorty advises that we should leave aside questions about the truth of things, the one best way of things, and "instead turn to the question of how to . . . broaden the size of the community" we seek to persuade. Doing so is not merely relevant to democratic politics, "it pretty much *is* democratic politics."

Tax-funded schools, seeking to produce public goods and not exclude, strike me as precisely the kind of social project that Rorty is talking about. And I think we can get more comfortable with collective bargaining when it is viewed as an obligation to talk to one another, with reasons that justify our beliefs, to find "unforced agreement." Collective bargaining formally includes others in decisions and thereby passes the exclusion test. Moreover, a duty among educators to talk to one another, about matters important enough to be in a scope of bargaining, frees schools from the hypocrisy of authoritarian employment relationships among people working to prepare future citizens for antiauthoritarian lives.[83]

Skeptics may still counter: Doctors and lawyers don't have unions or collective bargaining. If teachers seek to professionalize their work, shouldn't unionization and collective bargaining go away? Perhaps in time, when a Publicization Project is fully realized and people freely commit to talk to each absent any legal obligation to do so, because it produces more of the common goods we seek. But until then, it should suffice to point out that professional practices of doctors and lawyers still have enforceable obligations to one another. Partners can't rid themselves of partners, at will.

NEXT-STAGE TEACHER UNIONISM

Green Dot New York was more proof that a different mode of collective bargaining is possible and can lead to a contract unconstrained by the industrial paradigm. Nor was this some obscure experiment. It occurred within the largest school system in the country, amidst heated education reform politics, resulting in a meaningfully different kind of agreement signed by one of the nation's most prominent labor leaders and commended to her membership as a model. But the innovation didn't take. Our timing was off.

Barr invited his Los Angeles neighbor, the filmmaker Davis Guggenheim, to include Green Dot's New York school in a documentary Guggenheim was making about education reform. The film was expected to be as influential as his Oscar-winning work with former Vice President Al Gore on the climate crisis, *An Inconvenient Truth,* and we wanted in. We toured his producer and crew around the school. They interviewed Barr and Weingarten and filmed South Bronx streets for B-roll. Charitably, our hospitality was thanked in the closing credits. But we were naïve to think that Guggenheim, a documentarian, would tell the story straight. Nor did we do enough diligence on his backers, which included the conservative Anschutz Film Group.[84]

Guggenheim told a two-dimensional story of heroes and villains. He left on his cutting room floor the footage *he had in hand* of Green Dot's promising third-way approach to union and charter politics and the UFT's embrace of a professionalizing, school-based contract.[85] Instead, the film was a "paean" to privatization project reformers, starring charismatic education and civil rights leader Geoff Canada.[86] Its title, *Waiting for Superman,* was inspired by Canada's moving childhood story of watching the 1950s show and hoping for a savior.[87] Of course, such narratives need antagonists, and Guggenheim cast the teacher unions and Weingarten in the role. The film caused a short-lived flurry of publicity but did nothing to advance productive change. Instead, it unhelpfully hardened people and their positions. It also left in the shadows the young innovations that Green Dot, the UFT, and other AFT locals were cultivating.

Around the same time, Diane Ravitch published her influential book critical of education reform, recanting many of the privatizing views she had once advocated.[88] It was a provocative volte-face, which she promoted in book talks across the country, including one I attended in Hartford, hosted by AFT-Connecticut. She gave expert voice to teachers' feelings and frustrations against the privatization project, one that couldn't be ignored.

Avant-garde leaders of the type called for by Hargreaves and Fullan, particularly of membership organizations, can move only so fast and so far ahead of their constituents. Weingarten had been demonized on the big screen. Her members were rallying around Ravitch's call to arms. We received no reciprocal risk-taking from charter and reform leaders like KIPP on innovations like school-based contracts, or even support for common interests like the Campaign for Fiscal Equity. Weingarten did not need to be the preternatural student of politics that she is to feel the headwinds. The moment for any counterintuitive play, to "out-reform the reformers," had passed, if it was ever present. All that was left to do was to dig in and fight privatization, in political battles that the union would wage throughout the 12 long years of the Obama and subsequent administration.

But a hopeful question remains: If, at the time, Weingarten's leadership was premature and the conditions too much to overcome, is the time right, *now*, given the resurgence of progressive politics in American life? Within, as I've recommended, a Publicization Project that takes up the mantle of leadership in this moment of opportunity?

School-based bargaining should be an important part of this change, as it can serve to professionalize teaching by replacing industrial assumptions that impede a more equitable Intellectual-Emotional Paradigm. What else might "next-stage" teacher unionism entail?

We've already discussed the unions' role in professional accountability, by being an important voice in the setting of national teaching standards in dialogue with other stakeholders. We've also discussed the benefits of such well-defined practices for employment accountability, within a regime of mutual responsibility.

Digging into questions of due process, in good faith with others, is necessary, too. The Publicization Project will also need the unions' continued advocacy for sufficient resources by holding elected officials accountable, and for learning standards and charter authorizing that embraces an underlying philosophy of facts and the fact-making norms.

As I've argued, a Publicization Project is premised on political, rather than market-based, decision-making. This requires collective *action*, and no group is better at mobilizing educators than their unions. The Project will need this infrastructure and know-how. It should also learn from the unions' internal processes to better hear, heed, and edify the Project's stakeholders. Doing so can generate the shared commitments the Project seeks, motivating people to act in political processeses that determine school funding; hold elected officials accountable to provide this requisite support; add diverse perspectives to matters of education policy and law; and determine, at any given moment, what it means to be an educated American. Plus, assuming that the unions find self-interest in more professionalizing, school-based labor arrangements, their collective influence will be necessary to dismantle the national, state, and local regulatory regimes fortifying the industrial paradigm.

Imagine, then, teacher unions whose members come from *every* tax-funded school, district *and* charter. Teachers freely choose to be members, as is already required today by law, because the unions make clear the value they deliver to all educators, regardless of the type of school in which they work, and because of the unions' determination to make *all* schools more public. In national and state discussions, this more unified voice ensures that the perspectives and interests of the profession, across all tax-funded schools, are heard.

Also imagine, at a national level, stakeholders including the unions and elected officials agreeing to employment fundamentals for every educator.

Senator Bernie Sanders's recent proposal for a national minimum $60,000 teacher salary is an example.[89] Presumably it is fundable, too, as I argued in Chapter 1, if the federal share of school funding increases with taxes already due to Washington. To both I'd add reimagined due process, applicable nationwide, with each of its constituent parts designed to promote greater professionalism denoted by the quality of one's teaching practice. Such moves ensure that we will have a *national* teaching force that is well supported and up to the task, to prepare students in what we decide it means to be an educated American.

With major employment issues like pay and due process collectively determined and funded on a much broader scale, the scope of local and school-based discussions can focus on educational issues, decided among stakeholders closest to the work, and memorialized through school-based compacts and agreements. Such authority would be matched with school-based accountability, determined with evidence fit for the purpose, against a good-faith standard of effort. This kind of arrangement, within a regime of mutual accountability, takes teachers off the assembly line and asks them, instead, to be practitioners of a profession.

These ideas also make a clear distinction between unions' *macro* role, in matters of national and state policy, funding, and employment fundamentals applicable to all tax-funded schools, versus the more *micro* work entrusted to their members in schools' day-to-day operations. With such a demarcation, district leaders and reformers can no longer fall back on the old saw of union contracts micromanaging a principal's every last decision. Nor can unions protect members unable or unwilling to meet their own profession's expectations of good practice, in the tangle of rules and regulations defined through an ever-expanding scope of collective bargaining and an impractical burden of proof.

And, yes, there must be discussion. *More* of it, with explanations and reasons aimed to persuade each other. Some matters will be important enough to *require* conversation—collective bargaining—our duty to be in conversation together. Not simply because we have inherited labor laws and contracts. Or because a Publicization Project is deliberately incrementalist. But because we choose to bind ourselves in common cause, unwilling to defect, modeling the deliberation that, in a democracy, future citizens need to see.

CHAPTER 9

Conclusion

The right to have rights . . . should be guaranteed by humanity itself. It is by no means certain whether this is possible.

—Hannah Arendt, *The Origin of Totalitarianism*[1]

What is "public education"? It is an idea. It is very much like a right: first conceived, then nurtured by many fathers and mothers, raised across an extended family through common conviction, cared for and developed over generations. There is nothing intrinsic about it, no essential foundation on which the idea is natural, preordained, or self-evident that we are somehow trying to discover and achieve. What that education is, and the extent to which it is enjoyed by all, very much depends on us.

As Arendt presented with clinical dispassion, the right to an education that's public, like any right, is by no means certain and has a long and imperfect history. Alongside two centuries of achievements that expanded this right to more people are shameful chapters that keep it constrained. Of late, these imperfections have given some people cause to turn against the right itself, to only pursue more of schooling's private purposes.

To reinvigorate this right, we first need to agree on what we mean when we say "public education." These pages have aimed to persuade you that an education is "public" when it produces public goods and doesn't exclude. This means schools that prepare young people to advance the common benefits we've long asked of them: a healthy democracy, shared prosperity, social comity, and (more recently) the planet's habitability, and to do so in a way that doesn't exclude people from the effort, thereby making schools themselves a public good.

How can we know when this is happening? By appreciating that the publicness of schooling is dynamic, subject to our choices, with the help of tools like the exclusion test, and by examining education across key domains, to see where publicness can be strengthened, as it pertains to schooling that is:

- Free, funded by tax dollars sufficient to meet society's expectations, with fairness, so that the education enjoyed by one child is comparable to education of another and adequate to meet that child's needs, regardless of where they live or who they are

- Based on an underlying philosophy of facts and knowledge-making norms of evidence, fallibility, and persuasion, that still honors and contextualizes values and opinion.
- Governed inclusively through shared decision-making, to allow the diversity of stakeholders to collectively and regularly be in dialogue on what it means to be an educated American.
- In service of expected learning objectives that result from the unforced agreement among stakeholders regarding what is taught and how.
- Within a compact of mutual accountability among all stakeholders, who hold themselves and one another to a good-faith standard, based on evidence fit for each purpose.
- And, finally, equitable in the deepest sense, by ending the industrial sorting of children along assembly lines of race, ethnicity, class, gender, orientation, and place of birth, and in its stead, embracing a humanistic paradigm that develops the intellectual and emotional capacities innate to us all.

None of these ideas are new. But what is new is the language needed to hold them all together, through which we can act, in a project of *publicization*.

Schools that meet these criteria earn the right to be called public. With such schools, "public education" ceases to be a compound noun. "Public" becomes rightfully an adjective, an honorific, befitting any school that meets such commitments. This is the pragmatist's frame, as Rorty explains, to end our thinking about public education as corresponding to some underlying "nature of things," and instead begin considering it as a "commendatory term for well-justified beliefs" about what such schools do.[2]

This definition and six criteria are exploratory tools, to understand schooling and make it more public. To illustrate their usefulness, I've applied them to the two cases I know best: charter schools and the teacher unions. Both happen to be on the front lines of education politics. Both are key to the success of a Publicization Project.

Intentionally, I've not relitigated debates about whether charter schools are better or worse than district schools. Typical answers depend on metrics from an illegitimate industrial paradigm that itself needs to go. Plus, charters exist in sufficient numbers, have political permanence, and enroll millions of students who can most benefit from a quality education. In Weingarten's words more than a decade ago, these schools are a part of the "education landscape." The task is for charter leaders and others, together, to make *chartering* more public.

Nor, intentionally, did I debate the effects of teacher unions on schools and students. It's a nearly impossible question to answer, given the absence of like-for-like union to nonunion comparisons, with any contrasts confounded by "spillover effects."[3] Like charters, the unions exist. They have strengths that a Publicization Project needs, particularly for collective action. Some colleagues have shared that collective *action* should be sufficient, obviating the need for collective *bargaining*. But as I've argued, this mutual and binding obligation to talk, persuade, and decide on things together models in schools the deliberative relationships a democracy requires among citizens who are, like it or not, similarly bound together as Americans.

This definition and criteria can likely help us see and strengthen the publicness of education where we might not expect it, too. For example, the New York City school system pays tuition for students with special needs to attend privately operated schools that have particular expertise in educating these children. The arrangement is, for all intents and purposes, a voucher, to educate a student in ways that the school district cannot or may choose not to, in light of what the private school offers. In this, or any case involving school vouchers, to what extent does the private school meet the six criteria of publicness? And if it does, isn't it just as much a part of the enterprise of "public education" as any district or charter school? And if not, why?

WHAT IF IT COMES OUT "WRONG"?

Over the course of writing this book, I've been asked by colleagues: What if a Publicization Project leads to things I don't agree with? Such as resourcing schools at a level I think too rich or too poor? Or that doesn't add environmental stewardship to its overarching purposes, alongside schools' longstanding civic, social, and economic aims? Or that doesn't interrogate the nation's racism as part of the ongoing remaking of our national narrative? What if the deniers win?

I suppose I could always "exit" and send my kids to a private school that suits my tastes. Or say, with privileged flippancy, that "I'll move to Canada." But these are only temporary escapes, and I am reminded of Jean-Paul Sartre's insight that there is *no exit*[4] from an uninhabitable planet, the social effects of local and global poverty, or a return to an authoritarian, tribal world order.

Meaning, as it pertains to the vast majority of people, I ask my colleagues in return: How well does our *current* approach address the objections you raise? When was the last time you were in a conversation about what it means to be an educated American? How does the current resourcing of schools meet the material conditions in which you want your children to learn, particularly if they were randomly assigned to a school somewhere in America? Do you support the pressure that students are under to race ahead, as fast and as far as they can?

And might being part of a Publicization Project, with its commitment to deliberation and mutual accountability, increase the odds that we can find more satisfactory ways forward? And even when, at times, the Project isn't to your liking, stay in the conversation to change it? This does ask that we trust one another enough to talk, listen, moderate, and find unforced agreements. Fortunately, doing so, again and again, helps to build that very trust.

Or again from Sartre and the pragmatists: Instead of hell being other people, we choose to perceive others as our hope.

Another skeptical colleague said: "'Fiscal equity,' sign me up. A 'fact-based epistemology'? By all means. Ditto for 'respectful conversation,' and the 'Intellectual-Emotional Paradigm.' Again, *sign me up*." But he then pressed: How, precisely, do we make these things come about? In the world of American *realpolitik*?

Indeed. There is no shortage of educational *ideas* and precedents and books full of pie-in-the-sky recommendations to improve schools in ways that make them more public. What is needed are new *politics*, a durable political coalition, strong enough to shape the future of education in democratic ways to bring about these ideas.

The preceding pages also offer some hope as to why it is in the particular interest of one group or another to coalesce around publicization: the union leader who can better meet his members' desire for greater professionalism; the charter donor who can spend less of his private wealth for greater public impact; the parents and students stressed out and exhausted by assembly-line schooling; the employers who aren't getting workers prepared in the ways they seek; the champions of equity who know the current system is beyond repair and can't beat something with nothing; the citizens rightly worried about the future of our democracy and planet.

Rick Hess recently wrote that the previous coalition of the Clinton-Bush-Obama years has "come undone in today's polarized, populist era." Today's political reality requires "a pretty different tack from the one educational leaders, advocates, and funders are pursuing in their efforts to 'get the band back together' and reassemble the vintage coalition of the No Child Left Behind or Race to the Top days."[5]

Hess, a friend, is a senior fellow at the conservative American Enterprise Institute, where he directs education policy studies. He spent years advocating for the privatization project. Yet his recent essay acknowledges the need for change. In trying to understand why those who embrace testing "are no longer sure how to make their case," Hess writes that an answer lies in first "appreciating that testing has real shortcomings," that tests "aren't designed to improve instruction," given that "the results don't come back for months and parents don't get any actionable feedback." He calls on reformers "to think anew about how to make the case." Agreed, and these pages offered one such proposal: less testing, through sampling, alongside different ways of knowing, with evidence fit for its purpose, in a regime of mutual accountability.

Hess and I agree on the need for a new coalition. Might one that coalesces around a Publicization Project even find an ally at AEI, to move us past this current "distrustful era"?[6] Can the Project afford to not try to find out?

Without question, the founders and champions of a Publicization Project have an extraordinary amount of work to do, particularly when compared to the easier road traveled by the privatization project. We live in a world of markets and transactions. We're comfortable judging the value of something for ourselves, to meet our own private needs. Such choices are, as they say, "frictionless," and we prize the freedom that lets us do so. In recent decades, two generations have been raised in an era that glorified the private sector. Our mythologized rugged individualism makes self-interest and -reliance a cultural default. Doing what's best for ourselves and our own family not only comes naturally, it's *American*.

But we also live in communities. We gather together in churches and parks, at games and on sports teams, within civic associations, and at our jobs. In these groups we talk and deliberate and find ways to make things work, getting *through the friction*, until we need to talk and deliberate some more. Today we are also connected as a global community, sending messages, uploading posts, and scrolling feeds delivered to us at light speed. Although we may only ever deeply interact, over the course of our lives, with a handful of people, we still have an extraordinary, and ancient, ability to imagine what it means to be part of a larger community, spanning huge distances, with a shared identity.[7] Surely we have it in us to better imagine, together, what it means to be an American and the schools that can get us there.

MAKING A MOVEMENT

The nation *is* at risk. But unlike the eponymous 1983 report that placed *economic* woes at the feet of schools, it is now our *democracy* that is at risk. If left unattended, our deep divisions will shred the fabric of our country. This peril puts an even greater responsibility on schools to prepare citizens who will heal and sustain our democratic form of government, in service of a *whole* nation.[8]

The work of a Publicization Project is to find, create, and expand our common interests. I am not so naïve as to think that all of the many interests in American life will suddenly see the virtue, and necessity, of coming together in conversation, to strengthen the interests we share and dialogue through those that we don't. I have lived the *realpolitik* in which daring educational ideas flourish or fade. Plus, getting started won't be easy. It asks both stalwart champions of privatization and vigilant defenders of public education to *talk*. But the alternative—sustaining political skirmishes and stalemates—only strengthens the authoritarianism in our midst, as each side seeks to win its own vision of schooling through political force.

I've endeavored to make a case that is persuasive enough, or at least intriguing enough, to both sides. I've pointed to instances, small as they were, of risk and innovation, when something different happened. Change, by its very nature, is an outlier, and the courage to try something new needs to be honored and nurtured.

It will take a political and social movement, the Publicization Project, led by those who have spent their lives already championing these ideas, those who start to see their existing beliefs in a new light, and those fatigued, bored, or worried enough to give something new a try. Movements need their own language and intellectual frameworks, too, such as what is offered in these pages. Thomas Kuhn cautions that the new ideas that animate movement from one paradigm to another are often at first misunderstood and challenged. They need time to gain support and show how they solve more problems than the paradigm they displace, meaning that champions of this effort need the patience to be in it for the long haul.

Movements also need infrastructure, provided by existing organizations that are allied to the Project's aims, along with new entities purpose-built to aid the effort. It will take resources, from contributors large and small, for the organizing, white papers, advocacy, and proof points required for this proposed successor to privatization to be more than a book with an odd title. As Elizabeth Popp Berman concludes, champions of publicization will need to "build institutions that will help to support . . . [and] advocate–without apology." Her all-hands-on-deck *project.*[9]

Most importantly, movements need champions. Today there is no shortage of leaders and organizations who support American education in all of its various forms and toward their own preferred ends. If you've hung with me this far, how do *you* see yourself in the ideas of a Publicization Project? If you do, how will you advance and adjust your existing efforts to move the Project forward? So that when my colleague say, "Sign me up," there's something, somewhere for him to join? Or if you don't see yourself in this project, why not? What would you do differently to help schools better produce the common goods we need and be less exclusive in the process?

Let me end with a story. A friend described a recent effort to get charter school advocates and union leaders to combine their considerable advocacy powers and ensure sufficient COVID relief aid for all tax-funded schools—charter and district. The effort fizzled, despite aligned interests, largely for lack of trust or any practice working together.

I spent much of my early career trying to find some common ground between these two groups, and perhaps it's a quixotic hope. But as I thought about his anecdote, I put the deliberative, pragmatic values of a Publicization Project to the test. Did the stakeholders come to the table taking their own fallibility seriously, willing to listen to one another, open to reasons and persuasion, to seek out commonalities, in a belief that differences might improve one another's point of view? Was it a one-off, high-stakes game involving huge sums of money? Or might they have come together with a commitment to do so again and again, to achieve smaller shared wins that cultivate, over time, the collaboration needed to address thornier differences? Might we all just be tired enough of the old back-and-forth, the authoritarian attempts to end, rather than sustain, the conversation? Might we be ready, and even inspired, about something new, and turn our attention to a project that, in its broadest sense, makes America's schools more public?

Endnotes

Introduction

1. Examples include Steven Brill, *Class Warfare: Inside the Fight to Fix America's Schools* (New York: Simon & Schuster, 2011); Diane Ravitch, *The Great School Wars: A History of the New York City Public Schools* (Baltimore: Johns Hopkins University Press, 1974); National Alliance for Public Charter Schools, *Chartering 2.0: Leadership Summit Proceedings Document*, 2006, https://publiccharters.org/newsroom/publications/chartering-2-0-summit-proceedings-document/; Lydia Rainey, Andrew J. Rotherham, and Paul T. Hill, "A One-Day Ceasefire: What Charter School and Teacher Union Leaders Say When They Meet," in *Hopes, Fears, and Reality: A Balanced Look at American Charter Schools,* Robin J. Lake and Paul T. Hill (Seattle: National Charter School Research Project Center on Reinventing Public Education, Daniel J. Evans School of Public Affairs, University of Washington, 2006), 25–35; "Public Schooling Battle Map," Cato Institute, accessed 2/14/2023, https://www.cato.org/education-fight-map; and Paige Williams, "Class Warfare: How School Boards Are Being Attacked by Partisan Saboteurs," *The New Yorker,* November 7, 2022, 52–63.

2. "Fast Facts," National Center for Education Statistics, accessed 5/21/2021, https://nces.ed.gov/fastfacts/display.asp?id=84.

3. Christopher Jencks, "Giving Parents Money for Schooling: Education Vouchers," *Phi Delta Kappan* 52, no. 1 (September 1970): 49–52; Eric Rofes and Lisa M. Stulberg, eds., *The Emancipatory Promise of Charter Schools: Toward a Progressive Politics of School Choice* (Albany: State University of New York Press, 2004); Lisa M. Stulberg, "What History Offers Progressive Choice Scholarships," in *The Emancipatory Promise of Charter Schools: Toward a Progressive Politics of School Choice,* eds. Eric Rofes and Lisa M. Stulberg (Albany: State University of New York Press 2004), 7–54.

4. James W. Guthrie, "A Political Case History: Passage of the ESEA," *Phi Delta Kappan* 49, no. 6 (1968): 302–306.

5. National Commission on Excellence in Education, *A Nation At Risk: The Imperative for Educational Reform* (Washington, DC: NCEE, 1983).

6. David Osborne and Ted Gaebler, *Reinventing Government: How the Entrepreneurial Spirit Is Transforming the Public Sector from the Schoolhouse to Statehouse, City Hall to the Pentagon* (Reading, MA: Addison-Wesley, 1992).

7. The term "privatization project" has been used in various ways, for example by the Carnegie Council for Ethics in International Affairs; "Privatization Project," accessed 2/27/2023, https://www.carnegiecouncil.org/media/series

/privatization-project; and by the Human Rights and Privatization Project, which "works to examine how the privatization of essential sectors and services affects the realization of human rights, particularly for low-income people"; "Human Rights and Privatization Project," Center for Human Rights and Global Justice, accessed 2/26/2023, https://chrgj.org/all-projects/human-rights-and-privatization-project/. A useful summary of the bipartisan support for privatization policies is provided by Marilyn Cochran-Smith et al., *Reclaiming Accountability in Teacher Education* (New York: Teachers College Press, 2018), 9, 15–20.

8. Thomas Philippon, *The Great Reversal: How America Gave Up on Free Markets* (Cambridge, MA: The Belknap Press of Harvard University, 2019); Jonathan Tepper with Denise Hearn, *The Myth of Capitalism: Monopolies and the Death of Competition* (Hoboken, NJ: John Wiley & Sons, 2019); Anand Giridharadas, *Winners Take All: The Elite Charade of Changing the World* (New York: Alfred A. Knopf, 2018); Jonathan Hopkin, *Anti-System Politics: The Crisis of Market Liberalism in Rich Democracies* (Oxford, UK: Oxford University Press, 2020), Ian Haney López, *Merge Left: Fusing Race and Class, Winning Elections, and Saving America* (New York: The New Press, 2019), Thomas Piketty, *Time for Socialism: Dispatches from a World on Fire, 2016–2021*, trans. Kristin Couper (New Haven, CT: Yale University Press, 2021).

9. Elizabeth Popp Berman, *Thinking Like an Economist: How Efficiency Replaced Equality in U.S. Public Policy* (Princeton, NJ: Princeton University Press, 2022), 3, 229–230.

10. Popp Berman, *Thinking Like an Economist*, 4.

11. For example, Marilyn Cochran-Smith and colleagues generally refer to "public *and private* charter schools" (emphasis added), which is arguably a contradiction in terms, in *Reclaiming Accountability in Teacher Education* (New York: Teachers College Press, 2018), 9.

12. Personal correspondence with Harry Brighouse, one of the conveners, January 2022.

13. "Publicization (n.) 'act of publicizing,' 1962, noun of action from publicize. There is a 1907 use in the sense 'a making public' (of bridges built privately, etc.)." From "Publicization," Online Etymology Dictionary, accessed 8/11/2021, https://www.etymonline.com/word/publicization#etymonline_v_47542; also in academic use, such as Sarah Schindler, "The 'Publicization' of Private Space," *Iowa Law Review* 103, no. 3 (March 15, 2018): 1093–1153.

14. Richard Hofstadter, *Anti-Intellectualism in American Life* (New York: Random House, 1962), 305.

15. Popp Berman, *Thinking Like an Economist,* 232, emphasis added.

16. Sonya Douglass Horsford, Janelle T. Scott, and Gary L. Anderson, *The Politics of Education Policy in an Era of Inequality: Possibilities for Democratic Schooling* (New York: Routledge, 2019), 96.

17. A recent example with one-sided reporting is by Jonathan Mahler, "The Most Dangerous Person in the World Is Randi Weingarten," *New York Times,* April 28, 2023.

18. Taisir Subhi Yamin and Sandra Linke, "Sally M. Reis Made Real and Sustainable Change in Schools and Classroom Practice," *International Journal for Talent Development and Creativity* 8, no. 1–2 (2022): 263–274.

19. Jonathan Gyurko and Molly Simmons, "After Apartheid," *Taft Bulletin* 67, no. 4 (Summer 1997): 2–9.

20. "Tiger Kloof—A Brief History," Tiger Kloof Educational Institution, accessed 2/27/2023, https://www.tigerkloof.org/history.

21. "MAP's History," Maru-A-Pula School, accessed 2/14/2023, https://www.maruapula.org/about-us/maps-history/.

22. Colorado's Brad Jupp and the UK's Michael Barber come to mind: Alyson Klein, "Brad Jupp Is Arne's New Two-for-One Teacher Guy," *Education Week*, May 12, 2009, https://www.edweek.org/policy-politics/brad-jupp-is-arnes-new-two-for-one-teacher-guy/2009/05; Arne Duncan, *How Schools Work* (New York: Simon & Schuster, 2018), 187; and "Michael Barber (educationist)," Wikipedia, last modified 2/25/2023, https://en.wikipedia.org/wiki/Michael_Barber_(educationist).

23. "Gold in Them Thar Hills (Edison Project)," *60 Minutes,* season 33, episode 34, produced by Deirdre Naphin Curran, reported by Morley Safer, aired May 27, 2001, CBS.

24. Michael J. Petrilli, "NAEP 2017: America's "Lost Decade" of Educational Progress," Thomas B. Fordham Institute, April 10, 2018, https://fordhaminstitute.org/national/commentary/naep-2017-americas-lost-decade-educational-progress; Jay Caspian King, "America's Falling Test Scores and the Power of Parental Anxiety," *The New Yorker*, October 28, 2022, https://www.newyorker.com/news/our-columnists/americas-falling-test-scores-and-the-power-of-parental-anxiety; Sarah Mervosh, "U.S. Students' Progress Stagnated Last School Year, Study Finds," *New York Times,* July 11, 2023.

25. Emma García, "Schools Are Still Segregated, and Black Children Are Paying a Price," *Economic Policy Institute*, February 12, 2020, https://www.epi.org/publication/schools-are-still-segregated-and-black-children-are-paying -a-price/; and Richard Rothstein. *The Color of Law: A Forgotten History of How Our Government Segregated America* (New York: Liveright, 2017).

The Exclusion Test

1. David Schmidtz describes the distinction slightly differently, between education as a public good versus a "positional good," in David Schmidtz and Harry Brighouse, *Debating Education: Is There a Role for Markets?* (Oxford, UK: Oxford University Press, 2020).

2. This "tragedy of the commons" argues that absent some controlling authority like a government or through total privatization, public goods will be depleted. But not in all cases, as Elinor Ostrom showed: Michelle Nijhuis, "The Miracle of the Commons," *Aeon*, May 4, 2021, https://aeon.co/essays/the-tragedy-of-the-commons-is-a-false-and-dangerous-myth; and Elinor Ostrom, *Governing the Commons: The Evolution of Institutions for Collective Action* (Cambridge, UK: Cambridge University Press, 1990).

3. Henry M. Levin, "Education as a Public and Private Good," *Journal of Policy Analysis and Management* 6, no. 4 (Summer 1987): 628–641; and David F. Labaree, "Public Goods, Private Goods: The American Struggle Over Educational Goals," *American Educational Research Journal* 34, no. 1 (Spring 1997): 39–81.

4. Lawrence A. Cremin, *American Education: The Colonial Experience 1607–1783* (New York: Harper & Row Publishers, 1970); Carl Kaestle, *Pillars of the Republic: Common Schools and American Society, 1780–1860* (New York: Hill & Wang, 1990); David Tyack, Thomas James, and Aaron Benavot, eds., *Law and the Shaping of Public Education* (Madison: University of Wisconsin Press, 1987); Lawrence

A. Cremin, *The American Common School: An Historic Conception* (New York: Teachers College Bureau of Publications, 1951); Allen Oscar Hansen, *Liberalism and American Education in the Eighteenth Century* (New York: Octagon Books, 1965); Abraham Blinderman, *American Writers on Education Before 1865* (Boston: G. K. Hall, 1975); and Lawrence A. Cremin, *American Education: The National Experience, 1783–1876* (New York: Harper & Row, 1980).

5. Hofstadter, *Anti-Intellectualism,* 299–300.

6. Hofstadter, *Anti-Intellectualism*, 325–325.

7. David Wallace-Wells, *The Uninhabitable Earth: Life After Warming* (New York: Tim Duggan Books, 2019).

8. Robert A. Caro, *The Power Broker* (New York: Alfred A. Knopf, 1974).

9. Thomas J. Campanella, "Robert Moses and His Racist Highway," July 9, 2017, https://www.bloomberg.com/news/articles/2017-07-09/robert-moses-and-his-racist-parkway-explained; Moses' biographer, Robert A. Caro, described him as "the most racist human being I had ever really encountered."

Part I: Criteria

1. Christopher J. Voparil and Richard J. Bernstein, ed., *The Rorty Reader* (West Sussex, UK: Wiley-Blackwell, 2010), 17.

Chapter 1: Funding

1. *Key & Peele*, season 5, episode 4, "Teaching Center," directed by Peter Atencio and Payman Benz, featuring Keegan-Michael Key and Jordan Peele, aired July 29, 2015, on Comedy Central, https://www.cc.com/video/aimepr/key-peele-teachingcenter.

2. Cremin, *The National Experience*; Tyack, James, and Benavot, *Law and the Shaping of Public Education*; Cremin, *The Colonial Experience*; Kate Rousmaniere, "In Search of a Profession: A History of American Teachers," in *Portrait of a Profession: Teaching and Teachers in the 21st Century,* ed. David M. Moss, Wendy J. Glenn, and Richard L. Schwab (Lanham, MD: Rowman and Littlefield Education, 2008); Darrel Drury and Justin Baer, *The American Public School Teacher: Past, Present and Future* (Cambridge, MA: Harvard Education Press, 2011); David Tyack, *The One Best System: A History of American Urban Education* (Cambridge, MA: Harvard University Press, 1974); Kim Tolley, "The Rise of the Academies: Continuity or Change?" *History of Education Quarterly* 41, no. 2 (2001): 225–239; and Kim Tolley and Margaret A. Nash, "Leaving Home to Teach: The Diary of Susan Nye Hutchinson, 1815–1841," in *Chartered Schools: Two Hundred Years of Independent Academies in the United States, 1724 to 1925,* ed. Nancy Beadie and Kim Tolley (New York: Routledge Falmer, 2002).

3. Hofstadter, *Anti-Intellectualism*, 313.

4. Alexis de Tocqueville, *Democracy in America* (New York: Penguin, 2003).

5. Kaestle, *Pillars of the Republic,* 3–4.

6. Tyack, James, and Benavot, *Law and the Shaping of Public Education,* 134–147.

7. David Tyack and Elisabeth Hansot, *Managers of Virtue: Public School Leadership In America, 1820–1980* (New York: Basic Books, 1987); Kaestle, *Pillars of the Republic*; Tyack, James, and Benavot, *Law and the Shaping of Public Education*; Joseph P. Ferrie, "The Impact of Immigration on Natives in the Antebellum U.S.

Labor Market, 1850–60," *National Bureau of Economic Research*, Historical Working Paper No. 93, September 1996; Tyack, *One Best System*; and Cremin, *The National Experience.*

8. Hofstadter, *Anti-Intellectualism*, 302.

9. Kim Tolley and Nancy Beadie, "Reappraisals of the Academy Movement," *History of Education Quarterly* 41, no. 2 (Summer 2007), 220; Tolley, "The Rise of the Academies"; Theodore Sizer, *Age of the Academies* (New York: Teachers College Press, 1964); Nancy Beadie and Kim Tolley, eds., *Chartered Schools: Two Hundred Years of Independent Academies in the United States, 1727–1925* (New York: Routledge Falmer, 2002); and Hofstadter, *Anti-Intellectualism,* 325.

10. Rousmaniere, "In Search of a Profession," 12–13; Tyack and Hansot, *Managers of Virtue*, 112; Tyack, *One Best System,* 29; Tyack, James, and Benavot, *Law and the Shaping of Public Education*, 109–113; Tyack and Hansot, *Managers of Virtue*, 130–140; and Raymond E. Callahan, *Education and the Cult of Efficiency* (Chicago: The University of Chicago Press, 1964).

11. Louis Menand, *The Free World: Art and Thought in the Cold War* (New York: Farrar, Straus & Giroux), 301.

12. Menand, *Free World,* 616.

13. Hofstadter, *Anti-Intellectualism,* 316–322.

14. Michael Berkman and Eric Plutzer, *Ten Thousand Democracies: Politics and Public Opinion in America's School Districts* (Washington, DC: Georgetown University Press, 2005), 111–127.

15. Steven Skowronek, *Building a New American State: The Expansion of National Administrative Capacities 1877–1920* (Cambridge, UK: Cambridge University Press, 1982).

16. A fine description of the region's past industrial glory is Simon Winchester, *The Perfectionists: How Precision Engineers Created the Modern World* (New York: HarperCollins, 2018).

17. "Accreditation May Be at Stake if No Action Taken to Address Torrington High School Infrastructure Failures," *Waterbury Republican American,* October 11, 2020.

18. RJ Scofield, "Greenwich Billionaires Among Richest in US: Forbes," *Patch,* April 7, 2021, https://patch.com/connecticut/greenwich/greenwich-billionaires-among-richest-u-s-forbes; and "Racial Balance Plan," Greenwich Public Schools, accessed 2/15/2023, https://www.greenwichschools.org/district-information/district-priorities/racial-balance-plan.

19. Valerie Straus, "Report: Public Schools More Segregated Now Than 40 Years Ago," *Washington Post*, August 29, 2013, https://www.washingtonpost.com/news/answer-sheet/wp/2013/08/29/report-public-schools-more-segregated-now-than-40-years-ago/; Alvin Chang, "The Data Proves That School Segregation Is Getting Worse," *Vox*, March 5, 2018, https://www.vox.com/2018/3/5/17080218/school-segregation-getting-worse-data; and Keith Meatto, "Still Separate, Still Unequal: Teaching About School Segregation and Educational Inequality," *New York Times*, May 2, 2019, https://www.nytimes.com/2019/05/02/learning/lesson-plans/still-separate-still-unequal-teaching-about-school-segregation-and-educational-inequality.html.

20. Trinity Lutheran Church of Columbia, Inc. v. Comer, 788 F. 3d 779 U.S. (2017); and Carson v. Makin, 596 U.S. (2022).

21. "Private School Enrollment," National Center for Education Statistics, last modified May 2022, https://nces.ed.gov/programs/coe/indicator_cgc.asp.

22. "Landmark US Cases Related to Equality of Opportunity in K-12 Education," Stanford University, accessed 2/15/2023, https://edeq.stanford.edu/sections/landmark-us-cases-related-equality-opportunity-education.

23. David Rohde, "Victory in Schools Suit Spotlights Need for Free Legal Work," *New York Times,* January 22, 2001.

24. Michael Rebell, "The School Equity Fight Isn't Won," *The Daily News*, April 13, 2021, https://www.nydailynews.com/opinion/ny-oped-the-school-equity-fight-isnt-won-20210413-6wfsugvfvzewloc2m7l4lwzowa-story.html.

25. Rebell, "School Equity."

26. "Fiscal Accountability Summary (2017–2018)," Bedford CSD, *New York State Education Department*, accessed 2/15/2023, https://data.nysed.gov/fiscal.php?year=2018&instid=800000035721.

27. "Fiscal Accountability Summary (2017–2018)," NY Chancellor's Office, New York State Education Department, accessed 2/15/2023, https://data.nysed.gov/fiscal.php?year=2018&instid=800000048663.

28. "Bedford Central School District," Education, U.S. News, accessed 2/15/2023, https://www.usnews.com/education/k12/new-york/districts/bedford-central-school-district-106355; and "KWIC Indicator: Children Receiving Free or Reduced-Price School Lunch—Public Schools," Kids' Well Being Indicator Clearinghouse, New York State, February 15, 2023, https://www.nyskwic.org/get_data/indicator_profile.cfm?subIndicatorID=52.

29. Rachel Wimpee, "Funding a Social Movement: The Ford Foundation and Civil Rights, 1965–1970," Rockefeller Archive Center, accessed 2/27/2023, https://resource.rockarch.org/story/philanthropy-social-movements-ford-foundation-civil-rights-1965-1970/; and "A Legacy of Social Justice," Ford Foundation, accessed 8/16/2021, https://www.fordfoundation.org/about/about-ford/a-legacy-of-social-justice/.

30. ACORN was the target of a famous sting by Fox News that forced its closure and reimagining as a network of affiliated community organizations including New York Communities for Change. Joshua Rhett Miller, "Filmmakers Show Video of ACORN 'Sting' in Philadelphia," Fox News, May 16, 2015, https://www.foxnews.com/story/filmmakers-show-video-of-acorn-sting-in-philadelphia;and "New York Communities for Change," NYCommunities, accessed 2/15/2023, https://www.nycommunities.org/.

31. Hofstadter, *Anti-Intellectualism,* 305.

32. Hofstadter, *Anti-Intellectualism,* 281.

33. Horsford, Scott, and Anderson, *Politics of Education Policy*, 12, 210.

34. NCES, "Private School Enrollment."

35. Ginia Bellefante, "In the Budget, a Victory for Compassion," *The New York Times,* April 11, 2021.

36. Bruce D. Baker, Matthew Di Carlo, and Mark Weber, *The Adequacy and Fairness of State School Finance Systems* (Washington, DC: Albert Shanker Institute and Rutgers Graduate School of Education, 2019).

37. Melanie Hanson, "U.S. Public Education Spending Statistics," EducationData.org, June 15, 2022, https://educationdata.org/public-education-spending-statistics#new-york.

38. Daniel Estrin, Alejandra Marquez Janse, and Amy Isakson, "The IRS Misses Billions in Uncollected Tax Each Year. Here's Why," *All Things Considered,* NPR (New York: WNYC), April 19, 2022.

39. "U.S. School System Current Spending Per Pupil by Region: Fiscal Year 2020," United States Census Bureau, accessed 4/21/2021, https://www.census.gov/content/dam/Census/library/visualizations/2022/comm/school-system-finance.pdf.

40. A. C. Grayling, *The History of Philosophy* (New York: Penguin Press, 2019); and John Rawls, *A Theory of Justice* (Cambridge, MA: Belknap, 1999).

41. John Dewey, *The School and Society* (Chicago: University of Chicago Press, 1907) 19.

42. Horsford, Scott, and Anderson, *Politics of Education Policy*, 9.

Chapter 2: Facts and Beliefs

1. "People Are Entitled to Their Own Opinions But Not to Their Own Facts," Quote Investigator, last modified March 17, 2020, https://quoteinvestigator.com/2020/03/17/own-facts/.

2. Jill Lepore, *These Truths* (New York: W. W. Norton & Company, 2018).

3. David A. Graham, "The Wrong Side of 'the Right Side of History,'" *The Atlantic*, December 21, 2015, https://www.theatlantic.com/politics/archive/2015/12/obama-right-side-of-history/420462/.

4. Schmidtz and Brighouse, *Debating Education*, 178.

5. Jeffrey R. Henig, *Rethinking School Choice: Limits of the Market Metaphor* (Princeton, NJ: Princeton University Press, 1994).

6. Katherine Stewart, *The Power Worshippers: Inside the Dangerous Rise of Religious Nationalism* (New York: Bloomsbury Publishing, 2019): 186, quoted in Diane Ravitch, "The Dark History of School Choice," *New York Review of Books*, January 14, 2021, 37.

7. Tyack and Hansot, *Managers of Virtue,* 57; and Kaestle, *Pillars of the Republic*, 79–80.

8. Tyack, James, and Benavot, *Law and the Shaping of Public Education*, 14, 24; and Kaestle, *Pillars of the Republic*, 70–72, 95–96.

9. Tyack and Hansot, *Managers of Virtue*, 72–82; Ravitch, *The Great School Wars*; and Ian Lovett, "Catholic Schools Are Losing Students at Record Rates, and Hundreds Are Closing," *The Wall Street Journal,* May 10, 2021, https://www.wsj.com/articles/catholic-schools-are-losing-students-at-record-rates-and-hundreds-are-closing-11620651600#:~:text=Today%2C%20about%201.6%20million%20students,schools%2C%20according%20to%20the%20NCEA.

10. Linda Greenhouse, "Grievance Conservatives Are Here to Stay," *New York Review of Books*, July 1, 2021, 34.

11. Ravitch, "Dark History," 36.

12. Nick Martin, "Is America Ready to Face the Truth of Atrocities Against Indigenous Children?," *New Republic,* June 24, 2021, https://newrepublic.com/article/162821/america-ready-face-truth-atrocities-indigenous-children; "Searching for the Unmarked Graves of Indigenous Children," *The New York Times*, produced by Nilo Tabrizy, accessed 4/12/2021, https://www.nytimes.com/interactive/2021/10/20/video/indigenous-graves-children-canada-video.html; and Mark Walker, "Report Catalogs Abuse of Native American Children at Former Government Schools," *The*

New York Times, May 11, 2022, https://www.nytimes.com/2022/05/11/us/politics /native-american-children-schools-abuse.html.

13. Samuel Bowles and Herbert Gintis, *Schooling in Capitalist America: Educational Reform and the Contradictions of Economic Life* (New York: Basic Books, 1977).

14. Ivan Illich, *Deschooling Society* (London: Marion Boyars Publishers, 2000).

15. E. E. Schattschneider, *The Semi-Sovereign People* (New York: Holt, Rinehart and Winston, 1960), 35; and Kay Lehman Schlozman, Sidney Verba, and Henry E. Brady, *The Unheavenly Chorus: Unequal Political Voice and the Broken Promise of American Democracy* (Princeton, NJ: Princeton University Press, 2012).

16. "State Education Practices," National Center for Education Statistics, accessed 4/16/2021; https://nces.ed.gov/programs/statereform/tab5_1.asp.

17. Mark Danner, "Reality Rebellion," *New York Review of Books*, July 1, 2021, 12.

18. Jonathan Rauch, *The Constitution of Knowledge: A Defense of Truth* (Washington, DC: Brookings Institute, 2021), 9.

19. Rauch, *Constitution of Knowledge*, 100.

20. Theodore R. Sizer, "On the Habit of Informed Skepticism," in *Teaching for Intelligence*, ed. Barbara Z. Presseisen (Thousand Oaks, CA: Corwin Press, 2008), 8–16; and "An Education Visionary, Progressive Thinker—and 'Incredible Connector,'" Harvard Graduate School of Education, accessed 2/16/2023, https://www.gse.harvard.edu/hgse100/story/education-visionary-progressive-thinker-and-incredible-connector.

21. Daniel Kahneman, *Thinking, Fast and Slow* (New York: Farrar, Straus & Giroux, 2011).

22. Rauch, *Constitution of Knowledge*, 88–89.

23. Louis Menand, *The Metaphysical Club* (New York: Farrer, Straus, & Giroux, 2002); and Louis Menand, ed., *Pragmatism: A Reader* (New York: Vintage, 1997).

24. Rauch, *Constitution of Knowledge*, 60.

25. Hannah Arendt, *The Origins of Totalitarianism* (New York: Harvest, 1976), 333.

Chapter 3: Governance

1. Emily Brooks, "McAuliffe Says Parents Shouldn't Tell Schools What to Teach, Handing Youngkin a Campaign Ad," *Washington Examiner*, September 29, 2021; and Brittany Bernstein, "McAuliffe Argues Parents Shouldn't Have Control Over Public School Curriculum," *National Review*, September 29, 2021.

2. Hofstadter, *Anti-Intellectualism,* 127.

3. Nel Noddings, *Educating for Intelligent Belief or Unbelief* (New York: Teachers College Press, 1994).

4. Horsford, Scott, and Anderson, *Politics of Education Policy,* 89–92.

5. Amy Gutmann, *Democratic Education* (Princeton, NJ: Princeton University Press, 1987), 28.

6. Diane Ravitch, "Whatever Happened to Common Core and What Happened to Classic Literature?" *Diane Ravitch's Blog,* July 28, 2018, accessed 7/27/2023, https://dianeravitch.net/2018/07/23/whatever-happened-to-common-core-and-what-happened-to-classic-literature/.

7. Horsford, Scott, and Anderson, *Politics of Education Policy*, 89; Eva Gold, Jeffrey R. Henig, and Elaine Simon, "Calling the Shots in Public Education: Parents, Politicians, and Educators Clash," *Dissent Magazine*, Fall 2011; and Jeffrey R. Henig, *The End of Exceptionalism in American Education: The Changing Politics of School Reform* (Cambridge, MA; Harvard University Press, 2013).

8. Williams, "Class Warfare," 57; and Gabriella Borter, Joseph Ax and Joseph Tanfani, "School Boards Get Death Threats Amid Rage Over Race, Gender, Mask Policies," Reuters, February 15, 2022, https://www.reuters.com/investigates/special-report/usa-education-threats/.

9. Karl E. Weick, "Educational Organizations as Loosely Coupled Systems," *Administrative Science Quarterly* 21, no. 1 (March 1976): 1–19.

10. Horsford, Scott, and Anderson, *Politics of Education Policy*, 91.

11. David Tyack and William Tobin, "The 'Grammar' of Schooling: Why Has It Been So Hard to Change?," *American Education Research Journal* 31, no. 3 (Autumn 1994): 453–479.

12. Hofstadter, *Anti-Intellectualism,* 316.

13. Horsford, Scott, and Anderson, *Politics of Education Policy*, 89; Rousmaniere, "In Search of a Profession," 12–13; Tyack and Hansot, *Managers of Virtue*, 112, 117, 126; Tyack, *One Best System,* 29; Wayne Urban, *Why Teachers Organized* (Detroit: Wayne State University Press, 1982), 26; Callahan, *Education and the Cult of Efficiency*; Tyack, James, and Benavot, *Law and the Shaping of Public Education*, 109; Marjorie Murphy, *Blackboard Unions: The AFT and the NEA (1900–1980)* (Ithaca, NY: Cornell University Press, 1990), 23–45; Ravitch, *The Great School Wars*; Lawrence A. Cremin, *The Transformation of the School: Progressivism in American Education* (New York: Alfred Knopf, 1962); and Ira Katznelson and Margaret Weir, *Schooling for All* (Berkeley: University of California Press, 1985), 94.

14. Hofstadter, *Anti-Intellectualism,* 199.

15. National Commission on Excellence in Education, *A Nation at Risk.*

16. E. D. Hirsch, *Cultural Literacy: What Every American Needs to Know* (New York: Vintage, 1988); Diane Ravitch, *Left Back: A Century of Battles Over School Reform* (New York: Touchstone, 2000), 419–426; "More NCTM Standards," National Council of Teachers of Mathematics, accessed 10/22/2023, https://www.nctm.org/Standards-and-Positions/More-NCTM-Standards/, "History Standards," UCLA History Public History Initiative, accessed 10/22/2023, https://phi.history.ucla.edu/nchs/history-standards/, "Standards," National Council of Teachers of English, accessed 10/22/2023, https://ncte.org/resources/standards/ncte-ira-standards-for-the-english-language-arts/.

17. Ravitch, *Left Back*, 419–426.

18. Hofstadter, *Anti-Intellectualism,* 197–229; and Garry Wills, *A Necessary Evil: A History of American Distrust of Government* (New York: Simon & Schuster, 1999).

19. *Common Core State Standards,* Council of Chief State School Officers, accessed 3/2/2022, https://learning.ccsso.org/common-core-state-standards-initiative; and "Common Core," Wikipedia, last modified 2/1/2023, https://en.wikipedia.org/wiki/Common_Core.

20. Duncan, *How Schools Work*, 8.

21. Caitlyn Emma, "Jindal Sues Over Common Core," *Politico*, August 29, 2014, https://www.politico.com/story/2014/08/bobby-jindal-common-core-lawsuit-110377; and Duncan, *How Schools Work*, 144.

22. Horsford, Scott, and Anderson, *Politics of Education Policy*, 75.

23. Duncan, *How Schools Work*, 44–45.

24. Duncan, *How Schools Work*, 149, 132.

25. Duncan, *How Schools Work*, 143.

26. Duncan, *How Schools Work*, 95, 96, 100.

27. Duncan, *How Schools Work*, 105, 129.

28. Duncan, *How Schools Work*, 146.

29. Israel Ortega, "Common Core: Doubling Down on a Failed Strategy," The Heritage Foundation, October 5, 2013, https://www.heritage.org/education/commentary/common-core-doubling-down-failed-strategy.

30. Albert O. Hirschman, *Exit, Voice and Loyalty: Responses to Decline in Firms, Organizations, and States* (Cambridge, MA: Harvard University Press, 1970).

31. I am not suggesting that politics has been absent. We need look no further than Brown v. Board of Education and the long campaign of case law and well-organized sit-ins, boycotts, and other political activity that achieved this landmark. It made schools more of a public good, by no longer excluding Black students from all-White schools. The Elementary and Secondary Education Act, Title IX rights for women, the Individuals with Disabilities Education Act, and other legislative achievements resulted from political activism. But as this chapter demonstrates, privateness, as expressed through both parent choice and expert voice, still dominates the decisions that govern schools.

32. Gloria Ladson-Billings and William Tate, "Toward a Critical Race Theory of Education," *Teachers College Record* 97, no. 1 (Fall 1995): 58; and Horsford, Scott, and Anderson, *Politics of Education Policy*, 39.

33. Political commentator Walter Lippman and philosopher John Dewey famously debated this point from the 1920s through the 1950s. Sam Illing, "Intellectuals Have Said Democracy Is Failing for a Century. They Were Wrong," *Vox*, December 20, 2018, https://www.vox.com/2018/8/9/17540448/walter-lippmann-democracy-trump-brexit; Walter Lippman, *Public Opinion* (New York: Free Press, 1997); Tony DeCesare, "The Lippmann-Dewey Debate Revisited: The Problem of Knowledge and the Role of Experts in Modern Democratic Theory," *Philosophical Studies in Education*, 43 (2012): 106–116; and John Dewey, *The Public and Its Problems* (Athens, OH: Sparrow, 1954).

34. Marilyn Cochran-Smith et. al., *Reclaiming Accountability in Teacher Education*, 7.

35. Gary L. Anderson, "Toward Authentic Participation: Deconstructing the Discourse of Participatory Reforms," *American Educational Research Journal*, 35 no. 4 (Winter 1998): 571–606; and Horsford, Scott, and Anderson, *Politics of Education Policy*, 167.

36. Helpful research on this issue with a case study of the Common Core can be found in Lorraine M. McDonnell and M. Stephen Weatherford, *Evidence, Politics, and Education Policy* (Cambridge, MA: Harvard Education Press, 2020).

37. Leo Casey, "Triumphant Managerialism and the Strategy of Intellectual Non-Engagement and Avoidance," *Edwize*, December 16, 2005, http://edwize.org.

38. Williams, "Class Warfare," 52–56.

39. Williams, "Class Warfare," 55; Amelie Nierenberg, "The Conservative School Board Strategy," *The New York Times*, last modified February 15, 2023, https://www.nytimes.com/2021/10/27/us/the-conservative-school-board-strategy.html.

40. Williams, "Class Warfare," 52, 61.

41. Jonathan Zimmerman, remarks delivered at the National Higher Education Teaching Conference, New York City, June 22, 2023.

42. Rauch, *Constitution of Knowledge*, 3.

43. Theodore Sizer and Nancy Faust Sizer, *The Students Are Watching: Schools and the Moral Contract* (Boston: Beacon, 1999).

44. Robert Axelrod, *The Evolution of Cooperation* (Cambridge, MA: Basic Books, 2006); and James Carse, *Finite and Infinite Games* (New York: Simon & Schuster, 1986).

45. Danielle S. Allen, *Talking to Strangers: Anxieties of Citizenship Since Brown v. Board of Education* (Chicago: The University of Chicago Press, 2004), xix.

46. Allen, *Talking to Strangers,* 28–29.

47. Duncan, *How Schools Work*, 133, 147–148.

48. "Our Partners," Bellwether, accessed 2/26/2023, https://bellwether.org/about-us/our-partners/.

49. Valerie Straus, "Trump's 'Patriotic Education' Report Excuses Founding Fathers for Owning Slaves and Likens Progressives to Mussolini," *The Washington Post*, January 19, 2021; https://www.washingtonpost.com/education/2021/01/19/trump-patriotic-education-report-slavery-fascists/.

50. Williams, "Class Warfare," 54.

51. Jacey Fortin, "Critical Race Theory: A Brief History," *The New York Times*, November 8, 2021, https://www.nytimes.com/article/what-is-critical-race-theory.html.

52. Max Eden, "A New Front in the Fight Against Critical Race Theory in Schools," American Enterprise Institutes, May 19, 2021, https://www.aei.org/society-and-culture/a-new-front-in-the-fight-against-critical-race-theory-in-schools/; Benjamin Fearnow, "Texas GOP Passes Bill to Ban Critical Race Theory, Stop 'Blaming White Children' for Slavery," *Newsweek*, May 22, 2021, https://www.newsweek.com/texas-gop-passes-bill-ban-critical-race-theory-stop-blaming-white-children-slavery-1593923; "States That Have Banned Critical Race Theory 2023," World Population Review, accessed 2/17/2023, https://worldpopulationreview.com/state-rankings/states-that-have-banned-critical-race-theory; and David A. Lieb, "GOP States Targeting Diversity, Equity Efforts in Higher Ed," *Associated Press*, April 17, 2023, https://apnews.com/article/diversity-equity-inclusion-legislation-7bd8d4d52aaaa9902dde59a257874686.

53. Willem Roper, "Black Americans 2.5X More Likely Than Whites to Be Killed by Police," Statista, June 2, 2020, https://www.statista.com/chart/21872/map-of-police-violence-against-black-americans/; Brad Brooks, "Victims of anti-Latino hate crimes soar in U.S.: FBI report," Reuters, November 12, 2019, ttps://www.reuters.com/article/us-hatecrimes-report/victims-of-anti-latino-hate-crimes-soar-in-u-s-fbi-report-idUSKBN1XM2OQ; and Nikole Hannah-Jones, Caitlin Roper, Ilena Silverman, and Jake Silverstein, eds., *The 1619 Project* (New York: One World, 2021).

54. Thomas S. Kuhn, *The Structure of Scientific Revolutions* (Chicago: The University of Chicago Press, 2012), 151.

55. Kuhn, *Scientific Revolutions*, 92–93, 150.

56. Ibram X. Kendi, *How to Be an Antiracist* (New York: One World, 2023); and Cobb, "The Man Behind Critical Race Theory."

57. Allen, *Talking to Strangers*, 30, 41, 45.

58. Allen, *Talking to Strangers*, 63, 118.

59. Menand reminds us in *The Free World* that Thurgood Marshall "changed the law," but it was Martin Luther King Jr.'s "crusade" of political action that "changed the country in places that the law [had] not touched." Years passed between the Brown decision and the actual integration of schools, forced by the direct actions of the Civil Rights Movement; Menand, *Free World*, 619–621.

60. Sasha Issenberg, *The Engagement: America's Quarter-Century Struggle Over Same-Sex Marriage* (New York: Vintage, 2022); and Eric Servini, "How the Religious Right Made Same-Sex Marriage a Gay Rights Crusade," *The New York Times*, June 1, 2021, https://www.nytimes.com/2021/05/30/books/review/the-engagement-sasha-issenberg.html.

61. John Fabian Witt, "How the Republican Party Took Over the Supreme Court," *New Republic*, April 7, 2020, https://newrepublic.com/article/156855/republican-party-took-supreme-court; and Michael D. Shear, "Biden Signs Bill to Protect Same-Sex Marriage Rights," *The New York Times,* December 13, 2022, https://www.nytimes.com/2022/12/13/us/politics/biden-same-sex-marriage-bill.html.

62. "Book Ban Busters," Red Wine & Blue, accessed 3/1/2022, https://www.redwine.blue/bbb.

63. Kuhn, *Scientific Revolutions*, 137.

64. Eric Foner, "The Complicity of the Textbooks," review of *Teaching White Supremacy: America's Democratic Ordeal and the Forging of Our National Identity* by Donald Yacovone, *New York Review of Books*, September 22, 2022.

65. Allen, *Talking to Strangers*, xiii—xix.

66. Rauch, *Constitution of Knowledge*, 208, 255–257.

67. Allen, *Talking to Strangers*, 153; and Arendt, *Totalitarianism*, 290–302.

68. Arendt, *Totalitarianism*, 302.

69. Allen, *Talking to Strangers*, 98.

70. Melissa De Witte, "Stanford Students Put Deliberative Democracy Into Action," Stanford News, June 21, 2021, https://news.stanford.edu/2021/06/21/putting-deliberative-democracy-action/.

71. Antjie Krog, *Country of My Skull: Guilt, Sorrow, and the Limits of Forgiveness in the New South Africa* (New York: Three Rivers Press, 2000).

72. Sarah Soulie, "Does America Need a Truth and Reconciliation Commission?," *Politico,* August 16, 2021, https://www.politico.com/news/magazine/2020/08/16/does-america-need-a-truth-and-reconciliation-commission-395332.

73. Richard J. Bernstein, "Pragmatism, Pluralism, and the Healing of Wounds," in *Pragmatism, A Reader*, ed. Louis Menand (New York: Vintage, 1997), 397–401; and Richard J. Bernstein, *The Pragmatic Turn* (Cambridge, UK: Polity, 2010).

Chapter 4: Standards and Testing

1. *Lawrence of Arabia*, directed by David Lean (1962, Columbia Pictures: Sony Pictures Home Entertainment, 2008), DVD.

2. John Merrow, personal email to author, March 18, 2021.

3. Stanley Meisler, "Governors Bring Years of Concern to Education Summit: Bush Calls a Meeting of All State Leaders for Only 3rd Time in History," *Los Angeles Times*, September 27, 1989, https://www.latimes.com/archives/la-xpm-1989-09-27-mn-160-story.html.

4. M. A. Vinovskis, *Overseeing the Nation's Report Card: The Creation and Evolution of the National Assessment Governing Board* (Washington, DC: National Assessment Governing Board, 1998).

5. Alyson Klein, "Historic Summit Fueled Push for K-12 Standards," *Education Week,* September 23, 2014, https://www.edweek.org/teaching-learning/historic-summit-fueled-push-for-k-12-standards/2014/09; Drury and Baer, *American Public School Teacher,* 12; Ravitch, *Left Back,* 422.

6. Tyack and Cuban, *Tinkering Towards Utopia,* 45, 81.

7. Vinovskis, *Overseeing the Nation's Report Card.*

8. Marilyn Cochran-Smith et. al., *Reclaiming Accountability in Teacher Education,* 19; and Eric A. Hanushek, "The Economics of Schooling—Production and Efficiency in Public Schools," *Journal of Economic Literature* 24, no. 3 (September 1986): 1141–1177.

9. "The History of Abbott v. Burke," Education Law Center, accessed 2/27/2023, https://edlawcenter.org/litigation/abbott-v-burke/abbott-history.html

10. Popp Berman, *Thinking Like an Economist*, 3–4, 13–19.

11. John Maynard Keynes, decades before Popp Berman, drew attention to the same issue, complaining that cost-benefit analysis had turned political language and public deliberation into an "imbecile idiom." Corey Robin, "The Trouble With Money," *The New York Review of Books,* December 22, 2022, 75–76.

12. Popp Berman, *Thinking Like an Economist*, 66, 116–117.

13. "Alice Rivlin," Wikipedia, last modified June 26, 2023, https://en.wikipedia.org/wiki/Alice_Rivlin.

14. Eric A. Hanushek, "The Economics of Schooling: Production and Efficiency in Public Schools," *Journal of Economic Literature,* September 1986; Duncan, *How Schools Work*, 175.

15. Elizabeth Evitts Dickinson, "Coleman Report Set the Standard for the Study of Public Education," *Johns Hopkins Magazine,* Winter 2016, https://hub.jhu.edu/magazine/2016/winter/coleman-report-public-education/; James S. Coleman, "Equality of Educational Opportunity," National Center for Educational Statistics, July 2, 1966, https://files.eric.ed.gov/fulltext/ED012275.pdf.

16. "Evaluating the Success of the Great Society," *The Washington Post,* May 17, 2014, https://www.washingtonpost.com/wp-srv/special/national/great-society-at-50/; and Sar A. Levitan and Robert Taggart, "The Great Society Did Succeed," *Political Science Quarterly*, 91, no. 4 (Winter, 1976–1977): 601–618.

17. Marilyn Cochran-Smith et al., *Reclaiming Accountability in Teacher Education,* 15.

18. Marilyn Cochran-Smith et al., *Reclaiming Accountability in Teacher Education,* 21.

19. Nelson Lichtenstein, *State of the Union: A Century of American Labor* (Princeton, NJ: Princeton University Press, 2013); and Evelyn S. Taylor, *P.A.T.C.O. and Reagan: An American Tragedy* (Bloomington, IN: AuthorHouse, 2011).

20. Popp Berman, *Thinking Like an Economist,* 89–93.

21. Tyack, James, and Benavot, *Law and the Shaping of Public Education,* 114–124; and Rousmaniere, "In Search of a Profession," 13, 18.

22. With due respect to the late John Candy. *Planes, Trains, and Automobiles*, directed by John Hughes (1987; Burbank, CA: Warner Home Video, 2009), DVD.

23. Richard M. Ryan and Edward L. Deci, "Facilitating and Hindering Motivation, Learning, and Well-Being in Schools: Research and Observations From Self-Determination Theory," in *Handbook of Motivation at School (2nd edition)*, ed. Kathryn Wentzel and David B. Miele (New York: Routledge, 2016), 96–119; Daniel H. Pink, *Drive: The Surprising Truth About What Motivates Us* (New York: Riverhead, 2009); and Yoon Jik Cho and James L. Perry, "Intrinsic Motivation and Employee Attitudes: Role of Managerial Trustworthiness, Goal Directedness, and Extrinsic Reward Expectancy," *Review of Public Personnel Administration* 32, no. 4 (November 2, 2011): 382–406.

24. Joe Feldman, *Grading for Equity: What It Is, Why It Matters, and How It Can Transform Schools and Classrooms* (Thousand Oaks, CA: Corwin, 2019), 29; and John Hattie, *Visible Learning: The Sequel* (New York: Routledge, 2023).

25. Andy Hargreaves and Michael Fullan, *Professional Capital: Transforming Teaching in Every School* (New York: Teachers College Press, 2012), 15–16.

26. Peter Edelman, "The Worst Thing Bill Clinton Has Done," *The Atlantic,* March 1997, https://www.theatlantic.com/magazine/archive/1997/03/the-worst-thing-bill-clinton-has-done/376797/.

27. Matthew Di Carlo, "The 5–10 Percent Solution," Shanker Blog, Albert Shanker Institute, December 16, 2010, https://www.shankerinstitute.org/blog/5-10-percent-solution; and Eric A. Hanushek, "Teacher Deselection," in *Creating a New Teaching Profession*, ed. Dan Goldhaber and Jane Hannaway (Washington, DC: Urban Institute, 2009).

28. Despite my general critique, there is some merit here worth noting. Value-added analyses can identify positive teaching effects that might otherwise go unnoticed, such as two teachers whose students have the same increase in test scores. On closer examination, one teacher works with low-income students who attend a resource-poor school and is likely having a stronger impact.

29. Valerie Straus, "Weingarten Slams Teacher Evaluation by Student Test Scores," *The Washington Post*, January 13, 2014, https://www.washingtonpost.com/news/answer-sheet/wp/2014/01/13/weingarten-slams-teacher-evaluation-by-student-test-scores/.

30. Hofstadter, *Anti-Intellectualism*, 339. The episode is a classic example of Goodhart's Law, where data cease to be useful *measures* of performance because the data themselves *became* performance targets. "Goodhart's Law," Wikipedia, last modified January 29, 2023, https://en.wikipedia.org/wiki/Goodhart%27s_law. A similar critique was made by psychologist Donald T. Campbell, in what has become known as Campbell's Law: "Campbell's Law," Wikipedia, last modified November 30, 2022, https://en.wikipedia.org/wiki/Campbell%27s_law.

31. Craig LeMoult, "National Teachers' Union President Calls New Haven a National Model," NPR (Fairfield, CT: WSHU), September 8, 2014; Melissa Bailey/The Hechinger Report, "In New Haven, a Teachers Union Embraces Change," *Time*, June 11, 2014, https://nation.time.com/2013/06/11/in-new-haven-a-teachers-union-embraces-change/; "The New Haven Model," Editorial, *The New York Times*, May 3, 2010.

32. Ken Dixon, "Malloy Learned to Compromise in Second Legislative Session," *CT Insider*, May 14, 2012, https://www.westport-news.com/news/article/Malloy-learned-to-compromise-in-second-3556260.php.

33. Diane Ravitch, "The Connecticut Corporate Reform Gravy Train," Diane Ravitch's Blog (blog), May 22, 2013, https://dianeravitch.net/2013/05/22/the-connecticut-corporate-reform-gravy-train/; Diane Ravitch, *Reign of Error: The Hoax of the Privatization Movement and the Danger to America's Public Schools* (New York: Vintage Books, 2014).

34. Don Pesci, "Malloy Reforms Whipped," *New Haven Register*, April 4, 2012, https://www.nhregister.com/news/article/DON-PESCI-Malloy-reforms-whipped-11549298.php.

35. Jonathan Gyurko, "The Trouble With 'Teacher Voice,'" *Politics of Education Association* 38, no. 2 (Spring 2014): 1.

36. Kathleen Megan and Daniela Altimari, "House Unanimously Passes Education Reform Bill," *Hartford Courant*, May 9, 2012, https://www.courant.com/news/connecticut/hc-xpm-2012-05-09-hc-house-education-reform-0509-20120508-story.html.

Chapter 5: Accountability

1. James Baldwin, "Nothing Personal," *Contributions in Black Studies* 6, no. 1/5 (September 2008): 12. Baldwin's text was reprinted in *Contributions in Black Studies* with the author's permission, from his 1964 collaboration with photographer Richard Avedon, *Nothing Personal.*

2. President Ronald Reagan, "Inaugural Address" (United States Capitol, Washington, DC, January 20, 1981).

3. Robert Doer, "Is the Era of Big Government Back?," American Enterprise Institute, April 11, 2021, https://www.aei.org/op-eds/is-the-era-of-big-government-back/?mkt_tok=NDc1LVBCUS05NzEAAAF8fnYYEun0dLjegHVYDSNW0uvL7AhOYqq1ai5Qv06fR7bSXyjbO23n0lFmBOXbUltz8BaueaNO_vNwzMa001aI0Y0NMZKXaFWYsrQr-h2rNPw.

4. John Chubb and Terry Moe, *Politics, Markets and America's Schools* (Washington, DC: Brookings Institute, 1990); Milton Friedman, "The Role of Government in Education," in Robert Solo, ed., *Economics and the Public Interest* (New Brunswick, NJ: Rutgers University Press, 1955), 123–144; Milton Freidman, *Capitalism and Freedom* (Chicago, IL: University of Chicago Press, 1962); Horsford, Scott, and Anderson, *Politics of Education Policy*, 111; and Popp Berman, *Thinking Like an Economist*, 198.

5. Henig, *Rethinking School Choice*, 62–116; Seymour Fliegel, *Miracle in East Harlem: The Fight for Choice in Public Education* (New York: Random House, 1993); Chubb and Moe, *Politics, Markets and School Reform,* 217; and Jonathan Gyurko, *Teacher Voice (*PhD diss., Columbia University, 2012), Academic Commons, https://doi.org/10.7916/D8542VJ7.

6. Geoff Decker, "Facing Own Teacher Eval Deadline, Charter Schools Just Say No," *Chalkbeat*, December 12, 2012, https://ny.chalkbeat.org/2012/12/12/21094959/facing-own-teacher-eval-deadline-charter-schools-just-say-no.

7. Sebastian Buckup, "The End of Neoliberalism?," World Economic Forum, July 17, 2017, https://www.weforum.org/agenda/2017/07/this-is-what-the-future-of-economic-liberalism-looks-like-its-time-to-rethink-it; Jeremy Lent, "Coronavirus

Spells the End of the Neoliberal Era. What's Next?," Open Democracy, April 12, 2020, https://www.opendemocracy.net/en/transformation/coronavirus-spells-the-end-of-the-neoliberal-era-whats-next; Ganesh Sitaraman, "The Collapse of Neoliberalism," *The New Republic,* December 23, 2019, https://newrepublic.com/article/155970/collapse-neoliberalism, accessed 10/23/2023; "Biden: The End of Neoliberalism?," trans. Tom Walker, Watching America, April 2, 2021, https://watchingamerica.com/WA/2021/04/02/biden-the-end-of-neoliberalism/; and Grace Blakeley, "Covid-19 Is Not the End of Neoliberalism," *Tribune Magazine,* April 28, 2021, https://tribunemag.co.uk/2021/05/covid-19-is-not-the-end-of-neoliberalism.

8. Popp Berman, *Thinking Like an Economist*, 4–5, 14.

9. Marilyn Cochran-Smith et al., *Reclaiming Accountability in Teacher Education,* 9.

10. Horsford, Scott, and Anderson, *Politics of Education Policy*, 41, 170; Marilyn Cochran-Smith et al., *Reclaiming Accountability in Teacher Education,* 6.

11. Lani Guinier, *The Tyranny of the Meritocracy: Democratizing Higher Education in America* (Boston: Beacon Press, 2015), xi.

12. Duncan, *How Schools Work*, 172–175.

13. Hargreaves and Fullan, *Professional Capital,* xi, 44, 115.

14. Madeline Will, "States Crack Open the Door to Teachers Without College Degrees," *Education Week*, August 2, 2022, https://www.edweek.org/teaching-learning/states-crack-open-the-door-to-teachers-without-college-degrees/2022/08.

15. Marilyn Cochran-Smith et al., *Reclaiming Accountability in Teacher Education*, 76, 90.

16. Quoted in Duncan, *How Schools Work*, 170; Marilyn Cochran-Smith et al., *Reclaiming Accountability in Teacher Education*, 139.

17. Robert J. Marzano, *The New Art and Science of Teaching* (Bloomington, IN: Solution Tree Press, 2017), Charlotte Danielson, *The Framework for Teaching Evaluation Instrument* (2013), Doug Lemov, *Teach Like a Champion* (San Fransisco: Jossey-Bass, 2010).

18. Aaron M. Pallas and Anna Neumann, *Convergent Teaching: Tools to Spark Deeper Learning in College* (Baltimore: Johns Hopkins University Press, 2019).

19. "More Than 3,800 Teachers Achieve National Board Certification—Bringing National Total to More Than 125, 000 teachers," National Board for Professional Teaching Standards, December 9, 2019, https://www.nbpts.org/newsroom/more-than-3800-teachers-achieve-national-board-certification-bringing-national-total-to-more-than-125000-teachers/#:~:text=More%20than%203%2C800%20teachers%20achieve,profession%20that%20shapes%20America's%20future.

20. Dana Goldstein, "In the Fight Over How to Teach Reading, This Guru Makes a Major Retreat," *The New York Times*, May 22, 2022, https://www.nytimes.com/2022/05/22/us/reading-teaching-curriculum-phonics.html.

21. Marilyn Cochran-Smith et al., *Reclaiming Accountability in Teacher Education*, 3.

22. A similar, and successful, process was led 10 years ago to define and gain broad acceptance for collegiate teaching standards. It was led by my organization, the Association of College and University Educators (ACUE), which conducted an extensive literature review and spent more than a year working with higher education experts, institutional leaders, faculty, and professional associations. The resulting Effective Practice Framework was then independently reviewed and refined with a

panel of experts from UC Berkeley, Cal State Los Angeles, UMass-Amherst, Southern Methodist, and others convened by the American Council on Education (ACE), higher education's leading trade association. These standards, and the ACUE methods courses that prepare faculty to meet them, are now accepted as a standard for quality teaching at hundreds of college campuses. Nationwide adoption is being encouraged through collaborations with the National Association of System Heads, the Thurgood Marshall College Fund, the Council of Independent Colleges, and other organizations.

23. Susan A. Ambrose, Michael W. Bridges, Michele DiPietro, Marsha C. Lovett, and Marie K. Norman, *How Learning Works: Seven Research-Based Principles for Smart Teaching* (San Francisco: Jossey-Bass, 2010); and Daniel T. Willingham, *Why Don't Students Like School?: A Cognitive Scientist Answers Questions About How the Mind Works and What It Means for the Classroom* (San Francisco: Jossey-Bass, 2021).

24. Richard Elmore, "Improvement of Teaching at Scale" (plenary, National Science Foundation Conference, January 30, 2006).

25. Marilyn Cochran-Smith et al., *Reclaiming Accountability in Teacher Education*, 20, 21.

26. David F. Labaree, "The Trouble With Ed Schools," *Educational Foundations*, Summer 1996, https://davidlabaree.wordpress.com/2022/03/21/the-trouble-with-ed-schools/accessed 7/31/2023; David F. Labaree, *The Trouble With Ed Schools* (New Haven, CT: Yale University Press, 2004); Duncan, *How Schools Work*, 172–175; Hofstadter, *Anti-Intellectualism*, 319.

27. "Deborah Loewenberg Ball," School of Education, University of Michigan, accessed 2/21/2023, https://deborahloewenbergball.com/bio-intro#bio; and "Harnessing the Power of Teaching to Create a More Just Society," Teaching Works, accessed 2//22/2023, https://www.teachingworks.org/.

28. I am optimistic that leaders of a Publicization Project can organize a coalition around such de facto national teaching standards. Foundational teaching practices, sometimes called general pedagogy, are largely agnostic to subject matter. They address how and not what to teach, thereby avoiding curricular debates endemic in a pluralist society. The pioneering work of Lee Schulman on Pedagogical Content Knowledge does show that pedagogy and curriculum are intertwined. But at a minimum, there should be a foundation of best practice in every class.

29. Duncan, *How Schools Work*, 175, 176.

30. Casey, *Teacher Insurgency*.

31. Hargreaves and Fullan, *Professional Capital*, 16, 82, 44; Pasi Sahlberg, *Finnish Lessons: What Can the World Learn from Educational Change in Finland?* (New York: Teachers College Press, 2011).

32. Hargreaves and Fullan, *Professional Capital*, xiv, 106.

33. "The Creation of the Cambridge Network," Instructional Rounds Plus, accessed 2/21/2023, https://instructionalrounds.com/Cambridge.html.

34. "The New Haven Model," Editorial, *The New York Times*, May 3, 2010.

35. "Excerpts From Bush's Speech on Improving Education," *The New York Times*, September 3, 1999; Robert C. Johnston, "Bush Warns Against the 'Soft Bigotry of Low Expectations,'" *Education Week*, September 22, 1999; and George W. Bush, "Campaign Speech" (plenary, NAACP 91st Convention, Baltimore, MD, July 20, 2000).

36. Anthony S. Bryk, Louis M. Gomez, Alicia Grunow, and Paul G. LeMahieu, *Learning to Improve: How America's Schools Can Get Better at Getting Better* (Cambridge, MA: Harvard Education Press, 2017).

37. See years of research about the "degree premium" on average lifelong earnings from the Georgetown University Center on Education and the Workforce, https://cew.georgetown.edu/.

38. "Good Faith," Wikipedia, last modified February 10, 2023, accessed 2/21/2023, https://en.wikipedia.org/wiki/Good_faith.

39. "Good Faith Law and Legal Definitions," USLegal, accessed 2/21/2023, https://definitions.uslegal.com/g/good-faith-effort/.

40. Anthony S. Bryk, "Organizing Schools for Improvement," *The Phi Delta Kappan* 91, no. 7 (April 2010): 23–30; Anthony S. Bryk, Penny Bender Sebring, Elaine Allensworth, Stuart Luppescu, and John Q. Easton, *Organizing Schools for Improvement: Lessons From Chicago* (Chicago: University of Chicago Press, 2009); "John Q. Easton," University of Chicago Consortium on School Research, accessed 3/3/2022, https://consortium.uchicago.edu/about/staff/john-q-easton; and Duncan, *How Schools Work*, 67.

41. Bryk, "Organizing Schools," 24 (emphasis added).

42. *Waiting for Superman*, directed by Davis Guggenheim (Los Angeles, CA: Walden Media, 2010); *Stand and Deliver*, directed by Ramón Menéndez (Burbank, CA: Warner Brothers, 1988), DVD; *Freedom Writers,* directed by Richard LaGravenese (Hollywood, CA: Paramount Pictures, 2007); and *The Great Debaters*, directed by Denzel Washington (Beverly Hills, CA: Metro-Goldwyn-Mayer, 2007).

43. Abigail Thernstrom and Stephen Thernstrom, *No Excuses: Closing the Racial Gap in Learning* (New York: Simon & Schuster, 2003).

44. "Identifying and Implementing Educational Practices Supported by Rigorous Evidence: A User Friendly Guide," National Center for Education Evaluation and Regional Assistance, December 2003, https://ies.ed.gov/ncee/pubs/evidence_based/randomized.asp.

45. Elizabeth A. Stuart, Catherine P. Bradshaw, and Philip J. Leaf, "Assessing the Generalizability of Randomized Trial Results to Target Populations," *Prevention Science* 16, no. 3 (April 2015): 475–485; Antti Malmivaara, "Generalizability of Findings From Randomized Controlled Trials Is Limited in the Leading General Medical Journals," *Journal of Clinical Epidemiology* 107 (March 2019): 36–41; and Bryk, Gomez, Grunow, and LeMahieu, *Learning to Improve.*

46. Bryk, Gomez, Grunow, and LeMahieu, *Learning to Improve.*

47. Kathryn E. Joyce and Nancy Cartwright, "Bridging the Gap Between Research and Practice: Predicting What Will Work Locally," *American Educational Research Journal* 57, no. 3 (June 2020): 1045–1082.

48. Quoted in Duncan, *How Schools Work*, 170.

49. "W. James Popham," Association for Supervision and Curriculum Development, accessed 3/3/2022, https://www.ascd.org/people/james-popham accessed 3/3/2022; Robert Pondiscio, "It's Time to End the Testing Culture in America's Schools—And Start Playing the Long Game to Produce Better Life Outcomes for At-Risk Kids," *The 74*, November 20, 2018, https://www.the74million.org/article/pondiscio-its-time-to-end-the-testing-culture-in-americas-schools-and-start-playing-the-long-game-to-produce-better-life-outcomes-for-at-risk-kids/; and Feldman, *Grading for Equity.*

50. Gary King, Robert O. Keohane, and Sydney Verba, *Designing Social Inquiry: Scientific Inference in Qualitative Research* (Princeton, NJ: Princeton University Press, 2021).

51. Henry E. Brady and David Collier, *Rethinking Social Inquiry: Diverse Tools, Shared Standards (2nd Edition)* (Lanham, MD: Rowman & Littlefield, 2010); John Gerring, *Case Study Research: Principles and Practices* (Cambridge: Cambridge University Press, 2006), and Kristin Monroe, *Perestroika!: The Raucous Rebellion in Political Science* (New Haven, CT: Yale University Press, 2005).

52. Richard Rorty, *Pragmatism as Anti-Authoritarianism* (Cambridge, MA: Belknap Press, Harvard University, 2021), 19, 20.

Chapter 6: Equity

1. Franz Boas, *Anthropology and Modern Life* (Abingdon-on-Thames, UK: Routledge Revivals, 2014), 75; and "Franz Boas," Columbia 250, accessed 2/21/2023, https://c250.columbia.edu/c250_celebrates/remarkable_columbians/franz_boas.html.

2. Karen Belsha and Sarah Darville, "A New National Effort to Promote School Integration Is Underway. More Than Two Dozen School Districts Want In," *Chalkbeat*, October 9, 2020, https://www.chalkbeat.org/2020/10/9/21509770/new-national-effort-school-integration-bridges-collaborative-desegregation.

3. "D15 Diversity Plan," NYC Department of Education District 15, accessed 2/21/2023, https://d15diversityplan.com/; and Christina Veiga and Amy Zimmer, "A Push to Integrate Brooklyn Middle Schools Is Starting to Show Results, According to New Data," *Chalkbeat*, November 14, 2019, https://ny.chalkbeat.org/2019/11/14/21121770/a-push-to-integrate-brooklyn-middle-schools-is-starting-to-show-results-according-to-new-data.

4. "Violence Erupts in Boston Over Desegregation Busing," History, last updated September 12, 2019, https://www.history.com/this-day-in-history/violence-in-boston-over-racial-busing.

5. Saraya Wintersmith, "Arab Americans Say the Census and Other Forms Don't Consider Their Roots," NPR Morning Edition (New York: WNYC), March 9, 2022.

6. Valerie E. Lee and David T. Burkham, *Inequality at the Starting Gate: Social Background Differences in Achievement as Children Begin School* (Washington, DC: Economic Policy Institute, 2002), 1, 2.

7. Callahan, *Education and the Cult of Efficiency.*

8. Lynne M. Wiley, *Somewhere Between a Network and a Secret Society: The Cleveland Conference and Elite Policymaking in American Education* (Seattle: Annual Meeting of the American Educational Research Association, April 2001).

9. Callahan, *Education and the Cult of Efficiency*, 124.

10. Feldman, *Grading for Equity*, 20, 33–35, 40.

11. For a good example see Lawrence A. Cremin, *The Wonderful World of Ellwood Patterson Cubberley* (New York: Teachers College Press, 1965).

12. Carl Glickman, *Those Who Dared: Five Visionaries Who Changed American Education* (New York: Teachers College Press, 2008); and Henry Levin, *Accelerated Schools for At-Risk Students* (New Brunswick, NJ: Center for Policy Research in Education, August 21, 2017).

13. Thomas R. Gusky, "The Case Against Percentage Grades," *Educational Leadership* 71, no. 1 (September 2013), 68–72; Ken O'Connor, *A Repair Kit for*

Grading: 15 Fixes for Broken Grades (New York: Pearson, 2010); and Douglas B. Reeves, "The Case Against Zero," *Phi Delta Kappan* 86, no. 4 (December 2004): 324–325.

14. Feldman, *Grading for Equity*, xxiii, 6, and 39–58.

15. Jack Schneider, *Excellence for All: How a New Breed of Reformers Is Transforming America's Public Schools* (Nashville, TN: Vanderbilt University Press, 2011), 132–133.

16. Guinier, *Tyranny,* 21

17. Paulo Freire, *Pedagogy of the Oppressed* (New York: Penguin Books, 1970, 1993), 53.

18. Guinier, *Tyranny,* xi

19. Duncan, *How Schools Work*, 101.

20. Emma Dorn, Bryan Hancock, Jimmy Sarakatsannis, and Ellen Viruleg, "COVID-19 and Education: The Lingering Effects of Unfinished Learning," McKinsey & Company, July 27, 2021, https://www.mckinsey.com/industries/public-and-social-sector/our-insights/covid-19-and-education-the-lingering-effects-of-unfinished-learning; Per Engzel, Arun Frey, and Mark D. Verhagen, "Learning Loss Due to School Closures During the COVID-19 Pandemic," *Proceedings of the National Academy of Sciences* 118, no. 17 (February 26, 2021), https://www.pnas.org/doi/full/10.1073/pnas.2022376118; and Sarah Mervosh, "The Pandemic Hurt These Students the Most," *The New York Times*, updated September 7, 2021, https://www.nytimes.com/2021/07/28/us/covid-schools-at-home-learning-study.html.

21. Sarah Mervosh, "The Pandemic Erased Two Decades of Progress in Math and Reading," *The New York Times*, September 1, 2022, https://www.nytimes.com/2022/09/01/us/national-test-scores-math-reading-pandemic.html.

22. Lizzie Widdicombe, "Why Learning Pods Might Outlast the Pandemic," *The New Yorker,* March 14, 2021, https://www.newyorker.com/news/annals-of-education/why-learning-pods-might-outlast-the-pandemic; and Ashley Jochim and Jennifer Poon, "Crisis Breeds Innovation: Pandemic Pods and the Future of Education," Executive Summary, Center on Reinventing Public Education, February 2022, https://crpe.org/wp-content/uploads/Pods-executive-summary.pdf.

23. Travis Pillow, "Reinventing on the Fly: How Learning Pods May Hint at a New Structure for Public Education," Center on Reinventing Public Education, August 2020, https://crpe.org/reinventing-on-the-fly-how-learning-pods-may-hint-at-a-new-structure-for-public-education/.

24. Eilene Zimmerman, "Meeting the Mental Health Challenge in School and at Home," *The New York Times,* October 6, 2022, https://www.nytimes.com/2022/10/06/education/learning/students-mental-health.html?searchResultPosition=4.

25. *Creating a Culture of Caring: Faculty Resource* (Washington, DC: Active Minds-ACUE, 2020); William Deresiewicz, *Excellent Sheep: The Miseducation of the American Elite* (New York: Free Press, 2014); Rachel Shin, "Elite College Students Are Doing It to Themselves," *The Atlantic*, September 5, 2023, and Feldman, *Grading for Equity*, 60.

26. "University of Chicago Laboratory Schools," Britannica, accessed 2/21/2023, https://www.britannica.com/topic/University-of-Chicago-Laboratory-Schools; and Kate Rousmaniere, *Citizen Teacher: The Life and Leadership of Margaret Haley* (Albany: State University of New York Press, 2005).

27. A. S. Neill and Erich Fromm, *Summerhill: A Radical Approach to Child Rearing* (Oxford, UK: Hart Publishing, 1960); and "A. S. Neill," Wikipedia, last modified February 12, 2023, accessed 2/21/2023, https://en.wikipedia.org/wiki/A._S._Neill.

28. Schneider, *Excellence for All*, 41–71.

29. Theodore Sizer, *Horace's Compromise: The Dilemma of the American High School* (Boston: Houghton Mifflin, 1984); Theodore Sizer, *Horace's School: Redesigning the American High School* (Boston: Houghton Mifflin, 1992); Theodore Sizer, *Horace's Hope: What Works for the American High School* (Boston: Houghton Mifflin, 1996); Deborah Meier, *The Power of Their Ideas: Lessons for America for a Small School in Harlem* (Boston: Beacon, 1995); and Deborah Meier, *Will Standards Save Public Education?* (Boston: Beacon, 2000).

30. "About CES," Coalition of Essential Schools, accessed 5/25/2021, http://essentialschools.org/about-ces/.

31. Horsford, Scott, and Anderson, *Politics of Education Policy*, 214.

32. C. Christensen, M. Horn, and C. Johnson, *Disrupting Class: How Disruptive Innovation Will Change the Way the World Learns* (New York: McGraw-Hill, 2008); Terry Moe and John Chubb, *Liberating Learning: Technology, Politics, and the Future of American Education* (San Francisco: Jossey-Bass, 2009).

33. Kalley Huang, "A.I. Is Doing Homework. Can It Be Outsmarted?," *The New York Times*, January 17, 2023.

34. Stephen Gaukroger, *The Failures of Philosophy, A Historical Essay*, (Princeton: Princeton University Press, 2020); Rauch, *Constitution of Knowledge*, 97.

35. Meier, *Power of Their Ideas*; Schneider, *Excellence for All*.

36. Ambrose et al., *How Learning Works*; Pallas and Neumann, *Convergent Teaching*.

37. "What Is Career Readiness?," National Association of Colleges and Employers, accessed 2/22/2023, https://www.naceweb.org/career-readiness/competencies/career-readiness-defined/; and "Essential Learning Outcomes," American Association of Colleges and Universities, accessed 2/22/2023, https://www.aacu.org/initiatives/value-initiative/essential-learning-outcomes.

38. "National Commission on Social, Emotional and Academic Development," The Aspen Institute, accessed 2/27/2023, https://www.aspeninstitute.org/programs/national-commission-on-social-emotional-and-academic-development/.

39. Lisa Damour, *The Emotional Lives of Teenagers: Raising Connected, Capable, and Compassionate Adolescents* (New York: Ballentine Books, 2023); and Lisa Damour, *Untangled: Guiding Teenage Girls Through the Seven Transitions Into Adulthood* (New York: Ballantine Books, 2017).

40. "Student-to-School-Counselor Ratios," American School Counselor Association, accessed 2/22/2023, https://www.schoolcounselor.org/About-School-Counseling/School-Counselor-Roles-Ratios.

41. Theodore R. Sizer and Nancy Faust Sizer, "A School Built for Horace," *Education Next* 1, no. 1 (Spring 2001).

42. "Harkness Teaching Tools," Phillips Exeter Academy, accessed 2/22/2023, https://www.exeter.edu/programs-educators/harkness-outreach/harkness-teaching-tools; and "Head of School Emily Jones Stepping Down in June 2022," The Putney School, accessed 2/22/2023, https://www.putneyschool.org/head-of-school-emily-jones-stepping-down-in-june-2022/.

43. "Admission Policy," Bronx Better Learning, accessed 3/14/2022, https://www.bronxbetterlearning.org/apps/pages/index.jsp?uREC_ID=756048&type=d&pREC_ID=1163215; and "Caleb Gattegno," Wikipedia, last updated October 6, 2022, https://en.wikipedia.org/wiki/Caleb_Gattegno.

44. "Hyde at a Glance," Hyde School, accessed 2/22/2023, https://www.hyde.edu/; Joseph W. Gauld, *Character First: The Hyde School Difference* (Roseville, CA: Prima Lifestyles, 1995); and "Leaders in Our Neighborhood," Lion Charter School, Hyde-Bronx, accessed 2/22/2023, https://lioncharterschool.org/.

45. Horsford, Scott, and Anderson, *Politics of Education Policy*, 214.

46. Callahan, *Education and the Cult of Efficiency*, 264.

Part II: Cases

1. Clem Adelman, "Kurt Lewin and the Origins of Action Research," *Educational Action Research* 1, no. 1 (1993): 7–24.

Chapter 7: Charter Schools

1. Sizer, *Chartered Schools,* p. xii.

2. "Act Now: Tell Congress to Stop Funding the Charter Schools Program," Take Action, Network for Public Education, last modified 4/9/2021, https://networkforpubliceducation.org/cspmoratorium/.

3. "What Is a Charter School?," National Charter School Resource, accessed 2/26/2023, https://charterschoolcenter.ed.gov/what-charter-school; and "50-State Comparison: Charter School Policies," Education Commission of the States, January 28, 2020, https://www.ecs.org/charter-school-policies/.

4. "Charter Schools Are Innovative Public Schools," National Alliance for Public Charter Schools, accessed 4/27/21, https://www.publiccharters.org/; Brief of Amicus Curiae, National Alliance for Public Charter Schools, Peltier et al. v. Charter Day School et al., No. 20–1001 (4th Cir., filed August 30, 2021); and Stephanie Klupinski, Lindsay Nichols, and Kevin Stanek, "Public Schools, Private Employers? A Closer Look at the Labor Relations of Public Charter Schools," *Illinois State Law, Education and Policy Journal* 32, no. 2 (March 2012): 22–35.

5. "Charter School Data Dashboard," National Alliance for Public Charter Schools, accessed 3/14/2022, https://data.publiccharters.org/; and "Charter School FAQ," National Alliance for Public Charter Schools, accessed 10/23/2023, https://publiccharters.org/about-charter-schools/.

6. Joe Reich, Carol Reich, and Joel Klein, *Getting to Bartlett Street: Our 25-Year Quest to Level the Playing Field in Education* (New York: February Books, 2012).

7. Norm Fruchter, *Urban Schools, Public Will: Making Education Work for All Our Children* (New York: Teachers College Press, 2007).

8. Peter Iglinski, "Charter Schools Are Not All Equal," University of Rochester News Center, August 6, 2019, https://www.rochester.edu/newscenter/charter-schools-not-all-equal-391792/.

9. Sarah Reckhow, *Follow the Money: How Foundation Dollars Change Public School Policy* (Oxford, UK: Oxford University Press, 2012).

10. "Public Charter Startup Grants," Walton Family Foundation, accessed 10/28/2021, https://www.waltonfamilyfoundation.org/grants/public-charter-startup-grants.

11. "Every Child Deserves a High-Quality Education," Charter School Growth Fund, accessed 10/28/2021, https://chartergrowthfund.org/about/.

12. Michael Kimmelman, "An Ice Factory From the 1900s Is Now a Spectacular New Bronx School," *The New York Times*, February 15, 2023, https://www.nytimes.com/2023/02/15/arts/design/dream-charter-school-bronx-ice-factory.html.

13. Within such lotteries, variations include a preference for students of low socioeconomic status, as measured by eligibility for federal free and reduced-price lunch, and the children of teachers at the school, among other factors.

14. Daniel Golden, "Many Christian Parents Opt for Religious Charter Schools," *The Wall Street Journal*, September 15, 1999, https://www.wsj.com/articles/SB937349673185553337.

15. "Debate Rages Over NYC Hebrew Charter School," NBC News, February 3, 2009, https://www.nbcnews.com/id/wbna28992198

16. "Hellenic Classical Charter School at a Glance, 2020–2021," Kings County, New York State Education Department, accessed 2/22/2023, https://data.nysed.gov/profile.php?instid=800000058308; and Marci J. Harr Bailey and Bruce S. Cooper, "The Introduction of Religious Charter Schools: A Cultural Movement in the Private School Sector," *Journal of Research on Christian Education* 18, no. 3 (2009): 272–289, https://doi.org/10.1080/10656210903345255.

17. "Charter Schools Program," No Child Left Behind, Department of Education, July 2004, https://www2.ed.gov/policy/elsec/guid/cspguidance03.pdf.

18. Michael J. Petrilli, "For Better or Worse, Religiously-Affiliated Charter Schools Are on Their Way," Thomas Fordham Institute, November 5, 2020, https://fordhaminstitute.org/national/commentary/better-or-worse-religiously-affiliated-charter-schools-are-their-way.

19. Juan Perez Jr., "Oklahoma Approves Nation's First Public Religious Charter School," *Politico,* June 5, 2023, accessed 8/8/2023, https://www.politico.com/news/2023/06/05/oklahoma-approves-public-religious-charter-school-00100269.

20. Evie Blad, "Church-Run Charter Schools? Supreme Court Argument Stirs the Discussion," *Education Week*, January 26, 2020, https://www.edweek.org/leadership/church-run-charter-schools-supreme-court-argument-stirs-the-discussion/2020/01.

21. Mitch McConnell, "Confirmation of Judge Amy Coney Barrett" (remarks, U.S. Capitol, Washington, DC, October 26, 2020).

22. Ray Budde, *Education by Charter: Restructuring School Districts* (Andover, MA: Regional Laboratory for Educational Improvement of the Northeast and Islands, 1988); Albert Shanker, *Trying to Improve Schools: The Second Reform Movement* (Washington, DC: National Press Club, 1988); Albert Shanker, "Restructuring Our Schools," *Peabody Journal of Education* 65, no. 3 (1988): 88–100; Albert Shanker, "Where We Stand: A Charter for Change," *New York Times*, July 10, 1988; Albert Shanker, "Where We Stand: A Charter for Change (Cont'd.)," *New York Times*, July 17, 1988; Joe Nathan, *Charter Schools: Creating Hope and Opportunity for American Education* (San Francisco: Jossey-Bass Inc., 1996); "Charter School Data Dashboard," NAPCS; and "Just the FAQs—Charter Schools," Center for Education Reform, accessed 2/22/2023, http://www.edreform.com/issues/choice-charter-schools/facts/.

23. Or so the argument went; at the time, we underappreciated the extent to which loyal parents would lobby to keep a school open. Moreover, whether charter

school closures are a positive measure of accountability or indication of failed reform remains a bone of contention; Valerie Straus, "New Report Finds High Closure Rates for Charter Schools Over Time," *The Washington Post*, August 6, 2020, https://www.washingtonpost.com/education/2020/08/06/new-report-finds-high-closure-rates-charter-schools-over-time/.

24. My office managed their conversion to and from charter status. Operating concerns also played a part in the decision, specifically whether their funding under the state's charter law would be sufficient to meet employer retirement obligations.

25. Robert Pondiscio, *How the Other Half Learns: Equality, Excellence, and the Battle Over School Choice* (New York: Avery, 2019).

26. Chubb and Moe, *Politics, Markets and America's Schools*, 217.

27. National Alliance for Public Charter Schools, *Chartering 2.0: Leadership Summit Proceedings Document* (Washington, DC: NAPCS, January 2006).

28. Janus v. AFSCME et. al., 585 U.S. (2018).

29. "NYC Charter School's $125,000 Experiment," *60 Minutes*, season 43, episode 22, produced by Jenny Dubin, reported by Katie Couric, aired March 13, 2011, CBS.

30. Moe, *Special Interest*.

31. "Effective Education," Atlantic Legal Foundation, accessed 10/31/2021, https://atlanticlegal.org/mission-areas/school-choice/; "Remaining UNION FREE: A Counter Organizing Simulation," Jackson Lewis, accessed 10/31/2021, https://www.jacksonlewis.com/unionfree; and Donna Murch and Amy Higer, "Tell Your Legislators to Fire Jackson Lewis," Rutgers AAUP, accessed 2/22/2023, https://rutgersaaup.org/tell-your-legislators-to-fire-jackson-lewis/.

32. Stephen Singer, "Every Charter School Must Be Closed Down-Every. Single. One," Gadflyonthewall (blog), September 8, 2019, https://gadflyonthewallblog.com/2019/09/08/every-charter-school-must-be-closed-down-every-single-one/.

33. "About Charter Schools," National Alliance for Public Charter Schools, accessed 4/27/2021, https://www.publiccharters.org/about-charter-schools.

34. Jonathan Gyurko and Jeffrey R. Henig, "Strong Vision: Learning by Doing, or the Politics of Muddling Through?," in *Between Public and Private: Politics, Governance, and the New Portfolio Models for Urban School Reform*, ed. Katrina E. Bulkley, Jeffrey R. Henig, and Henry Levin (Cambridge, MA: Harvard University Press, 2010), 91–126.

35. Erica Pandey, "Charter Schools Boomed During the Pandemic," Axios, September 22, 2021, https://www.axios.com/2021/09/22/charter-school-pandemic-enrollment-growth?_hsmi=162345239&_hsenc=p2ANqtz-_6ggXK8STmuSL3txIFKhwrXGxckX19CHCjtae8_5Vq-XF_ZkFqh7YyGihLI4XpLZyHlBQiEqDWu8AfDOlFDb2sIBkpkg; and Debbie Veney and Drew Jacobs, *Voting With Their Feet: A State-Level Analysis of Public Charter School and District Public School Enrollment Trends* (Washington, DC: National Allliance for Public Charter Schools, 2021).

36. Geoff Decker, "As Fariña Meeting Nears, a New Charter School Coalition Angles for Acceptance," *Chalkbeat*, February 20, 2014, https://ny.chalkbeat.org/2014/2/20/21093159/as-farina-meeting-nears-a-new-charter-school-coalition-angles-for-acceptance; Coalition of Public Independent Charter Schools, https://www.indiecharters.org/.

37. Ken Paulson, "UFT, Representing 200,000 Members, Endorses Bill de Blasio for NYC," *Staten Island Advance,* September 18, 2013, mayorhttps://www.silive.com/news/2013/09/uft_representing_200000_member.html.

38. Valerie Straus, "Michael Bloomberg Pledges $750 Million to Expand Charter Schools," *The Washington Post*, December 1, 2021, https://www.washingtonpost.com/education/2021/12/01/bloomberg-donates-750billion-charter-schools/.

39. Lyndsey Layton and Michael Alison Chandler, "De Blasio Aims to Reverse Education Policies in New York," *The Washington Post,* November 8, 2013, https://www.washingtonpost.com/local/education/de-blasio-aims-to-reverse-education-policies-in-new-york/2013/11/08/5de6d24c-47f2-11e3-b6f8-3782ff6cb769_story.html.

40. Daniel Bergner, "The Battle for New York Schools: Eva Moskowitz vs. Mayor Bill de Blasio," *The New York Times Magazine,* September 3, 2014, https://www.nytimes.com/2014/09/07/magazine/the-battle-for-new-york-schools-eva-moskowitz-vs-mayor-bill-de-blasio.html.

41. Katie Ash, "N.Y.C. Charter Groups Rally to Keep Rent-Free School Spaces," *Education Week*, March 11, 2014, https://www.edweek.org/leadership/n-y-c-charter-groups-rally-to-keep-rent-free-school-spaces/2014/03.

42. Eva Moskowitz, *The Education of Eva Moskowitz: A Memoir* (New York: HarperColllins, 2017).

43. Grace Rauh, "Examining Status of de Blasio Vow to Fight 'Tale of Two Cities,'" Spectrum News NY1, September 18, 2017, https://www.ny1.com/nyc/all-boroughs/politics/2017/09/18/bill-de-blasio-nyc-mayor-tale-of-two-cities-inequality-promise-status.

44. Seymour Fliegel, *Miracle in East Harlem: The Fight for Choice in Public Education* (New York: Random House, 1993); Alex Medler, "The Charter School Movement: Complementing or Competing with Public Education?," in *The Emancipatory Promise of Charter Schools: Toward a Progressive Politics of School Choice*, Eric Rofes and Lisa M. Stulberg, eds. (Albany: State University of New York Press, 2004); Rofes and Stulberg, *Emancipatory Promise*; Richard D. Kahlenberg and Halley Potter, *A Smarter Charter: Finding What Works for Charter Schools and Public Education* (New York: Teachers College Press, 2014); Isaac Gottesman, "Socialist Revolution: Samuel Bowles, Herbert Gintis, and the Emergence of Marxist Thought in the Field of Education," *Educational Studies* vol. 49, no. 1, 2013.

45. Fred Mogul and Julianne Welby, "De Blasio Softens Rhetoric on Charters," WNYC, March 23, 2014, https://www.wnyc.org/story/de-blasio-softens-rhetoric-charters/; and "History and Archives," The Riverside Church, accessed 2/23/2023, https://www.trcnyc.org/history/.

46. Fred Siegal and Robert Doar, "De Blasio's Welfare-Reform Reversal," *City Journal Magazine*, Spring 2015, https://www.city-journal.org/html/de-blasio%E2%80%99s-welfare-reform-reversal-13718.html; William Neuman, "De Blasio, in Reversal, Says New York Will Pay $2 Million for His Lawyers," *The New York Times,* June 30, 2017, https://www.nytimes.com/2017/06/30/nyregion/de-blasio-investigations-legal-fees.html; Erin Durkin, "De Blasio Reverses Course, Pledges Funding for New NYPD Precinct," *Politico*, April 20, 2021, https://www.politico.com/states/new-york/albany/story/2021/04/20/de-blasio-reverses-course

-pledges-funding-for-new-nypd-precinct-1376388; Justine Coleman, "De Blasio to Reopen New York Elementary Schools in Reversal," *The Hill*, November 29, 2020, https://thehill.com/homenews/state-watch/527889-de-blasio-to-reopen-new-york-elementary-schools-in-reversal; and Sydney Pereira and Nsikan Akpan, "In Reversal, De Blasio Pledges to Release Data on Vaccine Site Distribution," *Gothamist*, February 18, 2021, https://gothamist.com/news/reversal-de-blasio-pledges-release-data-vaccine-site-distribution.

47. "Mayor De Blasio Appoints Richard Buery as Deputy Mayor for Strategic Policy Initiatives," The Official Website of the City of New York, accessed 4/26/2021, https://www.nyc.gov/office-of-the-mayor/news/732-14/mayor-de-blasio-appoints-richard-buery-deputy-mayor-strategic-policy-initiatives-pre-k#/0.

48. Patrick Wall, "Principals, Charter Leaders, Real Estate Experts, and Others to Tackle School-Space Issues," *Chalkbeat*, April 4, 2014, https://ny.chalkbeat.org/2014/4/4/21103347/principals-charter-leaders-real-estate-experts-and-others-to-tackle-school-space-issues.

49. His successor, Mayor Eric Adams, likely needs the Project, too, as the announcement of his schools chancellor was full of the adversarial soundbites that have characterized the fights of recent decades: Georgett Roberts, Selim Algar, and Emily Crane, "Eric Adams Names David Banks as New DOE Chancellor," *New York Post*, December 9, 2021, https://nypost.com/2021/12/09/eric-adams-names-david-banks-as-new-doe-chancellor/.

50. Rich Lowry, "De Blasio's Attack on Gifted Education Was the Capstone to His Dismal Reign," *New York Post*, October 11, 2021, https://nypost.com/2021/10/11/de-blasios-attack-on-gifted-education-was-capstone-to-his-dismal-reign/; Ray Domanico, "Saving Gotham's Students," *City Journal Magazine,* 2021, https://www.city-journal.org/nycr-de-blasio-and-the-collapse-of-education-in-new-york; Jake Martinez, "De Blasio's Education Legacy," NYCLU, last updated August 10, 2021, https://www.nyclu.org/en/news/de-blasios-education-legacy; Alina Adams, "Sound and Fury, Signifying Nothing: NYC Mayor Bill DeBlasio's Education Legacy," *New York School Talk,* February 8, 2021, https://newyorkschooltalk.org/2021/02/sound-and-fury-signifying-nothing-nyc-mayor-bill-deblasios-education-legacy/; and Michael Elsen-Rooney, "NYC Schools Head Richard Carranza Resigns, Meisha Porter to Become System's First Black Woman Chancellor," *New York Daily News*, February 26, 2021, https://www.nydailynews.com/new-york/education/ny-nyc-doe-richard-carranza-resigns-20210226-jumhzwebc5f2zlkt5mpxp6wx7m-story.html.

51. Kimmelman, *The New York Times.*

52. Robbie Sequeira, "Bye, bye: U.S. Census Shows Bronx Suffered Fifth-Highest Population Decline," *Bronx Times*, March 31, 2023, https://www.bxtimes.com/bronx-fifth-highest-population-decline/#:~:text=The%20Bronx%20saw%20the%20fifth,a%20recent%20U.S.%20Census%20report; USA Facts, https://usafacts.org/data/topics/people-society/population-and-demographics/our-changing-population/state/new-york/county/bronx-county/#:~:text=How%20has%20Bronx%20County's%20population,when%20the%20population%20dropped%202.8%25, accessed 8/6/2023, and "Demographics of the Bronx," *Wikipedia,* last updated July 25, 2023, accessed 8/6/2023.

53. ACUE, the company I co-founded, is one.

54. This approach, with other examples, is well explained in Richard H. Thaler and Cass R. Sunstein, *Nudge: Improving Decisions About Health, Wealth, and Happiness* (New York: Penguin Books, 2009).

55. Hofstadter, *Anti-Intellectualism,* 197–229.

56. Rebecca Gau, Chester E. Finn Jr., and Michal J. Petrilli, *Trends in Charter School Authorizing* (Washington, DC: Thomas B. Fordham Institute, May 2006).

57. "Renewing the Compact: A Statement by the Task Force on Charter School Quality and Accountability" (Washington, DC: National Alliance for Public Charter Schools), August 9, 2005; "Research and Publications," accessed 10/23/2023, National Association of Charter School Authorizers, https://qualitycharters.org/research/.

58. Elizabeth Baylor, *State Disinvestment in Higher Education Has Led to an Explosion of Student-Loan Debt* (Washington, DC: Center for American Progress, 2014).

59. Rachel Cohen, "The Untold History of Charter Schools," *Democracy: A Journal of Ideas*, April 27, 2017, https://democracyjournal.org/arguments/the-untold-history-of-charter-schools/; Jonathan Gyurko, *The Grinding Battle With Circumstance: Charter Schools and the Potential of School-Based Collective Bargaining* (New York: National Center for the Study of Privatization in Education, 2008); Shanker, *Trying to Improve Schools*; Budde, *Education by Charter*; Shanker, "Restructuring Our Schools"; Shanker, "Where We Stand"; Shanker, "Where We Stand (Cont'd.)"; and Richard D. Kahlenberg, *Tough Liberal: Albert Shanker and the Battles Over Schools, Unions, Race, and Democracy* (New York: Columbia University Press, 2007).

60. Albert Shanker, "National Press Club Speech" (address, National Press Club, Washington, DC, March 31, 1988), 6–7; and Paul E. Peterson, "No, Al Shanker Did Not Invent the Charter School," *Education Next Blog*, July 21, 2010, https://www.educationnext.org/no-al-shanker-did-not-invent-the-charter-school/.

61. Nathan, *Charter Schools.*

62. Kahlenberg, *Tough Liberal.*

63. Thernstrom and Thernstrom, *No Excuses.*

64. Bryk, Gomez, Grunow, and LeMahieu, *Learning to Improve.*

Chapter 8: Teacher Unions

1. William Shakespeare, *The Tragedy of Macbeth* (New York: Simon & Schuster, 2013), 9.

2. Hargreaves and Fullan, *Professional Capital,* 7.

3. Stan Karp, "A Tale of Two Districts," *Rethinking Schools* 29, no. 3 (Spring 2015): 34–41; Richard Whitmire, "A 'Founders' Excerpt: How Joel Klein Found His Disruptive Force—And Reshaped NYC Education," *The 74*, November 22, 2016, https://www.the74million.org/article/a-founders-excerpt-how-joel-klein-found-his-disruptive-force-and-reshaped-nyc-education/; and Matthew Green, "How Charter Schools Became Such a Big Player in California's Education System," KQED California Report (San Francisco, CA: KQED), March 20, 2019.

4. Popp Berman, *Thinking Like an Economist,* 218; and "The Disarming Revolutionary," *The Economist*, September 21, 2000, https://www.economist.com/business/2000/09/21/the-disarming-revolutionary.

5. Robin J. Lake, *Seeds of Change in the Big Apple: Chartering Schools in New York City* (Washington, DC: Progressive Policy Institute, 2004), 18.

6. Diane Ravitch, "Who 'Owns' Charter Schools?," *Education Week,* July 12, 2007, https://www.edweek.org/technology/opinion-who-owns-charter-schools/2007/07.

7. Paul Hill, Lawrence C. Pierce, and James W. Guthrie, *Reinventing Public Education: How Contracting Can Transform America's Schools* (Chicago: University of Chicago Press, 1997); Joseph Schumpeter, *Capitalism, Socialism and Democracy*, (New York: Harper Perennial Modern Classics, 2008); Clayton M. Christensen, Michael B. Horn, and Curtis W. Johnson, *Disrupting Class: How Disruptive Innovation Will Change the Way the World Learns* (New York: McGraw Hill, 2008); Katrina E. Bulkley, Jeffrey R. Henig, and Henry Levin, eds., *Between Public and Private: Politics, Governance, and the New Portfolio Models for Urban School Reform* (Cambridge, MA: Harvard Education Press, 2010).

8. Deinya Phenix, Dorothy Siegel, and Norm Fruchter, *Virtual District, Real Improvement: A Retrospective Evaluation of the Chancellor's District, 1996–2003* (New York: New York University Institute for Education and Social Policy, 2004).

9. "Make Believe They're Charter Schools," NYC Educator (blog), February 17, 2010, http://nyceducator.com/2010/02/make-believe-theyre-charter-schools.html; Norman Scott, "Klein Criticized for Favoring Charter School," *The Wave*, August 13, 2010, https://www.rockawave.com/articles/klein-criticized-for-favoring-charter-school/; Joel Klein, "What I Learned at the Education Barricades," *Wall Street Journal,* December 4, 2010, https://www.wsj.com/articles/SB10001424052748704104575622800493796156; and "Klein on Charter Schools," Eduwonk (blog), May 21, 2004, http://www.eduwonk.com/archives/2004_05_16_archive.html.

10. Anna Phillips, "Chancellor Orders Troubled Brooklyn Charter School to Close," *Chalkbeat*, April 16, 2010, https://ny.chalkbeat.org/2010/4/16/21086586/chancellor-orders-troubled-brooklyn-charter-school-to-close.

11. "Joel Klein," Wikipedia, last modified November 16, 2022, https://en.wikipedia.org/wiki/Joel_Klein.

12. Maureen Kelleher, *New York City's Children First: Lessons in School Reform* (Washington, DC: Center for American Progress, 2014).

13. Ruth Ford, "What's Behind the Bill de Blasio-Eva Moskowitz Feud Over Charters," *City Limits*, November 5, 2015, https://citylimits.org/2015/11/05/whats-behind-the-bill-de-blasio-eva-moskowitz-feud-over-charters/.

14. "About the UFT," United Federation of Teachers, accessed 5/4/2021, https://www.uft.org/your-union/about-uft; "DOE Data at a Glance," NYC Department of Education, accessed 4/4/2021, https://www.schools.nyc.gov/about-us/reports/doe-data-at-a-glance#:~:text=the%20school%20system.-,Students,students%20are%20English%20Language%20Learners.

15. Kahlenberg, *Tough Liberal;* Richard D. Kahlenberg, "The History of Collective Bargaining Among Teachers," in *Collective Bargaining in Education: Negotiating Change in Today's Schools*, ed. Jane Hannaway and Andrew J. Rotherham (Cambridge, MA, Harvard Education Press, 2006), 7–26; Murphy, *Blackboard Unions;* Jerald E. Podair, *The Strike That Changed New York: Blacks, Whites, and the Ocean Hill-Brownsville Crisis* (New Haven, CT: Yale

University Press, 2002); Ravitch, *The Troubled Crusade*; Richard B. Freeman, "Unionism Comes to the Public Sector," *Journal of Economic Literature* 24, no. 1 (March 1986): 41–86.

16. "About Us," American Federation of Teachers, accessed 2/24/2023, https://www.aft.org/about; and "Purpose and Power in Community," National Education Association, https://www.nea.org/about-nea, accessed 5/4/21.

17. Rachelle Garbarine, "City Teachers' Union Gives a Lesson in Real Estate," *The New York Times*, September 15, 2002.

18. Beth Fertig, "The High, Low and Lowest Points Between a Mayor and a Union," NPR (New York: WNYC), February 3, 2013.

19. Brill, *Class Warfare*; Gyurko and Henig, "Strong Vision."

20. Abby Goodnough, "Teachers' Union Sues Klein, Claiming Bias in Layoffs of Aides," *The New York Times*, May 6, 2003, National Edition.

21. Gyurko, *Grinding Battle;* "The *New York Post Says* No to a UFT Charter School in New York," Eduwonk (blog), May 11, 2004, http://www.eduwonk.com/archives/2004_05_09_archive.html#108429710520402913; "Good News-Bad News From NY . . . And a Great Point From MA," Eduwonk (blog), May 8, 2004, http://www.eduwonk.com/archives/2004_05_02_archive.html#108397373052444958.

22. "Teacher Strike Over Charter Schools Shuts Down Detroit Schools," *The Michigan Daily*, Sept. 25, 2003; Laura A. Bischoff, "Charter School Moratorium Divides," *Dayton Daily News*, March 15, 2007; and Martin Carnoy, Rebecca Jacobsen, Lawrence Mishel, and Richard Rothstein, *The Charter School Dust-Up: Examining the Evidence on Enrollment and Achievement* (New York: Economic Policy Institute and Teachers College Press, 2005).

23. Joe A. Stone, "Collective Bargaining and Public Schools," in *Conflicting Missions? Teachers Unions and Educational Reform,* ed. Tom Loveless (Washington, DC: Brookings Institution Press, 2000); Susan M. Johnson and Morgaen L. Donaldson, "The Effects of Collective Bargaining on Teacher Quality," in *Collective Bargaining in Education: Negotiating Change in Today's Schools,* ed. Jane Hannaway and Andrew J. Rotherham (Cambridge, MA: Harvard Education Press, 2006), 111–140.

24. Joel Klein, "The Failure of American Schools," *The Atlantic,* June 2011, https://www.theatlantic.com/magazine/archive/2011/06/the-failure-of-american-schools/308497/; Moe, *Special Interest;* Frederick M. Hess and Andrew P. Kelly, "Scapegoat, Albatross, or What? The Status Quo in Teacher Collective Bargaining," in *Collective Bargaining in Education: Negotiating Change in Today's Schools,* ed. Jane Hannaway and Andrew J. Rotherham (Cambridge, MA: Harvard Education Press, 2006), 53–88; Dan Goldhaber, "Are Teachers Unions Good for Students?," in *Collective Bargaining in Education: Negotiating Change in Today's Schools,* ed. Jane Hannaway and Andrew J. Rotherham (Cambridge, MA: Harvard Education Press, 2006), 141–158; F. Howard Nelson and Michael Rosen, *Are Teachers Unions Hurting American Education? A State-by-State Analysis of the Impact of Collective Bargaining Among Teachers on Student Performance* (Milwaukee: Institute for Wisconsin's Future, 1996); Lala C. Steelman, Brian Powell, and Robert M. Carini, "Do Teacher Unions Hinder Educational Performance? Lessons Learned from State SAT and ACT Scores," *Harvard Educational Review* 70, no. 4 (December 2000), 437–

467; Terry Moe, "Collective Bargaining and the Performance of the Public Schools," *American Journal of Political Science* 53, no. 1, (January 2009): 156–174; Caroline Hoxby, "How Teachers' Unions Affect Education Production," *Quarterly Journal of Economics* 111 (August 1996): 671–718; Tom Loveless, ed., *Conflicting Missions? Teachers Unions and Educational Reform* (Washington, DC: Brookings Institution, 2000); Jane Hannaway and Andrew J. Rotherham, eds., *Collective Bargaining in Education: Negotiating Change in Today's Schools* (Cambridge, MA: Harvard Education Press, 2006); and Terry Moe, "Union Power and the Education of Children," in *Collective Bargaining in Education: Negotiating Change in Today's Schools,* ed. Jane Hannaway and Andrew J. Rotherham (Cambridge, MA: Harvard Education Press, 2006), 229–256.

25. Moe, *Special Interest.*

26. Tanay Warerkar and Reuven Blau, "United Federation of Teachers Charter Schools Are a Tale of Two Cities," *New York Daily News,* November 19, 2013, https://www.nydailynews.com/new-york/bronx/uft-charters-tale-cities-article-1.1522676.

27. Randi Weingarten, "Chartering Educational Excellence: Why Teachers Matter Most," Eduwonk (blog), August 24, 2007, http://www.eduwonk.com/archives/2007_08_19_archive.html; and Randi Weingarten, "It's Time to Take the Politics Out of Charter Schools," paid advertisement in *The New York Times,* December 2006, http://www.uft.org/news/randi/ny_times/what_matters_most4.pdf.

28. Thomas Carroll, "Randi's Big Gamble: UFT's Bid for a Charter School," *New York Post,* December 7, 2004.

29. Randi Weingarten, "2009 AFT Quest Conference" (address, AFT, Washington, DC, July 13, 2009), https://www.aft.org/sites/default/files/media/2015/sp_weingarten071309.pdf accessed 2/26/2023.

30. "Closed Charter Schools by State, National Data 2009," EdReform, accessed 2/24/2023, https://edreform.com/wp-content/uploads/2013/03/Closed-charters-by-state-2009.pdf; and Carl Campanile, "Levy Shuts Failing Charter School," *New York Post*, July 3, 2002, https://nypost.com/2002/07/03/levy-shuts-failing-charter-school/.

31. Office of the New York State Comptroller, *Monitoring of Charter School Performance Report 2005-N-8* (Albany, NY: OSC, 2005), 14.

32. Charter School Leadership Council, "CSLC Applauds New York City Teachers Union to Vote to Create Two Public Charter Schools in Brooklyn," statement, February 10, 2005; and Elissa Gootman, "Official to Advise Union on Schools," *The New York Times*, August 5, 2004, https://web.archive.org/web/20050405051501/http://www.charterschoolleadershipcouncil.org/archive.asp.

33. Erik Robelen, "A School of Their Own," *Education Week* 25, no. 24 (February 22, 2006): 41–44.

34. "Poverty in New York City Council Districts," Institute for Children, Poverty & Homelessness, accessed 2//24/2023, https://www.icphusa.org/wp-content/uploads/2016/04/Poverty.pdf.

35. Howard Megdal, "UFT Charter School Film," *The Chief*, May 4, 2006, https://thechiefleader.com/news/news_of_the_week/uft-charter-school-film/article_af750923-64d4-5681-9eb7-94c08e84c967.html; and "5th Annual Tribeca Film Festival," Getty Images, accessed 2/24/2023, https://www.gettyimages.com/photos/5th-annual-tribeca-film-festival-climbing-to-the-crest-premiere.

36. "Steve Barr (educator)," Wikipedia, last modified September 7, 2022, https://en.wikipedia.org/w/index.php?title=Steve_Barr_(educator)&action=history; and Douglas McGray, "The Instigator," *The New Yorker*, May 11, 2009: 66.

37. Gary Kopycinski, "Chicago ACTS, UNO Announce Agreement Guaranteeing Charter Educators the Free Choice to Form a Union," eNews Park Forest, March 8, 2013, https://www.enewspf.com/latest-news/chicago-acts-uno-announce-agreement-guaranteeing-charter-educators-the-free-choice-to-form-a-union/.

38. "Green Dot New York Charter School and the United Federation of Teachers Collective Bargaining Agreement," UFT, last modified June 19, 2002, https://www.uft.org/files/contract_pdfs/green-dot-contract-2008-2011.pdf.

39. Weingarten, "2009 AFT Quest Conference."

40. "Getting a Wedgie," *District 299* (blog), July 25, 2007, https://district299.typepad.com/district299/2007/07/yahoo-360—mik.html#comment-77230960; and "Montague Charter Academy," SEIU Local 99, accessed 3/17/2022, https://www.seiu99.org/workplaces/k-12/montague/.

41. Jennifer Medina, "Charter Schools Weigh Freedom Against the Protection of a Union," *The New York Times*, April 20, 2009, https://www.nytimes.com/2009/04/21/education/21kipp.html; and Steven Greenhouse and Jennifer Medina, "Teachers at 2 Charter Schools Plan to Join Union, Despite Notion of Incompatibility," *The New York Times,* January 13, 2009.

42. Nahal Toosi, "Union Run Charter School in New York Draws Scrutiny From All Sides of Debate," Associated Press, January 2006.

43. Carroll, "Randi's Big Gamble."

44. David Andreatta, "Union's Charter School Due for OK in Comeback," *The New York Post*, June 8, 2005.

45. Elizabeth Green, "UFT in a Race To Avert a School Revolt," *The New York Sun,* March 24, 2008, https://www.nysun.com/article/new-york-uft-in-a-race-to-avert-a-school-revolt; Mahsa Saeidi, "Controversial UFT Charter School in Brooklyn to Close Elementary and Middle Grades," NY1 News, February 28, 2015; "UFT to Close Its K-8 Charter; Seeks Renewal for High School," United Federation of Teachers, March 4, 2015, https://www.uft.org/news/news-stories/uft-close-its-k-8-charter-seeks-renewal-high-school.

46. Diane Ravitch, "Mary Butz: Hedge Fund Managers and Foundations Should Fund Catholic Schools," Diane Ravitch's blog, September 26, 2015, https://dianeravitch.net/2015/09/26/mary-butz-hedge-fund-managers-should-fund-catholic-schools/; and Kevin Carey, "Diane Ravitch Is Not Telling the Truth. At All," Education Policy (blog), New America, November 28, 2015, https://www.newamerica.org/education-policy/edcentral/diane-ravitch-not-telling-truth/; both accessed 3/17/2022.

47. Geoff Decker and Philissa Cramer, "Opened to Prove a Point, UFT's Charter School Could Be Closed," *Chalkbeat*, October 9, 2012, https://ny.chalkbeat.org/2012/10/9/21089608/opened-to-prove-a-point-uft-s-charter-school-could-be-closed.

48. Alex Zimmerman, "After 15 Rocky Years, NYC's Teacher Union No Longer Wants to Run a Charter School," *Chalkbeat*, February 28, 2020, https://ny.chalkbeat.org/2020/2/28/21178679/after-15-rocky-years-nyc-s-teacher-union-no-longer-wants-to-run-a-charter-school.

49. "UPCHS Wins 2016 National Blue Ribbon Award," University Prep Public Schools, September 28, 2016, http://upchs.ss6.sharpschool.com/news_announcements/highlights/u_p_c_h_s_wins_2016_national_blue_ribbon_award.

50. Murphy, *Blackboard Unions*; and Clarence Taylor, *Reds at the Blackboard: Communism, Civil Rights, and the New York City Teachers Union* (New York: Columbia University Press, 2013).

51. Kahlenberg, *Tough Liberal,* 50–51; and Murphy, *Blackboard Unions.*

52. Chris Cillizza, "The Single Most Important Sentence in Joe Biden's Big Speech," CNN Politics, last modified April 29, 2021, https://www.cnn.com/2021/04/29/politics/biden-speech-congress-sotu/index.html; and President Joseph R. Biden, "State of the Union" (address, United States Capitol, Washington, DC, March 1, 2022).

53. Randi Weingarten, "Democracy in Education, Education for Democracy" (remarks, AFT TEACH 2019, Washington, DC, July 11, 2019).

54. John Dewey, *Democracy and Education: An Introduction to the Philosophy of Education* (New York: The Free Press, 1977).

55. Seymour Martin Lipset, Martin A. Trow, and James S. Coleman, *Union Democracy: The Internal Politics of the International Typographical Union* (Glencoe, Il: The Free Press, 1956).

56. "Board of Directors," National Board for Professional Teaching Standards, accessed 2/23/2023, https://www.nbpts.org/about/board/.

57. "National Board Certification," National Board for Professional Teaching Standards, accessed 5/13/2021, https://www.nbpts.org/national-board-certification/.

58. Jordan Weissman, "Former NYC Schools Head Joel Klein: We Need a Bar Exam for Educators," *The Atlantic,* November 14, 2012.

59. Nicholas Kristof, "The New Haven Experiment," *The New York Times,* February 15, 2012.

60. A good summation provided by UC Berkeley: "Seven Tests of Just Cause," Guide to Managing Human Resources, University of California Berkeley, accessed 2/24/2023, https://hr.berkeley.edu/hr-network/central-guide-managing-hr/managing-hr/er-labor/disciplinary/just-cause.

61. Linda Conner Lambeck, "Teacher Tenure Reform Plans Stir Debate," *Greenwich Time,* February 19, 2012, https://www.greenwichtime.com/local/article/Teacher-tenure-reform-plans-stir-debate-3341997.php, accessed 10/23/2023.

62. Hargreaves and Fullan, *Professional Capital,* 16.

63. Menand, *Free World,* 382–383.

64. Casey, *Teacher Insurgency*; and John Riley, "Florida House Passes Heinous 'Don't Say Gay' Bill," *Metro Weekly,* February 24, 2022, https://www.metroweekly.com/2022/02/florida-house-passes-dont-say-gay-bill/.

65. Susan Moore Johnson and Susan M. Kardos, "Reform Bargaining and Its Promise for School Improvement," in *Conflicting Missions? Teachers Unions and Educational Reform,* ed. Tom Loveless (Washington, DC: Brookings Institution Press, 2000), 7–46.

66. Joe Williams, "Revolution From the Faculty Lounge: The Emergence of Teacher-Led Schools and Cooperatives," *Phi Delta Kappan* 89, no. 3 (November 2007): 210–216; Priscilla Wohlstetter, Susan Albers Mohrman, and Peter J. Robertson, "Successful School-Based Management: Lessons for Restructuring Urban Schools," in *New Schools for a New Century: The Redesign of Urban Edu-*

cation, ed. Diane Ravitch and Joseph P. Vitteritti (New Haven, CT: Yale University Press, 1997), 201–225; and Priscilla Wohlstetter and Penny Bender Sebring, "School-Based Management in the United States," in *The Governance of Schooling: Comparative Studies of Devolved Management*, ed. Margaret A. Arnott and Charles D. Raab (London: Routledge, 2000), 161–179.

67. Charles Taylor Kerchner, Julia E. Koppich, and Joseph G. Weeres, *United Mind Workers: Unions and Teaching in the Knowledge Society* (San Francisco: Jossey-Bass, 1997); its title is also a pun on United Mine Workers, founded by John L. Lewis.

68. "Adam Urbanski," Influence Watch, accessed 2/24/2023, https://www.influencewatch.org/person/adam-urbanski/; see also https://www.turnweb.org/about/ for information about TURN and "RTA: A Union of Professionals," accessed 2/24/2023, https://rochesterteachers.org/about-us/.

69. *Teacher Professional Partnerships: A Different Way to Help Teachers and Teaching* (St. Paul, MN: Education Evolving, January 2004).

70. Stephen Sawchuk, "Gates Unveils First-Round Grants in New Education Strategy," *Education Week*, September 4, 2018, https://www.edweek.org/policy-politics/gates-unveils-first-round-grants-in-new-education-strategy/2018/09.

71. Andy Hargreaves and Michael Fullan, *Professional Capital: Transforming Teaching in Every School* (New York: Teachers College Press, 2012).

72. John L. Lewis, AFL-CIO, https://aflcio.org/about/history/labor-history-people/john-lewis, accessed 8/8/2023.

73. "American Federation of Labor," *Wikipedia,* https://en.wikipedia.org/wiki/American_Federation_of_Labor, accessed 8/8/2023.

74. Ryan Sager, "Kicking Klein to the Curb," *New York Post*, October 27, 2004.

75. Elizabeth Green, "With Union Decision Imminent, KIPP Is Ready to Start Bargaining," *Chalkbeat*, April 23, 2009, https://ny.chalkbeat.org/2009/4/23/21085238/with-union-decision-imminent-kipp-is-ready-to-start-bargaining.

76. Jay Mathews, *Work Hard. Be Nice.: How Two Inspired Teachers Created the Most Promising Schools in America* (Chapel Hill, NC: Algonquin Books, 2009).

77. Horsford, Scott, and Anderson, *Politics of Education Policy*, 79; "John Fisher," KIPP: Public Schools, accessed 3/19/2022, https://www.kipp.org/board-of-director/john-fisher/; and "News, Events & Press Releases," KIPP: Public Schools, accessed 3/19/2022, https://www.kipp.org/news/60-minutes-mike-wallace-reports/.

78. Leo Casey, "The Warped Logic of School Privatization," review of *Education and the Commercial Mindset* by Samuel Abrams, *Dissent*, Summer 2017.

79. Casey, "Warped Logic."

80. Sam Dillon, "Maverick Leads Charge for Charter Schools," *The New York Times,* July 24, 2007; and Randi Weingarten, "A Unique Partnership for a New School Year," paid advertisement in *The New York Times,* September 2007, http://uft.org/news/randi/ny_times/uft_wmm_Sept07_v3.pdf.

81. Frederick M. Hess, *Spinning Wheels: The Politics of Urban School Reform* (Washington, DC: Brookings Institute, 1998).

82. Rorty, *Pragmatism as Anti-Authoritarianism*, 9, 19, 2, 21, 59.

83. Allen explores how "rituals to solidify social order inevitably involve children in politics, however one might wish the case otherwise." The question becomes, in what kind of politics will they be involved? Allen, *Talking to Strangers*, 25–28.

84. Barbara Miner, "Supersized Dollars Drive Waiting for Superman Agenda," *NOT Waiting for Superman*, Rethinking Schools, October 20, 2010, https://notwaitingforsuperman.org/articles/20101020-minerultimatesuperpowe/.

85. Jonathan Gyurko, "On Guggenheim's Cutting Room Floor," HuffPost, September 28, 2010, https://www.huffpost.com/entry/on-guggenheims-cutting-ro_b_742345.

86. John Heilemann, "Schools: The Disaster Movie," *New York Magazine,* September 3, 2010; Ilana Garon, "Still Waiting: Davis Guggenheim's Manipulative and Short-Sighted *Waiting for Superman,*" *Dissent,* November 12, 2010, accessed 3/19/2022, https://www.dissentmagazine.org/online_articles/still-waiting-davis-guggenheims-manipulative-and-short-sighted-waiting-for-superman; and Paul Tough, *Whatever It Takes: Geoffrey Canada's Quest to Change Harlem and America* (Boston: Mariner Books, 2008).

87. Trip Gabriel, "Remedial Study for Failing Public Schools," *The New York Times,* September 19, 2010; and Tough, *Whatever It Takes*.

88. Diane Ravitch, *The Death and Life of the Great American School System* (New York: Basic Books, 2010).

89. Staci Maiers, "NEA Supports Sanders' Bill Calling for $60,000 Minimum Teacher Salary," National Education Association, March 9, 2023, accessed 8/9/2023, https://www.nea.org/about-nea/media-center/press-releases/nea-supports-sanders-bill-calling-60000-minimum-teacher-salary#:~:text=The%20legislation%20calls%20to%20pay,the%20new%20Congress%20by%20Rep.

Chapter 9: Conclusion

1. Arendt, *Totalitarianism,* 298. For an interesting essay that deals directly with Arendt's assertion, see Seyla Benhabib, "Thinking Without Banisters," *New York Review of Books,* February 24, 2022, 26.

2. Richard Rorty, "Solidarity or Objectivity?" (1984), in *The Rorty Reader*, ed. Christopher J. Voparil and Richard J. Bernstein (West Sussex, UK: Wiley-Blackwell, 2010), 233.

3. Amber M. Northern, Janie Scull, and Dara Zeehandelaar Shaw, *How Strong Are U.S. Teacher Unions? A State-By-State Comparison* (Columbus, OH: Thomas B. Fordham Institute, October 29, 2012). I served as an advisor to this project, and researchers came to admit that state-to-state comparisons were much less useful than within-state comparisons to other interest groups, which the study did not examine.

4. Jean-Paul Sartre, *No Exit and Three Other Plays* (New York: Vintage International, 1989), 45; and Kirk Woodward, "The Most Famous Thing Jean-Paul Sartre Never Said," Rick on Theater (blog), July 9, 2010, http://rickontheater.blogspot.com/2010/07/most-famous-thing-jean-paul-sartre.html.

5. Frederick Hess, "What Does the Future Hold for School Accountability?," *Education Next*, accessed 3/21/2022, https://www.educationnext.org/what-does-the-future-hold-for-school-accountability/.

6. Hess, "What Does the Future Hold?"

7. David Graeber and David Wengrow, *The Dawn of Everything: A New History of Humanity* (New York: Farrar, Straus & Giroux, 2021), 276–281.

8. Allen, *Talking to Strangers*, 9–24.

9. Popp Berman, *Thinking Like an Economist*, 232.

Index

The letter *n* after a page number indicates an endnote.

About the Author

Jonathan Gyurko (pronounced GUR-koh) holds a PhD in politics and education from Teachers College, Columbia University, and was the inaugural Harber Fellow in Educational Innovation at Wesleyan University. From 2000 to 2014 he led public education reform efforts for the New York City Department of Education, the United Federation of Teachers, the Coalition of Public Independent Charter Schools, and as a board member of the National Association of Charter School Authorizers. He served as board secretary for DREAM Charter School and board vice president for the American Friends of Maru-a-Pula School in Gaborone, Botswana. He currently serves as president and co-founder of the Association of College and University Educators (ACUE), which awards the only nationally recognized certification in effective college instruction. Gyurko attended the University of North Carolina at Chapel Hill as a Morehead Scholar and began his career as an English and drama teacher at Tiger Kloof School in Vryburg, South Africa.